100 YEARS OF RUGBY LEAGUE

100 YEARS OF RUGBY LEAGUE

The Daily Telegraph

HarperSports
An imprint of HarperCollins*Publishers*

Harper*Sports*
An imprint of HarperCollins*Publishers*

First published in Australia by *The Daily Telegraph* in 1999
First published in book form in 1999
by HarperCollins*Publishers* Pty Limited
ACN 009 913 517
A member of HarperCollins*Publishers* (Australia) Pty Limited Group
http://www.harpercollins.com.au

This book is published in association with *The Daily Telegraph*

HarperCollins*Publishers*
25 Ryde Road, Pymble, Sydney NSW 2073, Australia
31 View Road, Glenfield, Auckland 10, New Zealand
77–85 Fulham Palace Road, London W6 8JB, United Kingdom
Hazelton Lanes, 55 Avenue Road, Suite 2900, Toronto, Ontario M5R 3L2
and 1995 Markham Road, Scarborough, Ontario M1B 5M8, Canada
10 East 53rd Street, New York NY 10022, USA

National Library of Australia Cataloguing-in-Publication data:

100 years of rugby league.
ISBN 0 7322 6525 8
1. Rubgy League Football – Australia. I. Sunday Telegraph
(Sydney, N.S.W.). II. Title: One hundred years of rugby league
796.33380994

Produced in Australia by The Australian Book Connection
Printed on 130gsm Impress Satin

6 5 4 3 2 1   99 00 01 02

Editor for *The Daily Telegraph*: Geoff Greenwood.

Design for *The Daily Telegraph*: Kevin Kearney.

Artwork for *The Daily Telegraph*: David Matthews.

Writers: Ian Heads, Peter Frilingos, Ray Kershler and David Middleton.

Additional writing: Tim Prentice, Tony Adams and Jon Geddes.

Statistics: David Middleton.

Book design: Maxco.

Special thanks: Ian Collis, Albert Clift, Ian Gately, Nicole Emanual, Peter Muhlbock, Shane Wallace and New Limited imaging staff, News Limited photo and reference library, Frant Stanton, Wally O'Connell, *Rugby League Week*, Alan Hill, Arthur Stanley and Mark Gately.

Photographers: all News Limited photographers who have got their knees dirty covering Rugby League, with a special mention to Barry McKinnon, Graeme Fletcher, Warwick Lawson, Phil Merchant, Stuart Menzies, Graeme Noad, Geoff Henderson, John Burney, Barry Norman, Peter Kurnick, Wayne Jones, Anthony Weate, Anthony Moran, Bob Barker, Gregg Porteous, Mark Evans, Phil Hillyard, Roy Haverkamp, Trent Parke, Jay Town, Andrew Darby, Rob McKell, Gary Graham, Ray Strange, Michael Jones and David Crosling — without whose efforts this publication would not have been possible.

Congratulations to *The Daily Telegraph* for what promises to be an absorbing book saluting the game of rugby league.

Rugby league is one of our greatest games. It continues to enthral millions of Australians. The devotion for the game held by Australians from all walks of life serves as a great reminder that those things that bind us together – such as a love of sport – are far greater than our differences.

League has a strong sense of tradition, with many of its fans continuing to follow the same team throughout their lifetimes. It also, however, has a sense of dynamism, and a willingness to adapt to the times. Recent years serve as a reminder of league's great capacity to emerge from difficult times, stronger than ever.

Since 1908, when the Sydney first grade premiership was inaugurated, the game of rugby league has engaged generations of fans in Australia, particularly in New South Wales and Queensland. The premiership has, of course, spread well beyond its original base in Sydney, with the advent of the Melbourne Storm.

From 1980, State of Origin matches between New South Wales and Queensland have assumed a major place on the nation's sporting calendar. In many respects they have matched, and even surpassed, Test matches against nations like Great Britain as the prime events of the league year.

Of course, representing Australia remains the greatest honour league players seek.

The game faces a number of challenges as it looks to the future. The standard of rugby league, however, has never been higher and the premiership is as tightly contested as it has ever been.

I look forward to reading *The Daily Telegraph's* '100 Years of Rugby League' and know it will be in line with the newspaper's usual excellent league coverage.

John Howard
Prime Minister

'NOW I can die happy.' With those five words way back in 1912 Australian rugby league captain Chris McKivatt proclaimed his unbridled joy at beating England on their soil in a three-Test Ashes series.

It was an unashamed response from a man who had just made rugby league history, a celebration of the significance of his team's achievement. To McKivatt, this was more than a game. It was akin to war and deserved recognition as such.

For most of this century rugby league in Australia has ridden just such an emotional journey. *The Daily Telegraph*, through its recent series '100 Years of Rugby League', captured the spirit of the greatest game of all. From the night the Australian game began in a Sydney hotel to the player strike of 1917, Brian Bevan's 'try of the century' in 1948 and the most famous Test of all when Australia won the Ashes for the first time in 30 years. Right through to a world record crowd of over 107,961 fans who packed Stadium Australia for the the last grand final this century between Melbourne and St George-Illawarra.

Such was the success of the '100 Years of Rugby League' series that it was decided to reproduce the work in book form, the ultimate chronicle of the games history. The game that started as a revolution in the north of England at the end of the last century — an upstart breakaway from the establishment rugby union — soon forged support on the other side of the globe, in working class Sydney.

Born from disenchantment and resentment, the new game sought and won the support of rugby union icon of the day, Herbert Henry 'Dally' Messenger — and the rest, as they say, is history. But what a history. Test matches bathed in blood and glory.

Intense interstate rivalry that has grown into a national sporting institution. A club competition, described as the toughest in the world, that has undergone its own revolutions — only to emerge seemingly stronger and more resilient. And through it all the players — the gladiators — have left their indelible imprint on the lives of hundreds of thousands of fans. For it is the players who have made rugby league the great game that it is. Messenger, Horder, Brown, Churchill, Gasnier, Langlands, Fulton, Beetson, Lewis, Sterling, Langer, Johns, Daley and Fittler. Names woven into the fabric of our sporting culture.

'100 Years of Rugby League' is dedicated to their memory and their deeds. Their legacy is etched in the words and pictures that follow.

Let the game begin ...

Steve Howard

Editor, *The Daily Telegraph*

LEAGUE
AUSTRALIAN RUGBY LEAGUE
WORLD TOUR
1929-30
N.S.W
1927
1927
AUSTRALIAN TOUR
SECOND TEST
NEW ZEALAND v AUSTRALIA
THIRD
HERBERT HENRY
1927-28-29-30-32
RUGBY LEAGUE
1907-57
JUBILEE
WORLD CUP
AUSTRALIAN
N.S.W.R.F.L
NRL
CLASSIC
ST. GEORGE
ILLAWARRA

CHAPTER ONE

Let the Game begin

BY IAN HEADS

The way we were...

1900: Swimmer Freddy Lane wins two gold medals at the Paris Olympic Games. He was the first Australian swimmer to compete in the modern Olympics.

1901: Mass celebrations as Australia is welcomed into the Commonwealth of Nations. One hundred and three people die as Sydney is gripped by bubonic plague. **Queen Victoria** dies aged 82.

I was there...

'Dally Messenger wasn't a footballer, he was a wizard. I first saw him play when I was about seven or eight years old and I couldn't take my eyes off him. He was the top player of the day, the superstar, and he was the brainiest footballer I've ever seen. The man had a touch of genius about him and rugby league owes a great debt to The Master.'

Harry 'Mick' KADWELL, the oldest living Kangaroo tourist, until his death at 96 in October, 1999

Let the Game begin

MOMENTOUS events often have small beginnings. And so it was with the hard game that came long ago to Australia from the mines and milltowns of England's north. Rugby league. Its early signposts: a whisper on the wind – of a new game, played far away... a red-haired forward with a dodgy shoulder ... the simmering age-old discontent of workers with conditions offered by their employers ... an afternoon taxi ride from downtown Sydney to Double Bay ... a man with a handlebar moustache, and a dream... a great cricketer, who shared that dream. These things are rugby league's ancient building blocks – the disparate threads that somehow entwined into what became one of the truly remarkable sporting sagas of the 20th century. Without even one of them we may never have seen such sights as these: dazzling, masterful Dally Messenger; brilliant, courageous Clive Churchill; the Magic Dragon, Reg Gasnier, gliding majestically over Kogarah's green spaces; Keith Barnes kicking impossibly long-range goals on his "tin legs"; Bob Fulton running this way and that, rebounding from tacklers ... rebounding again; John Ferguson leaping high to steal a grand final from Balmain's fingertips; Ricky Stuart sending Mal Meninga away for a miracle try in Old Trafford's late afternoon glow; Alfie Langer dodging, probing ... relentless; Paul Harragon and Mark Carroll colliding like titans – with even the grandstands shuddering. These things, and a million more, are the memories of the rugby league century. In this book, a tribute to a remarkable game. *The Daily Telegraph* will take you on a deluxe journey, past great and momentous sporting afternoons and nights, revisiting with a fresh eye legendary wins and losses, days of drama ... and despair, champion players, breathtaking courage, skulduggery ... and sadness.

The single great coup ... the signing of the most famous rugby union player of the time, Herbert Henry 'Dally' Messenger, in action below, was a significant catalyst in 1907 for the formation of the new game

The birth of all the stories we will tell took place in the winter of 1907 in Sydney (population then 118,215) and came via complex events that criss-crossed each other, each one adding weight daily to the start of a revolution.

THE NEW GAME: The miners and millhands of Yorkshire and Lancashire had played 'Northern Union' (rugby league) since 1895. Fresh and first-hand news of the game reached Sydney in March, 1906, brought by All Black (rugby union) players returning home from a UK tour. Those contacts represented the first stirring.

THE RED-HAIRED FORWARD: Alex 'Bluey' Burdon busted a shoulder while playing (rugby union) for Australia against England in 1904. Off work for many weeks, he received no compensation from the wealthy Union establishment. Then, on July 22, 1907, in a match at Wingham, in northern NSW, Burdon suffered a further shoulder dislocation. Once again there was no financial support to get him through and amidst rumblings of discontent 'Bluey' Burdon became a *cause celebre* among those working for the new movement.

DISCONTENT AMONG THE 'WORKERS': In 1907 the NSW Rugby Union was a wealthy body, reaping huge sums from a successful All Blacks tour that year. Yet, despite rumours of 'secret' payments it showed no inclination to look after injured players – and especially the likes of 'Bluey' Burdon and NSW captain Harold Judd, who lay in St Vincent's Hospital with a broken leg. It was this very issue that led to the breakaway of 1907.

THE TAXI RIDE: The story comes from the heart of the Messenger family – of how James Giltinan and Victor Trumper, the men flying the flag highest for the new game, took a cab to Double Bay on an afternoon in early August 1907 – to the home of the most famous rugby union player of his time, Herbert Henry 'Dally' Messenger. There, with the blessing of Dally's strong-willed mum, Mrs Annie Messenger, Trumper and Giltinan secured Messenger's signature for the upcoming games against Albert Baskiville's New Zealand All Golds – the games which effectively kicked off rugby league in Australia.

Messenger's signing was the single great coup of the whole exercise. Ninety years on, his sobriquet still says all that needs to be said about his standing in the game: The Master.

THE MAN WITH THE HANDLEBAR MOUSTACHE: There is no doubt that James Joseph Giltinan is rugby league's founding father. Cricket umpire, amateur walker, entrepreneur and, in 1907, an executive with a building firm, Giltinan was a man driven by his dream. It was his guarantee of 500 pounds which brought the All Golds to Sydney for the three matches (against NSW, under union rules) that began rugby league. It was Giltinan who bankrupted himself in taking the 1908 Kangaroos to England. The game, in its turn, kicked him out. A near-broken man, Giltinan was unceremoniously dumped from office by the NSWRL as he headed home aboard the steamship RMS India after the 46-match tour.

THE GREAT CRICKETER: Victor Trumper, of whom Sir Neville Cardus wrote, 'he was the most gallant and handsome batsman of them all', was a true believer who stood alongside Giltinan in the face of furious opposition from the rugby union establishment. Trumper's sports store in Market Street was the new movement's hotbed and headquarters in 1907. Meetings stretching late into the night were held there, the participants seated on chairs borrowed from a nearby wine salon. In Messenger, rugby league had the great footballer of the day – in Trumper, the great cricketer. The pair of them were priceless assets. The game that rugby league became, and is today, as athletes of unprecedented size and power battle it out, made its way across stepping stones scattered down the seasons – each one of

The way we were...

1902: King Edward VII is coronated. **Harry Harbord 'Breaker' Morant** and Lt Peter Handcock face firing squad in Pretoria for shooting Boers who had surrendered. Artist Albert Namatjira is born. Australian women win right to vote. Mine explosion at Mt Kembla colliery leaves 94 dead.

1904: Prime Minister John Watson forms Australia's first Federal Labor ministry; bushfires claim 13 lives at Gippsland.

Birth of a club...

Six hundred people packed into the Balmain Town Hall in Darling Street on January 23, 1908, to form the Balmain Rugby League Club. In his new book *Tiger Tiger Burning Bright*, Ray Chesterton writes that at the gathering there was palpable anger directed against the Rugby Union and its indifferent attitude to injured players. A motion that the Balmain club be formed was carried with cheers and applause, especially when it was announced that 16 prominent rugby union players had agreed to join the club. Balmain played their first game on Easter Monday, April 20, at Birchgrove Oval, beating Western Suburbs 24-0.

COLOURS: The club's first jumper had black and gold horizontal bars, the same colours and design as the rugby union club.

NICKNAME: 'The Tigers' due to the jumper design. Early on the club was also known as the Watersiders.

them representing a marker post and a profound change, shifting the game's direction this way or that for the future. *100 Years of Rugby League* has identified seven of them; some will be revisited in detail in the chapters to follow. They are:

■ The signing, in 1909, of the majority of the current Wallaby (rugby union) team – and especially of skipper Chris McKivat, an under-appreciated and enormously influential figure in the kick-starting of rugby league. With most of rugby's stars on board, league gained a break on the 15-a-side code that was never surrendered.

■ League's decision to 'play on' during the two World Wars, and especially the Great War (1914-18) when huge pressure was mounted on sportsmen to 'play the other game'. Many league men went to war, and numbers were lost, including the NSWRL's first secretary, Edward Larkin, who fell at Gallipoli – but somehow the game kept going. Rugby union did not.

■ The arrival of radio in 1924 – with the Balmain-Souths final the first football match ever broadcast in Australia. Suddenly, the game had a new medium to spread the word.

■ The beginning of television coverage (1961) and, especially, colour TV (1974). No game suits the small screen better than rugby league, with its compressed nature and its mix of deft skills and fierce physical contact.

■ The introduction of limited tackle football in 1967 – first four tackles and then six (1971). In its 91 years league has had no greater on-field change than this one, designed specifically to combat the bash 'n' barge tactics under which one side in a match could dominate possession endlessly ... and increasingly did. Controversial at its beginning,

Dally (seated bottom right) gave rugby league credibility and the fans responded

limited tackle football proved to be the game's springboard for the future. The modern era began with the four-tackle rule in 1967.

■ The appointment, in 1980, of the former Battle of Britain pilot Jim Comans as chairman of the NSWRL judiciary. His supporters called him 'Gentleman Jim', his detractors believed him to be the 'Hanging Judge' – but the certainty was that Jim Comans had a deep and wise understanding that in an age of increasing TV focus, with the game beamed into the lounge rooms of the land, rugby league could no longer afford the excesses of violence that had once been accepted. In his quiet

Birthplace of the game ... Birchgrove Oval, where two of the first ever premiership matches were played

1900-09

APRIL 5, 1904: Less than nine years after the Northern Union breaks away from the Rugby Football Union in England to initiate the rugby league game, the code's first international match is played in Wigan. Other Nationalities, a team made up mainly of Welshmen and a few Scots, beat an English side 9-3.

1906: A series of rule changes begin to effect a noticeable distinction between the two rugby codes. Teams are reduced from 15-a-side to 13-a-side; a tackled player is required to play the ball; and a scrum is formed at the point of kicking if the ball enters touch on the full.

AUGUST 8, 1907: The New South Wales Rugby League is formed at a meeting at Bateman's Crystal Hotel in George Street, Sydney. Henry Hoyle is elected president, **James J Giltinan** secretary and cricketing legend, Victor Trumper, treasurer.

AUGUST 10, 1907: The approximate date that legendary player Dally Messenger agrees to play with the new professional body. The story goes that when Giltinan and **Victor Trumper** came knocking at the door of Dally's Double Bay house, Messenger left the final decision on his future to his mother, Annie.

way Comans declared war on foul play, declaring that stiff-arm tackles, gouging, biting, use of elbows and spear tackles had no place on the sporting field. His own crash-tackles – via sentences long enough to shock, and in one or two cases to end careers – drove home a vitally needed message.

■ The Super League War of 1995-96-97. If rugby's internecine split of 1907-08 was a revolution – then this was the game's civil war, wreaking havoc as war tends to do, bringing vast change. As journalist Mike Colman commented when his fine 1996 book *Super League: The Inside Story* was launched – the full story of what took place, and the implications of what it

all meant may not be known for another decade. The 'war' was about a lot of things – about new technology (Pay TV) arriving in an old game, about festering discontent in some quarters at a NSWRL-ARL regime seen as too sleek and comfortable; perhaps even about an ancient seam of ill-feeling that had existed between NSW and Queensland for most of league's life. It was, after all, in the boardroom of the Broncos of Brisbane that the first seeds were sown. It is true that the robust interest of a major corporation (News Limited) in rugby league was in its own way a significant compliment to the game – evidence of what James J Giltinan's dream had grown into by 1994, when every indicator showed it at unprecedented levels of popularity. The words Super League are no longer in the lexicon – but the dramatic events that overtook the game in its name have changed rugby league forever.

The game's passing parade since 1908, when South Sydney won a competition which began on a gloriously sunny Easter Monday at Wentworth Park and Birchgrove Oval and when Dally Messenger dazzled and amazed wherever he went, has been a marvellously colourful story. Many words sit comfortably alongside those two at the core: RUGBY LEAGUE – drama, controversy, bravery and brilliance among them.

Once it was just a game that blokes played on a Saturday afternoon at the end of the working week. Today at its highest level it is a mix of sport-entertainment-business – packaged, marketed, promoted, hyped. Yet, for all of that, it is not so very different. Rugby league, as we enter the year 2000, is still essentially about 13 against 13 (even though drawn from 17 these days), an 80-minute game played on a grassed rectangle – a brave man with a whistle in the middle of the throng, somehow trying to make sense of it all, knowing he can never provide total satisfaction. Today's athletes are bigger, faster, stronger – by far – but their job is the same as it was for Messenger, McKivat, Howard Hallett and co back then – to score the tries, kick the goals and do your darndest to stop the other mob from doing the same.

Coaches were once the things that conveyed the teams to matches. Today they are the cutting edge, wired-for-sound, hands-on, clipboard-carrying, puppet masters of the game, imposing more influence by a fair space on rugby league's directions than any other group.

A time tunnel trip in 1999 past famous and infamous league moments would produce a kaleidoscope of images far too overwhelming for one mind to absorb. In a single sweep you'd see Harold Horder dodging; the Earl Park mob rioting; England and Australia locked in an endless life-and-death Test battle; Dave Brown sprinting; Churchill inspiring; St George dominating; referee Aub Oxford leaving kicking and punching Poms and Aussies to it at the SCG,

one afternoon in 1954; Johnny Sattler, jaw broken, refusing to say die; Johnny Raper scything; Frank Hyde roaring; Beetson blockbusting; Puig-Aubert turning his back – then kicking a goal; Brian Bevan, all bandages and baldness, scoring try after try; Ray Price praying; Jack Gibson wisecracking (with the emphasis on wise); the Cauldron crowd roaring; Wally Lewis controlling – so completely he could be in a dinner suit; Ron Coote striding; Ken Irvine sizzling; Brad Fittler swerving; Gorden Tallis steam-rolling; Darren Albert proving after all that miracles do happen; 88,000 at a State of Origin match and a world record league crowd of 107,961 at a grand final. That'd be just for starters!

In short, you'd see a helluva game – with a past so unbelievably colourful, that the 21st century future is, surely, guaranteed – notwithstanding the bumpy ride of the recent changing seasons. You'd see a game that won over the hearts and minds of the people of NSW and Queensland with astonishing speed in the early years – and never for an instant let loose the grip. You'd see a game that has been called the toughest body contact sport in the world, and probably is. You'd see what many Aussies are proud to call: our game. Recognising rugby league's place in the sporting winters of the Australian century, *The Daily Telegraph* begins a journey of celebration and acclaim for 'the greatest game'. Enjoy the experience as we revisit famous football days, famous men, and unforgettable games ...

Bigger, faster, stronger ... State of Origin players Brad Fittler and Allan Langer epitomised the modern footballer, but their job was not much different to the pioneers of yesteryear

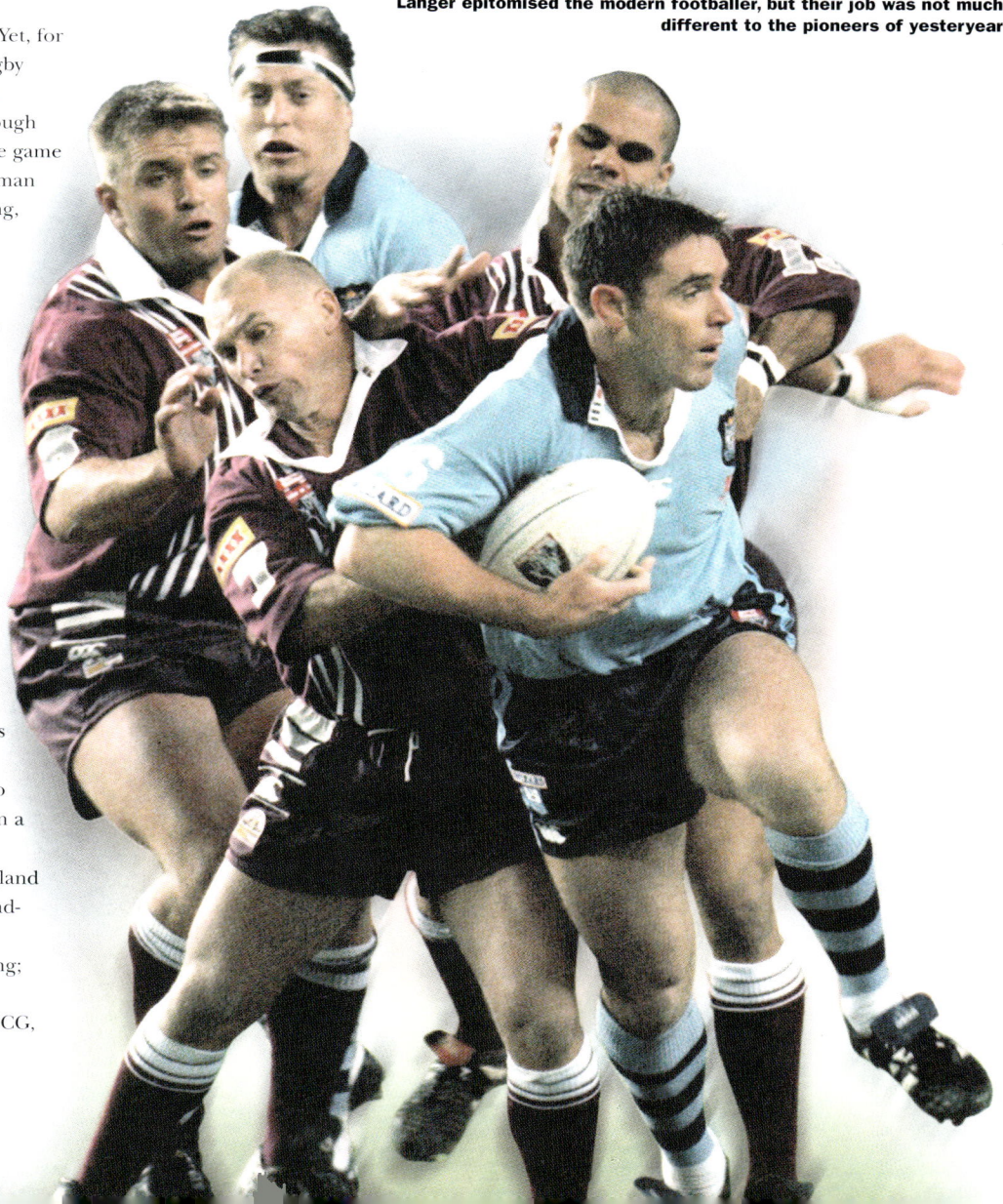

Master of courage

CLIVE Churchill – rugby league's Little Master – was a player whose skill and daring made him a legendary figure in the game.

But Churchill's brave performance for South Sydney one afternoon at Redfern Oval in the winter of 1955 ranks among the most courageous league has ever seen.

In one of the code's most amazing stories, Churchill played almost the entire game against Manly with a broken wrist.

And not only that, the plucky fullback, arm hanging limply by his side, somehow managed to boot a mighty sideline conversion in the dying seconds to earn the Rabbitohs a vital win.

For Souths, that win proved the catalyst to one of league's greatest comebacks. Second last at the halfway mark of the season, the Rabbitohs were written off by just about every critic in town.

But the Manly win proved a turning point in the Rabbitohs' season. Even without Churchill – sidelined for the rest of the season as a result of his injury – Souths won 11 sudden-death games in a row to claim the title.

But back to Redfern on that afternoon in June, 1955. Souths had lost seven of their first 10 matches and looked finished as a premiership force.

With a galaxy of star players like Churchill, Bernie Purcell, Jack Rayner and Col Donohoe, it was only a matter of time before Souths came good. They beat Newtown, Balmain, Canterbury, Parramatta, Easts and Wests and were fast gaining momentum.

But every game was a grand final and a loss to Manly would have effectively ended their season.

Just six minutes into the game, Churchill went in to make a tackle on Manly winger George Hugo and heard his wrist snap.

He knew the arm was broken but, in the era of no replacements, refused to come from the field in a move that would have left his team a man short.

Churchill was virtually a passenger and at halftime was urged not to return by club officials.

WHAT A GAME! SOUTHS v MANLY 1955

But Churchill would not hear of it. The club doctor put an ice cream stick on either side of his fractured wrist, holding them in place with an exercise book cover wrapped in tape.

The match was a tight one. Some 16 minutes from fulltime, Manly winger John Hobbs picked up a loose ball and sprinted 40m to score, putting the Sea Eagles ahead 7-4.

With less than five minutes on the clock, Souths finally drew level when lock Les Cowie barged over in the corner.

A draw was no good to Souths – they had to win to stay alive and skipper Rayner was unsure whether Churchill, in tremendous pain, was up to the conversion attempt.

After some deliberation, Rayner tossed the ball to 'The Little Master', who placed it on the mound with his good arm, calmly walked back and sent it sailing between the posts for a dramatic 9-7 win.

Churchill's courage gave Souths the impetus to go on with the job. They won their next three matches to reach the grand final and then disposed of Newtown 12-11 in a thrilling finale to the season. 🏉

The Little Master ... Clive Churchill's courage gave Souths the impetus to go on and win the 1955 title

1900-09

AUGUST 17, 1907: The first match is played under banner of the NSWRL. NSW meet A H Baskiville's **New Zealand 'All Golds'** at Sydney's Agricultural Ground (old Showground) under rugby union rules. New Zealand win the game 12-8, but fittingly, the great star of the Australian game, Dally Messenger, scores the first try and kicks the first goal.

JANUARY 9, 1908: Glebe become the first club side formed to play in the 1908 NSWRL premiership. A meeting is held at Glebe Town Hall and the club's first patron is **W M Hughes**, who became better known as Australian Prime Minister, Billy Hughes.

JANUARY 14, 1908: Newtown follows the lead of Glebe to become the second club side formed. One by one rugby players make the jump to the new game. Newtown rugby union club ceases to exist in 1912.

JANUARY 17, 1908: A meeting is held in the Redfern Town Hall to form the South Sydney club. Prominent rugby union player **Arthur Hennessy** had held meetings at his home in Chapman Street, Surry Hills, over the summer months of 1907-08 with a view to forming a district club. The support he generated led to an overwhelming vote in favour of a switch to the new game.

JANUARY 23, 1908: Around 600 people attend a 'rowdy' meeting at the Balmain Town Hall and local players Robert Hutcheson and Robert Graves move 'that the Balmain District Rugby League Football Club be now formed'. The motion is carried enthusiastically.

Man
'Dally' Messenger

THE arguments have raged for as long as the game has been played. Who was the better player – Dave Brown or Reg Gasnier? Howard Hallett or Clive Churchill? Bob Fulton or Wally Lewis?

Comparing players from different eras is a pastime fraught with danger. As soon as someone utters that the players of today are fitter, faster and stronger than their predecessors, the arguments begin.

Modern critics tell you that today's game is so fast and the players so highly skilled that the players of yesteryear could not compete. But what if the early players were afforded the same opportunities as today's?

How good would the great winger of the 1920s, Norths' Harold Horder, have been if he had been a fulltime professional? If he followed the weights and sprint training regime of today's players or undertook the same specialised diet?

They are questions without answers but it is always a tantalising talking point, no matter on which side of the fence you sit.

The game's greatest star of the early years was Herbert Henry 'Dally' Messenger, a centre without peer. It was his signature on the dotted line that virtually sealed the future of the movement that broke away from rugby union in Australia in 1907.

Many of Dally M's feats have become the subject of folklore. He is documented to have kicked goals from 65m, landed field goals while one leg was held by the opposition and dived over fullbacks to score tries.

Herbert Henry 'Dally' MESSENGER
Born: April 12, 1883.
Died: Nov 24, 1959.
Played: 1907-13.
Club: Eastern Suburbs.
Position: Centre.
Playing weight: 79kg (12st 6lb).
Height: 173cm (5ft 8in).
Tests: 10 (7 for Australia, 3 for NZ).
Career games: 140.
Career points: 998.

on Man
v Ryan Girdler

Messenger still holds the record for the most points scored in an interstate match – 32 in one game in 1910. But followers of the game today would be surprised to learn that Messenger wasn't much different in stature to Allan Langer. Dally M was slightly taller but the regular playing weight of the pair was almost identical.

Messenger would be dwarfed by most of today's centres. Take Penrith and NSW centre Ryan Girdler. He is about the average height and weight of a top class, modern-day centre.

Girdler stands at 182cm (6ft) and weighs 90kg (14st 6lb). By comparison, Messenger was 173cm (5ft 8in) and 79kg (12st 6lb).

Messenger, though, was not small for a player of his day. No member of the first Kangaroo touring side stood taller than 182cm (6ft) and the heaviest forward weighed just 99kg (15st 8lb).

Dally Messenger was the champion of his day. He stood head and shoulders above the other players of the era and it is safe to say, given the opportunities and circumstances of players in the 1990s, that he would be a champion today. But would he run rings around Ryan Girdler? We will never know. 🏉

Ryan GIRDLER
Born: September 19, 1972.
Played: From 1991.
Clubs: Illawarra, Penrith.
Position: Centre.
Playing weight: 93kg (14st 6lb).
Height: 182cm (6ft).
Tests: 1.
Career games: 152.
Career points: 1,110.

JANUARY 24, 1908: Paddington Town Hall is the scene for the formation of the Eastern Suburbs club. **Harry 'Jersey' Flegg** is appointed Easts' first captain – one of many hats he wore in that first season. He was the club's first secretary, first captain, delegate to the NSWRL and a foundation selector of the club. He later became a long-term president of the NSWRL.

FEBRUARY 4, 1908: The Western Suburbs club is formed at a meeting at the Ashfield Town Hall.

FEBRUARY 7, 1908: A meeting is held at the North Sydney School of Arts in Mount Street, North Sydney, where the seventh district club of the NSWRL is formed.

APRIL 9, 1908: A birth notice appears in The Newcastle Herald: 'League: NSW Rugby Football League of a son, born today, on Showground, baptised on Saturday. Both doing well.' A **Newcastle team** joins the seven Sydney-based clubs, with plans to travel to Sydney each weekend to play.

APRIL 20, 1908: The opening day of club rugby league in Australia. Double-headers are played at Wentworth Park and Birchgrove Oval, with around 3000 people turning up to both venues. At Wentworth Park, Easts beat Newtown 32-16 and Glebe down Newcastle 8-5. At Birchgrove, Souths beat Norths 11-7 and Balmain whitewash Wests 24-0.

⟨ **21** ⟩

The Evolution of Headquarters...

1900-09

On the same day, 23 members of the Western Suburbs Rugby Union Club meet at the Horse and Jockey Hotel at Flemington to form a ninth premiership club, Cumberland.

MAY 9, 1908: Australia play in their first Test match, against the New Zealand side, which had returned from its long tour to Great Britain. New Zealand win a thrilling match 11-10, with Dally Messenger missing a late goal which could have won the game for Australia.

JULY 11, 1908: New South Wales and Queensland meet at the Agricultural Ground in the game's first interstate clash. Referee Fred

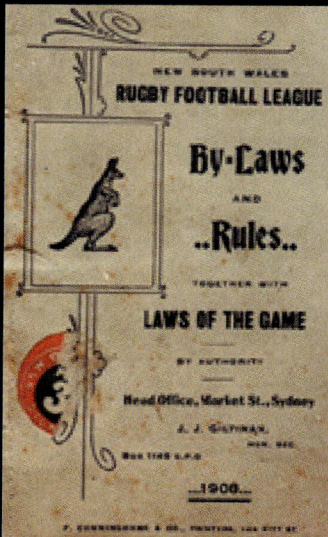

Henlen loses track of time and lets the first half run for 53 minutes. With a near Test line-up, NSW lead 20-0 at the break and go on to beat the novice Queenslanders 43-0.

AUGUST 15, 1908: The first Kangaroos, a team of 34 players and manager Jim Giltinan, sail for England aboard the SS *Macedonia*. The tourists would endure five months of ice, rain and severe economic hardships as well as a gruelling 46-match program.

The **Agricultural Ground** (above) at Moore Park was rugby league's early headquarters but some major fixtures were also played at Birchgrove Oval and Wentworth Park.

In 1911, the league hierarchy moved its big games to the adjacent **Sydney Cricket Ground**, a roomier venue which developed a special league flavour. The Saturday afternoon 'match of the day' became a wonderful tradition, packing the crowds in during the St George club's domination from the late 1950s to 1966. Some of the greatest Test matches of all time were played at the SCG and it was with much sadness that league vacated the ground to take up residence at the newly built **Sydney Football Stadium** (below left) in season 1988.

As the years rolled on, the SFS developed its own special character. It hosted a string of gripping State of Origin games and grand finals. The extra-time Balmain-Canberra decider of 1989 and the Newcastle-Manly thriller of 1997 are among the finest played in any era.

This year has seen the code adopt the ultimate home base: the fabulous, new **Stadium Australia** (below) at Homebush Bay. It's a space-aged, state-of-the-art complex which provides first-class facilities for up to 110,000 fans

Birth of a club...

A large crowd gathered at Redfern Town Hall on January 17, 1908 where the vote to start the South Sydney Rugby League Club was 'overwhelming'. Little did those present realise they had witnessed the birth of an Australian sporting institution. By March, Souths had training under way at Moore Park with an enthusiastic bunch of recruits. The club played its first competition game against Norths on Easter Monday, April 20, winning a dour game 11-7, with winger Tommy Anderson

scoring the club's first try. Souths won the first premiership final against Easts in 1908 by 14-12.

COLOURS

In its first year the club wore its famous cardinal and myrtle colours, the same as the rugby union team.

NICKNAME

Legend has it some members of the old South Sydney rugby union club were 'rabbitohs', who hawked rabbits through the district wearing their jerseys.

The way we were...

1906: Melbourne police are urged to take action against speeding motorists who travel at 20mph, instead of the legal 12mph. Bondi Surf Life Saving Club founded. Tennis coach Henry Christian (Harry) Hopman is born and wheat grower William Farrer dies.

1907: Future aviator **Charles Kingsford-Smith**, aged nine, is rescued in the surf off Bondi. Telephone trunk line opens between Sydney and Melbourne. Ernest Edward 'Weary' Dunlop, surgeon and soldier, is born. Left-handed Australian tennis player Norman Brookes becomes first foreigner to win Wimbledon.

1908: Cricketer **Donald Bradman** is born. French Government protests over Australia's use of the term 'champagne'. Rail collision at Sunshine, Victoria, kills 46, injures 414. Australian boys join Boy Scout movement, founded by Robert Baden-Powell. American fighter Jack Johnson beats Canadian Tommy Burns at Sydney Stadium to become the first black world heavyweight champion.

1909: Sydney journalist and engineer George Taylor becomes first Australian to fly when his 'heavier-than-air' biplane successfully takes off at Narrabeen Beach. Electricity used in sheep shearing for first time.

1900-09

AUGUST 29, 1908: South Sydney and Eastern Suburbs meet in the first premiership final. Although star players from both sides were already en route to England with the first Kangaroos, the match is hard-fought and entertaining. Easts winger Horrie Miller scores a try which covered the length of the field diagonally, but Souths become the first premiers winning 14-12.

OCTOBER 3, 1908: The Kangaroos play their first match, beating Welsh side Mid-Rhondda 20-6 at Tonypandy. A crowd of over 700 are enthralled by the war cry of the tourists.

DECEMBER 12, 1908: The first Ashes Test is played between Australia and England at London's Park Royal ground. The match finishes in a 22-all draw.

JANUARY 23, 1909: England defeat Australia 15-5 at St James Park, Newcastle, in the second Test match.

Team of the Decade...
1900-1909

Arthur 'Pony' Halloway

A team dominated by Eastern Suburbs players despite South Sydney capturing the first two New South Wales Rugby League premierships. 'Dally' Messenger, The Master, and the dominant force in the game in the early years, gives this Team of the Decade a touch of enduring class.

Fullback: Mick BOLEWSKI (Bundaberg).
Wingers: Dan FRAWLEY (Easts), Albert ROSENFELD (Easts).
Centres: 'Dally' MESSENGER (Easts), Jim DEVEREUX (North Sydney).
Five-eighth: Arthur BUTLER (Souths).
Halfback: Arthur 'Pony' HALLOWAY (Glebe, Easts).
Lock: Bill CANN (Souths).
Secondrowers: Robert GRAVES (Balmain), Tedda COURTNEY (Newtown, Wests).
Frontrowers: Alex BURDON (Glebe), Larry 'Jersey' O'MALLEY (Easts).
Hooker: 'Sandy' PEARCE (Easts).

'Sandy' Pearce

1900-09

FEBRUARY 15, 1909: With Dally Messenger missing through injury, Australia go down 6-5 to England in the deciding third Test at Birmingham's Villa Park.

MARCH 15, 1909: The NSWRL's founding management team of Hoyle, Trumper and Giltinan are dumped at an explosive meeting of the League in Sydney. The trio are thrown out amid accusations of mismanagement.

AUGUST 27, 1909: The NSWRL place their imprimatur on a privately run series of matches between the Kangaroos and the Wallabies. In one of the game's great coups, a large number of the country's most prominent rugby union players accept lucrative inducements to switch codes and play in a series of matches, underwritten by entrepreneur **James Joynton Smith**. The influx of top talent virtually seals the future of rugby league in Australia.

SEPTEMBER 4, 1909: A crowd of 18,000 watch the first of the Kangaroos-Wallabies matches at the Agricultural Ground.

SEPTEMBER 18, 1909: Controversy erupts when the fourth Kangaroos-Wallabies match is scheduled for the same day as the premiership final between Balmain and South Sydney. Balmain declare the League's decision to play the final as a preliminary to a representative match is an insult to the two club sides and refuse to play. Souths do not share the views of their opponents and they turn up, score a farcical try and are declared premiers.

WE SELECT THE BEST
The Great 100

COMPARING and ranking players from different eras rarely provides satisfaction for anyone other than family and friends of those nominated as the best.

Despite that inescapable position there are few exercises guaranteed to spark raging debate than publishing a list of rugby league's Top 100 Australian players.

The Daily Telegraph panel of Peter Frilingos, Frank Stanton, Wally O'Connell, Ian Heads and David Middleton agonised for weeks before producing what we believe to be the definitive list of the game's finest players.

So rich was the pool of talent that we could easily have come up with another 100 players from all eras who could credibly challenge our list.

Our panel had the capacity to go back to the 1940s to judge first hand the talents from those days and for earlier eras the resources of noted league historian Middleton through statistics and media reports provided an insight into the game way back when.

There were no definitive guidelines for ranking the players other than to take into account playing records at all levels of the game backed by that intangible factor – opinion.

Some of the players ranked highly in our 100 might have played only one or two Test matches while others with 20 internationals to their credit finished lower down the list.

For example two players from the 1940s and 1950s, Harry Bath and Brian Bevan, did not play for Australia yet rank among the game's greats.

Every era has had at least one and often two or three benchmark players, starting with Dally Messenger from 1908 and progressing to Frank Burge 1914-21, Joe 'Chimpy' Busch from the 1920s, Dave Brown from the 1930s and so on, all the way up to the Laurie Daleys and Brad Fittlers of today.

Messenger was named 'The Master' for his exploits and it wasn't until Clive Churchill exploded on the scene in the late 1940s that it was deemed appropriate to elevate another player to that status.

Churchill became known as the 'The Little Master' and now 14 years after his untimely death his position in the game's pantheon of greats remains unchallenged.

It was Churchill who perfected the fullback's running game. His injection into the South Sydney and Australian backline dazzled fans and frazzled opposition teams like no other fullback.

He also played through one of South Sydney's golden eras when the side won five premierships between 1950 and 1955 under the leadership of another great in powerful forward Jack Rayner.

After his retirement Churchill coached Souths to four premierships (1967-68 and 1970-71) as the era of limited tackle football changed the face of the game forever.

The late 1950s and 1960s saw a rash of talent emerge headed by St George players Reg Gasnier, Johnny Raper and Graeme Langlands.

They were all part of the world record St George team that won 11 straight premierships between 1956 and 1966.

OF THE CENTURY

Rugby league icon Norm Provan played in 10 of those 11 premiership teams and he also takes his place in the top 100 along with forward contemporaries like teammate Ian Walsh and Wests' Kel O'Shea.

In the 1960s there were many people willing to compare Gasnier, Raper and Langlands with Messenger and Churchill.

Gasnier or 'Puff the Magic Dragon', as he became known, accelerated with a silky smooth action that the game had never before, or ever again, experienced.

He scored three tries on his Test debut in England on the 1959 Kangaroo tour and his status as the Prince of Centres was never challenged until his premature retirement from a chronic knee injury in 1967.

Raper's resilience and uncanny ball skills were matched by Langlands's freakish sidestep and his ability to handle fullback, wing or centre at Test level.

Testimony to Langlands's ability came from 'The Little Master' himself who said 'Changa' Langlands was the best all-round footballer he had seen.

Like Langlands, Manly's Bob Fulton came from the Illawarra district at 18 to stamp himself as a player way above the ordinary.

At centre and five-eighth, Fulton led Australia to Ashes victory against Great Britain as a player and later as a coach.

Born in Warrington, England and moving to Australia as an infant, Fulton was the 'one who got away' from the Old Dart and had he stayed in the northern hemisphere who is to say he would not have achieved just as much playing and coaching over there.

Forwards Arthur Beetson, Ron Coote and Bob McCarthy came out of that 1960s period to earn recognition as the best in their positions at international level.

Beetson ranks with Raper as a skilful player and those talents coupled with his speed and bulk probably stand him in a class of his own as a prop or secondrower.

Pundits from the 1920s who saw Glebe forward Frank Burge play Test football would be likely to disagree.

On the 1921-22 Kangaroo tour the English press described Burge as "the greatest tryscoring forward in the world" and considering his 33 tries on that tour stands as a record for a forward, the rapturous praise was not surprising.

The 1970s saw Graham Eadie, Mick Cronin, Steve Rogers, Craig Young and Ray Price head a new breed of footballer who by the 1980s were to achieve world dominance for Australia.

In 1982 Frank Stanton coached the first Kangaroo side to go through a tour of England and France undefeated with players like Rogers, Price, Young, Brett Kenny and skipper Max Krilich in the vanguard.

Champion five-eighth Wally Lewis led Don Furner's 1986 Kangaroos down the same invincible path and went on to epitomise State of Origin football as Queensland's captain.

Lewis and Fulton usually go head-to-head for best-ever honours at five-eighth and this panel had difficulty in placing one in front of the other.

The current crop of stars lose little by comparison with players from previous eras with the recently retired Allan 'Alfie' Langer and **Glenn Lazarus** (pictured) heading the charge.

Was Langer a better halfback than Peter Sterling, Keith Holman or Duncan Thompson and Chimpy Busch from the 1920s?

Or are Brad Fittler and Laurie Daley superior to Lewis, Fulton, Pat Devery, Frank Stanmore or Brian Clay when they were in their prime?

Unanswerable questions maybe, but our top 100 will hopefully stimulate debate again as league's fabulous century draws to a close. 🏉

The Judges

PETER FRILINGOS
The Daily Telegraph's chief rugby league writer and the game's No 1 reporter. In a career spanning 35 years, he has covered four Kangaroo tours, three World Cups, every Origin series and the club matches that mattered since 1964.

IAN HEADS
Covered rugby league and major sport for *The Daily* and *The Sunday Telegraph* for 18 years, during a career which now spans 35 seasons. He has authored or co-authored 20 books on sport – including True Blue (official history of the NSWRL) and The Kangaroos (story of the league tours to England and France from 1908).

DAVID MIDDLETON
Recognised as rugby league's leading historian and statistician, Middleton has been editor of the official league yearbook since early 1988. Middleton worked at *Rugby League Week* for nine years before establishing his own agency, League Information Services. Also covers league for Channel Nine and 2UE.

FRANK STANTON
Former Kangaroo centre who has built a magnificent record as coach and administrator. Coached Manly to premierships in 1976 and '78 and was national coach from 1978-82. Has served as Manly's chief executive since December 1992.

WALLY O'CONNELL
A star five-eighth for Eastern Suburbs and Manly Warringah in the 1940s and early 50s. Played in five Tests on the 1948 Kangaroo tour and captained Australia in the first Test against England. Coached the Sea Eagles in 1966 and 1967.

EDITOR'S NOTE: Wally O'Connell was voted into The Great 100 by the other four judges and therefore takes his place on merit.

Glenn LAZARUS
Born: 1965

100 FEW players have enjoyed greater success over a longer period than Glenn Lazarus, who represented Australia in the front row in 20 Tests (1990-99). A Queanbeyan junior, Lazarus began his top grade career with Canberra in 1987 and played in the club's first two premiership-winning sides in 1989 and 1990 before transferring to Brisbane in 1992, where he tasted grand final success in '92 and '93. Lazarus was foundation captain of 1999 Premiers Melbourne Storm. Toured with the Kangaroos 1990, 1994.

Paul SIRONEN
Born: 1965

96 STANDING 194cm tall and weighing more than 110kg, Paul Sironen was a giant of the modern game. The hard-running secondrower made a huge impact for Balmain in his debut year in 1986 and represented Australia the same season. Made his third tour with the Kangaroos in 1994, a rare distinction for a forward. Sironen played a record 246 first grade games for Balmain and appeared in 14 State of Origin matches for NSW. 21 Tests (1986-94), Kangaroo 1986, 1990, 1994.

Frank McMILLAN
1889 - 1966

94 WHEN Frank McMillan died in 1966, Rugby League News described him as 'The Greatest Fullback of his Day'. McMillan was Australia's fullback from 1929-34 and played all nine of his Tests against the old foe, England. A tall, spindly player, McMillan was known as 'Skinny', but his slight frame belied his abilities. Had long career with Wests, playing in the club's first premiership win in 1930 and leading them to victory in 1934. Captained the Kangaroos in 1933-34. Nine Tests (1929-34), toured with the Kangaroos 1929-30, 1933-34.

Kevin RYAN
Born: 1934

99 KEVIN 'Kandos' Ryan had already walked the international stage as a rugby union player when he signed a league contract with St George in 1960. Ryan developed into one of the hardest, toughest forwards in one of the game's most physical eras. Played in seven winning grand finals for Saints before helping to plot their downfall in 1967 as captain-coach of Canterbury. Ryan's attack and defence carried a sledgehammer punch. Two Tests (1963-64), Kangaroo 1963-64.

THE Daily Telegraph

WE SELECT THE BEST OF THE CENTURY

John O'NEILL
1943 - 1999

93 IT is perhaps one of the game's great injustices that the Test career of John 'Lurch' O'Neill was limited to just two matches. One of the toughest and most fearsome forwards of his era, O'Neill carved out a superb career at the top level from 1965-75. He is remembered as a big-match performer and his display in the brutal World Cup final of 1970 was one of his best. O'Neill was also a grand final specialist, winning titles with Souths (1967-68-70-71) and Manly (1972-73). Two Tests (1973-74), toured with Kangaroos 1973.

Gene MILES
Born: 1959

98 GENE Miles began his career in the centres, but finished it as a damaging secondrower. Emerged on the representative scene in 1981 when he first played State of Origin for Queensland. Over next decade was a Maroons regular and played for Australia in 14 Tests. High point of career came in 1986 when he was centre partner to Brett Kenny on undefeated Kangaroo tour. 14 Tests (1983-87), Kangaroo 1982, 1986.

Wayne PEARCE
Born: 1960

97 THERE have been more skilful players to represent Australia, but few with greater dedication than Wayne 'Junior' Pearce. A wholehearted lock or second–rower, Pearce forged a towering career for Balmain, NSW and Australia through the 1980s. Set new standards for personal fitness, playing 192 top grade games for the Tigers, 15 Origin matches and 18 Tests. Cemented a place in the Test side with a superb Kangaroo tour in 1982. 18 Tests (1982-88), Kangaroo 1982.

The Great 100

Ernie NORMAN
1912 - 1993

95 PRODUCT of Easts juniors, Ernie Norman was only 20 when he played in the infamous 'Battle of Brisbane' in 1932. It was the toughest initiation imaginable for the young centre. A report said 'Norman was jumping around like a headless rooster, suffering concussion. He received a terrific hammering, but stood up to it as gallantly as a Trojan'. Norman was a member of the great Easts sides of the 1930s, a fine handler and a grand tackler. 12 Tests (1932-38), Kangaroo 1937-38.

Frank STANMORE
Born: 1919

92 SMALL, strongly built five-eighth, Stanmore formed a potent scrumbase combination with halfback Keith Holman for Wests, NSW and Australia during the early 1950s. Stanmore joined Wests from Cessnock in 1948 and played in premiership-winning sides for the Magpies in 1948 and 1952. Career highlight came in third Test against Great Britain in 1950, when Australia won the Ashes for the first time in 30 years. Represented in 10 Tests (1949-53) and toured with the Kangaroos 1952-53.

Wally O'CONNELL
Born: 1923

91 HE was described as the Wally Lewis of the 1940s. A tough, nuggety and highly skilled five-eighth, O'Connell developed into an outstanding leader at all levels of the game. Highlight of his career came on the Kangaroo tour of 1948-49, when he captained Australia in the first Test of the series. O'Connell's career began at Eastern Suburbs in 1942. Made his Test debut in 1948 and in 1951, as captain-coach of Manly, took the club to its first grand final appearance. Represented in 10 Tests (1948-51), toured with the Kangaroos 1948-49.

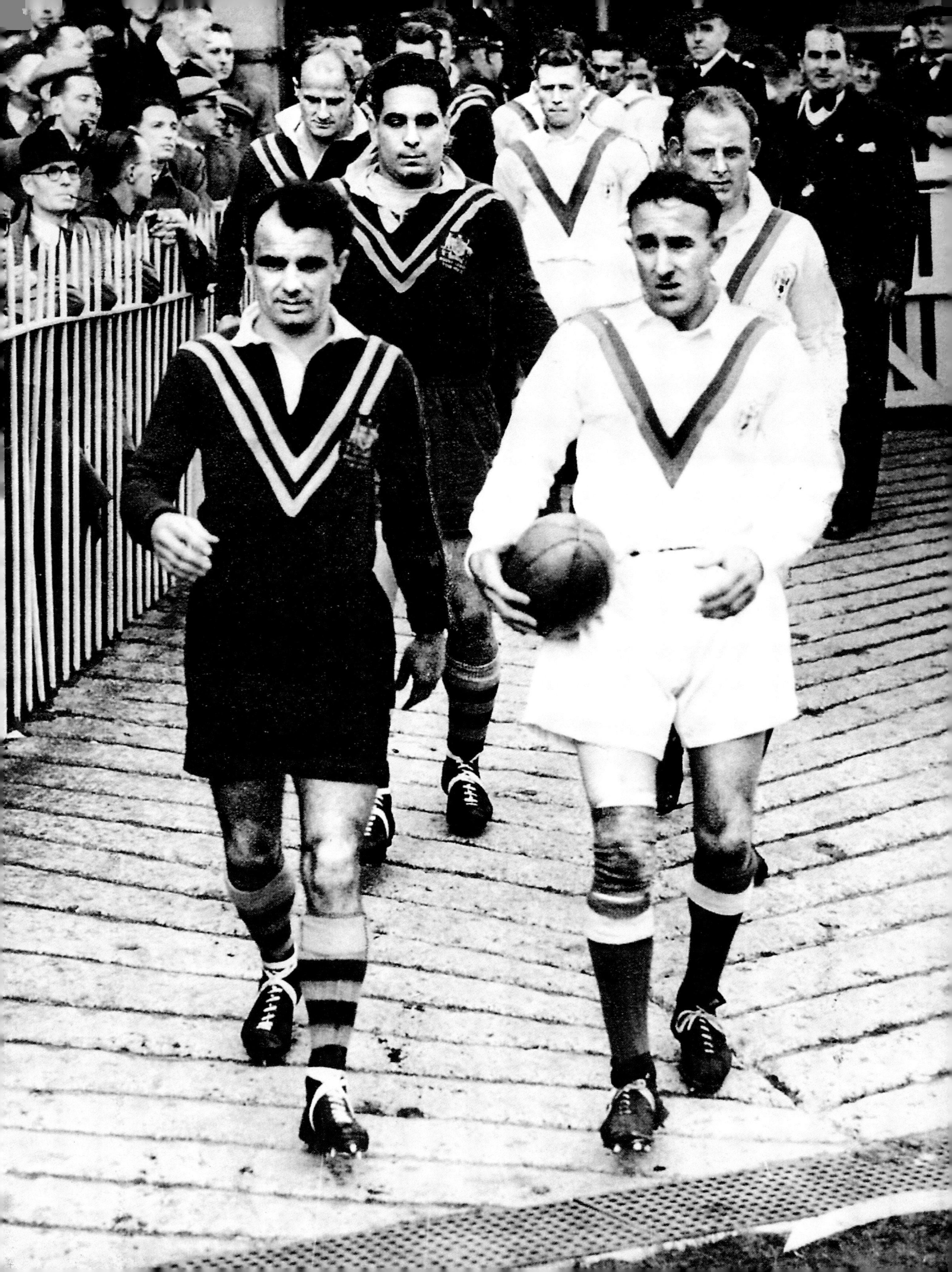

The Test of Men

BY RAY KERSHLER

1910-19

APRIL 30, 1910: Annandale join the eight-team NSWRL premiership, replacing Newcastle, who withdrew at the end of the 1909 season to form their own club competition. Local mayor Alfred Milson kicks off when North Sydney celebrate their first match at a new ground, North Sydney Oval.

MAY 10, 1910: A four-team club competition kicks off in Newcastle, featuring South, North, Central and West Newcastle.

MAY 24, 1910: The first English

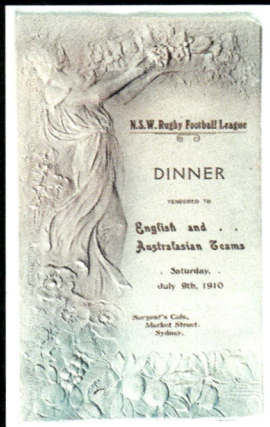

touring side arrives in Australia. Under the captaincy of Jim Lomas, the tourists play 14 matches in Australia and four more in New Zealand.

SEPTEMBER 17, 1910: Newtown and Souths meet in a dramatic premiership final at the Agricultural Ground (Showground). Souths look set to claim their third consecutive title when they lead 4-2 in the late stages. But Newtown centre Albert Hawkes calls 'mark' after catching the ball near halfway. Under the rules of the day, goals are allowable from marks and winger Charlie 'Boxer' Russell makes no mistake with the kick. The scores finish 4-all, but as minor premiers, Newtown are awarded the title.

The Test

# of Men

F ROM the moment Dally Messenger made his momentous decision in 1907 to defect from rugby union, a movement was set in train which would give birth to some of the greatest sporting contests in history.

For while club loyalty and State honours have meant a lot to rugby league players over the past 100 years, the chance to play for their country meant more.

The pride which enveloped a player when he pulled his national jersey over his head manifested itself on the field in a series of memorable clashes which could be, alternately, dazzling or dour, fair or ferocious.

While the first Tests were played between Australia and New Zealand, the clashes between the colonials from Australia and the players from the mother country were the ones which best illustrated the rivalry of the contest.

Generations of fans would become mesmerised by the sight of an England team which walked sombrely and menacingly on to the pitch while their Australian opponents sprinted and stepped and swerved on to the arena.

While the word 'professional' was associated with rugby league, the code's early days were anything but. The first Test match played on the Australian tour to England of 1908 featured one of the Australians, Albert Conlon, as a touch judge. He might otherwise have remained little known but for the fact he signalled a goal from Messenger which had drifted wide of the posts. The decision helped Australia to a 22-all draw.

Two years later, England toured Australia and New Zealand and again played against Messenger in two Tests and also in two matches against an Australasian team which included Maori players.

The England winger James Leytham helped cement an antagonism which lives to this day when he criticised Australian crowds:

'I have not been impressed by what I have seen so far of the Australian spectator. He is a one-sided individual, shouts with glee when we are put down, and hoots when a Britisher brings a colonial to the ground.'

Further antagonism was assured when the English management criticised the refereeing standards.

Leytham had said: 'The referee can see only one side and he interprets the rules badly.'

Insult was added to injury when the tour manager, Joe Houghton, on the way home, told reporters from, of all papers, the *Ceylon Sportsman*: 'We should have won matches even more decisively but for absolutely bad refereeing.'

From the moment those comments made their way back to Australia, refereeing controversies and crowd rivalry were forever interwoven into the game.

In pursuit ... Joe 'Chimpy' Busch chases down an Englishman in the fourth and deciding Test on the 1929-30 Kangaroo tour

The English underestimated the ability of the Australians to improve their game and Chris McKivat's tourists won an historic series undefeated in 1911-12.

McKivat returned serve when he said before returning home: 'I put down our successes chiefly to the fact the British player does not possess the pace of the colonials. Your men are too orthodox. Passing from man to man is pretty to watch, no doubt, but you want to perfect the cut-in and the inside passing to be a success.'

Australia had become a more powerful rugby league nation than England but the trick now was to maintain the gap.

Within a few short years of those somewhat tentative fixtures there was a game played which would set in blood a rivalry to last to the end of the millennium.

The Rorke's Drift Test match at the SCG in 1914 – a brutal affair – is the stuff of legend. Never after that game was played would either Australian or British teams take the field without the highest respect for each other.

By the 1920s the Test series were still creating history and Australia won the Ashes on Australian soil for the first time. Bill Richards, the Queensland forward, created a little bit of history of his own when he became the first Australian player to be sent off in an Ashes Test.

Australia's 1929-30 tour of England produced, quite remarkably, the only Ashes series in which four Tests were played.

A chance remark 'When's the replay?' to the Australian captain Tom Gorman after a 0-0 draw in the third Test tied the series, resulted in the English league arranging a deciding Test.

The Australians believed they had won the series when Joe 'Chimpy' Busch scored in the corner with two minutes to go.

Despite referee Bob Robinson conceding he thought it was a fair try, the touch judge Albert Webster ruled Busch had knocked over the corner flag first.

Busch would later emphatically claim he cleanly put the ball down half a metre inside the post.

The fourth Test was arranged because of the claim England were deemed to have kept the Ashes by being the holders. This became an accepted practice in later series, but in this case it was academic when England won the only fourth Test ever played 3-0.

Meanwhile, attempts to spread the game in France had been undertaken since 1921, but an Australian team did not play in the country until 1933, and on New Year's Eve on a frozen ground they beat England 63-13 in an exhibition match.

In 1937-38, Fred Gilbert made a name for himself by becoming the first Australian to score a try in a Test against France – a length-of-the-field intercept.

The brilliant Dave Brown, appointed at 22 as the youngest captain of Australia and being hailed as the Don Bradman of rugby league, led Australia in a home series in 1936 with war clouds hovering over Europe.

Brown's team lost the series 2-1, highlighted by the dismissal twice in three Tests of the rugged Australian prop Ray Stehr.

England successfully defended the Ashes against Wally Prigg's tourists in 1937, but another Test would not be played for 10 years as the world was engulfed in war.

Gus Risman, a veteran of campaigns in Libya and Italy, led the English tourists back to Australia after the war. Although local sporting contests, including rugby league, had been allowed to continue in Australia in the war years, Risman's tourists surprisingly triumphed.

The war had made no difference to tactics and the pre-war dominance of the scrums by England continued to be a problem for Australia.

The first Test at the SCG had been sold out and the overflow crowd in Moore Park listened to a description of the game.

In 1948 came the greatest selection shock in rugby league history when Len Smith, the incumbent captain, was left out of the Kangaroos touring team in what has been described as 'one of the greatest injustices ever done to any man in any sport'. Catholic-Mason rivalry was blamed.

Amazingly, in a tour of acrimony, a Test was played which would light up the game for generations.

War cry ... the 1956-57 Kangaroos announce their intentions before the Wigan Test

The way we were...

1910: Act of parliament creates Australian Navy. First Australian banknotes printed. Record crowd of 100,000 sees Comedy King (10/1) win Melbourne Cup at Flemington. Empire mourns death of **Edward VII**.

1911: Commonwealth Bank is established. Tragedy off coast of northern Queensland when Adelaide Steamship Company's *Yongala* is wrecked in a storm off Townsville and 122 die. Australia's population reaches 4,455,005.

Eccentric Frenchman ... goalkicking fullback Puig-Aubert thrilled the Sydney Cricket Ground crowd with his unorthodox style

Casting aside all animosity, the two nations thrilled the crowd with a match in which 12 tries were scored as Britain won 23-21 in a classic encounter.

Led by Colin Maxwell, the Australians again lost the series as the secretary of the Australian Board of Control, Keith Sharp, prepared to spend months in Britain trying to fathom the English supremacy in the game.

Two years later all such thoughts vanished as a muddy Ron Roberts scored the try which gave Australia a series victory for the first time in 30 years.

Australia let down their guard when France visited a year later. Led by the eccentric French fullback Puig-Aubert – who did not believe fullbacks should tackle and backed up his beliefs by inaction – the French beat Australia 2-1 in the series with Puig-Aubert proving one of the most popular footballers to tour this country.

In the '50s, Australia was involved in 14 tours. The dominance of the St George club side toward the end of the decade began to show through in the national side as players such as Norm Provan, Reg Gasnier and Johnny Raper established their reputations.

In 1959, Gasnier scored three tries in his first British Test but with the help of the unpopular English referee 'Sergeant Major' Eric Clay, Britain won the series 2-1, the last time Australia was to lose a series in England.

When in 1962 Ken Irvine kicked a goal from the touchline (with the help of referee Darcy Lawler who suggested a readjustment to his line), Australia was saved the embarrassment of a 3-0 whitewash.

In 1963 Australia played two Tests against South Africa, winning both comfortably. The strong South African rugby union and the increasing criticism of the country's apartheid policy ensured there would be no more, although an 86-6 Australian victory at the 1995 World Cup is officially classified as a Test and Australia's biggest victory.

I was there...

Australia v Great Britain, first Test, 1959

'They ended up calling him Puff The Magic Dragon and Reg Gasnier was certainly magical in his Ashes debut. The guy was just so fast off the mark and he scored three superb tries in the Swinton Test we won 22-14. Reg had been a sensation at club level for St George and it was obvious he was going to have an even greater impact in an Australian jumper.' **Noel Kelly** (who toured with Gasnier in 1959, '63 and '67).

The way we were...

1912: Sydney's **Fanny Durack** wins gold for 100 yard swim at Stockholm Olympics. Chicago architect Walter Burley Griffin wins first prize in international competition to design Canberra.

1913: Sydney quarantined and all travellers vaccinated due to smallpox epidemic. Bodies of Captain Robert Falcon Scott, Dr Wilson and Lieutenant Bowers found in snow-covered tent in Antarctic. Australia's basic wage is now eight shillings (80 cents) per day.

1914: First Coles variety store opened in Collingwood, Melbourne. Australia's first air mail arrives in Sydney from Melbourne.

The Last Call

Prime Minister Joseph Cook pledges full support to England after its declaration of war on Germany. 'Australia is now at war,' announces the PM and offers 20,000 troops.

1915: The courage and spirit of Australian and NZ troops (**ANZACS**) at Gallipoli wins lavish praise and so begins a proud tradition. BHP Steelworks open at Newcastle.

Late in 1963, Australia toured England and the second Test of a successful series became known as The Swinton Massacre as Australia overwhelmed Britain with superb football, winning 50-12.

Even the recall of referee Clay to help Britain win the third Test could not dim the lustre of that second Test victory.

In 1970 Great Britain reclaimed the Ashes, winning two Sydney Tests in front of 60,000 crowds, but they would not win another series this century.

For some of the greatest rugby league teams in Australian history were in their embryonic stages and Australia was about to dominate the game as never before.

Australia's march to the apex of rugby league competition began with a supreme effort in 1973.

Needing to win the third Test they encountered a ground covered in thick ice on a day when all other sport in Britain was cancelled.

The conditions were totally foreign to the Australians and the challenge ahead of the tourists was clear when English trainer, Paddy Armour, warned that 'heads could crack like egg shells' on the hard Wilderspool Stadium surface.

Led by Tommy Raudonikis, Australia scored five tries to one for a stunning 15-5 victory with Arthur Beetson, Gary Stevens and Ken Maddison starring.

Although Australia played its first Test matches against New Zealand back in 1908, the clashes became sporadic with at times a gap of 16 years and 11 years between engagements.

Australia has always been dominant other than a period in 1952 and 1953 when New Zealand strung together four Test victories in a row.

Tests

Yet England went to an 8-0 lead before the complexion of the game changed. Australia grabbed an 11-8 lead at halftime and then the game became 'deplorably one-sided' in the eyes of one English critic.

The win secured a place in history for McKivat's team. The 1911-1912 Kangaroos became the first team to win a Test match against Great Britain; the first team to take the Ashes away from Great Britain; and the the first team to complete a Test series undefeated.

In the bath after the Third Test victory McKivat *(pictured left)* told reporters: 'Now I can die happy'.

THE THIRD TEST
ENGLAND v AUSTRALASIA
at Villa Park, Birmingham
January 1, 1912

THIS match is not regarded by the British as one of the great clashes in rugby league history. But for the Australians, and certainly historically, the Kangaroos' triumph was one of the best.

Chris McKivat's tourists had already won the first Test 19-10, drew the second 11-11 and they would take the third resoundingly 33-8.

The game started badly for Britain when in the first minute the English forward Dick Ramsdale was hurt, leaving England a man short for the duration.

AUSTRALASIA: Howard Hallett, Dan Frawley, Viv Farnsworth, Herb Gilbert, Tom Berecry, Bill Farnsworth, Chris McKivat (c), Bill Noble, Bob Craig, Bill Cann, Bob Williams, Paddy McCue, Con Sullivan.
ENGLAND: Alf Wood, Bill Batten, Jim Lomas (c), Bert Jenkins, Albert Jenkinson, Will Davies, Fred Smith, Dick Ramsdale, Billy Winstanley, Doug Clark, Tommy Woods, Fred Harrison, Albert Avery.
AUSTRALASIA 33 (Berecry 2, McCue 2, Frawley 2, McKivat 2, V Farnsworth tries; Frawley 2, Gilbert goals.)
ENGLAND 8 (Lomas, Clark tries; Wood goal.)
Referee: Bob Robinson. Crowd: 4000.

In 1967 Australia played NZ in the first clashes under the four-tackle rule with Australia winning the series 3-0.

Since then New Zealand has never quite been able to consistently match the Australians, and tours to Britain with such stars as Steve Mortimer, Peter Sterling, Ray Price, Wayne Pearce, Brett Kenny, Mal Meninga and Wally Lewis returned with the tags The Invincibles and The Unbeatables.

As the century ends, the debate remains as fervent as ever. Which was the greatest Australian rugby league team?

The field can arguably be narrowed to four – the 1911-12, 1963, 1982 or 1986 Kangaroo tourists.

Perhaps it's best to say that in a century of football only four teams came close to perfection.

# of time

THE THIRD TEST
AUSTRALIA v GREAT BRITAIN
at the Sydney Cricket Ground
July 4, 1914

IN 1879, 139 British and colonial troops defended and held the ruins of Rorke's Drift, South Africa, for 12 hours against a horde of 4000 Zulu warriors in one of the legendary battles of British military history.

After this Test at the SCG, when 10 British players held out for a win against a full-strength Australia in one of league's bloodiest battles, the tag Rorke's Drift Test was attached to the match and the British players were later honoured with the initials RD after their name.

The game was prefaced by an antagonistic atmosphere brought about by a late change in Britain's tour schedule which saw them forced to play three Tests in eight days.

A British protest fell on deaf ears with the English League cabling their manager, John Clifford, to accede to Australia's wishes and, almost dismissively, that 'England expected every man to do his duty'.

The British team which had to make four changes from the second Test because of injury was fired up before the match by an inspirational speech by Clifford.

'You are playing in a game of football this afternoon,' he said. 'But more than that you are playing for England. And, more, even, you are playing right versus wrong. You will win because you have to win. Don't forget that message from home: "England expects every man to do his duty".'

What team could fail to be inspired? But fate took a hand. Before the first scrum the England winger Frank Williams hurt his leg and became a passenger. Yet England led 9-0 at halftime.

Early in the second half forward Duggie Clark broke his collarbone, centre Bill Hall was concussed and Williams was finally forced to leave the field. With 30 minutes to go England were playing with 10 men and at one stage only nine men in a defensive line when another player was winded.

Somehow England, guided by captain Harold Wagstaff, held out for a courageous 14-6 victory, despite the second half lasting an agonising 54 minutes because of injury time.

Birth of a club...

Unrest among rugby union players in the west was growing in 1907. The meeting – convened by a local painter named Charlie Elliot – which founded the Magpies was held at Ashfield Town Hall on February 4, 1908.

The club did not have a home ground in the area so matches were played at the RAS Showground, Birchgrove Oval and Wentworth Park. Wests were beaten 24-0 by Balmain in their first game.

COLOURS: The team wore black and white, the same as the Ashfield Metropolitan Rugby Union side.

NICKNAME: Fruitpickers and Cherrypickers, due to orchards in the west. It was the habitat of magpies and references to the team as 'The Magpies' can be traced to 1928.

I was there...

Australia v Great Britain, second Test, 1963

'I played at Swinton the day we smashed the Poms by a record score of 50-12. Our lock Johnny Raper was unbelievable. No one could control him. He ran and off-loaded passes at will – everything he touched turned to gold. He had a hand in nine of our 12 tries. It was the best game I ever saw Chook play.'

Graeme Langlands
(who toured with Raper in 1963 and 1967)

ENGLAND: Alf Wood, Frank Williams, Harold Wagstaff (c), Billy Hall, Willie Davies, Stuart Prosser, Fred Smith, Jack Chilcott, Dick Ramsdale, Duggie Clark, Dave Holland, Percy Coldrick, Albert Johnson.

AUSTRALIA: Howard Hallett, Bob Tidyman, Wally Messenger, Sid Deane (c), Dan Frawley, Charles Fraser, Arthur Halloway, Bill Cann, Bob Craig, Tedda Courtney, Con Sullivan, 'Sandy' Pearce, Frank Burge.

ENGLAND 14 (Davies, Johnson tries; Wood 4 goals.)

AUSTRALIA 6 (Messenger, Deane tries.) Referee: Tom McMahon. Crowd: 34,420.

THE THIRD TEST
AUSTRALIA v GREAT BRITAIN

at the Sydney Cricket Ground
July 22, 1950

THE unfashionable winger Ron Roberts scored the try which enabled Australia to win this Test match – and claim the Ashes for the first time in 30 years.

The try made Roberts a hero but, in truth, Australia's forwards did all the hard work that day.

Rain had swamped the SCG for a week and the British side was expected to revel in the conditions.

But the fitness and endurance of the Australians overcame the guile and experience of the English pack.

The Australian hooker Kevin Schubert convincingly beat Joe Egan in the scrums and forwards such as Bernie Purcell and 'Dutchy' Holland had sensational games.

The memorable try which was to etch Roberts' name into the record books came 16 minutes from the end – with the scores locked 2-all – after an orthodox backline movement. Orthodox on a dry day.

Slick hands astonished both the crowd and the Englishmen and by the time the ball safely reached Roberts he had 25m to run to the corner.

He dived over to scenes of jubilation and Australia prevailed 5-2.

Australia had beaten Britain in an Ashes series for the first time since 1920 and the crowd went wild, sweeping the players off the field and chanting the name of the captain 'Clive Churchill' outside the dressing rooms after the game. The Australian halfback Keith Holman *(pictured right)* established himself that day and the man who was given credit for masterminding the victory was a great of the game, the Australian coach Vic Hey.

Every man does his duty ... in what must be one of the earliest action pictures, Charles 'Chook' Fraser takes a fall in the Rorke's Drift Test at the SCG in 1914

AUSTRALIA: Clive Churchill (c), Ron Roberts, Keith Middleton, Doug McRitchie, Jack Troy, Frank Stanmore, Keith Holman, Len Cowie, 'Mick' Crocker, Bernie Purcell, Jack Holland, Kevin Schubert, 'Duncan' Hall.

GREAT BRITAIN: Jim Ledgard, Tom Danby, Ernie Ward (c), Ernest Ashcroft, Jack Hilton, Jack Cunliffe, Tommy Bradshaw, Harry Street, Doug Phillips, Fred Higgins, Elwyn Gwyther, Joe Egan, Ken Gee.

AUSTRALIA 5 (Roberts try; Churchill goal).
GREAT BRITAIN 2 (Ward goal). Referee: Tom McMahon. Crowd: 47,178.

THE FIRST TEST
AUSTRALIA v FRANCE
at the Sydney Cricket Ground
June 11, 1951

AUSTRALIANS had never seen an exhibition of rugby league the way France played the game on their first international tour.

And they had never seen a player like French fullback Puig-Aubert.

Australian spectators were enthralled at the French style. Australian players were equally amazed – and frustrated.

To say the French were unpredictable was to master understatement.

But it was the eccentric Puig-Aubert, a roly-poly, cigarette-smoking fullback and stand-in captain who could kick a goal with either foot, who seemed to typify the French attitude to the game.

Obsessed with defeating Great Britain (which they did the previous year), Australia were vulnerable to the frenetic French chain-passing style.

For all their colourful characters such as Louis Mazon, Jean Dop, Edouard Ponsinet and Elie Brousse the French form leading to the first Test was poor.

So inferior in fact, they were instructed to 'lift your game' by anxious Australian officials.

But a draw against NSW in which Puig-Aubert kicked a penalty from the touchline after the bell set up the Test and a crowd of 60,160 packed Sydney Cricket Ground.

1910-19

JANUARY 1, 1912: The Kangaroos win the Ashes for the first time. Captained by halfback **Chris McKivat**, the tourists remain undefeated in the three-Test series and secure the Ashes with a remarkable 33-8 victory in the third Test at Birmingham's Villa Park.

AUGUST 26, 1912: South Sydney's 18-year-old winger **Harold Horder** scores a superb 90-metre try in his debut game in first grade. The *Sydney Morning Herald* describes the try as 'brilliant' and tells how 'the cheers that followed it continued for minutes'.

SEPTEMBER, 1912: A New South Wales side tours New Zealand for the first time. The team plays nine matches, winning eight and losing one.

FEBRUARY 11, 1913: England's Northern Union (the forerunner of the English Rugby League), ban the importation of players from Australia and New Zealand. It is, effectively, the game's first international transfer ban and lasts 10 years.

The way we were...

France's entertaining style belied their determination and the first scrum ended in a punch-up. Puig-Aubert won the Test for France by kicking seven goals from nine attempts.

France jumped out to an 11-0 lead and led 16-2 at halftime. Australia clawed back to 16-15 but two more French tries sealed their famous win on a tour which was truly an expression of champagne football.

AUSTRALIA: Clive Churchill (c), Johnny Bliss, Gordon Willoughby, Noel Hazzard, Johnny Graves, Frank Stanmore, Keith Holman, Noel Mulligan, 'Mick' Crocker, Brian Davies, 'Duncan' Hall, Kevin Schubert, Denis Donoghue.
FRANCE: Puig-Aubert (c), Vincent Cantoni, Gaston Comes, Jean Crespo, Raymond Contrastin, Charles Galaup, Jean Dop, Rene Duffort, Elie Brousse, Edouard Ponsinet, Paul Bartoletti, Gabriel Genoud, Louis Mazon.
FRANCE 26 (Cantoni 2, Contrastin, Genoud tries; Puig-Aubert 7 goals.)

AUSTRALIA 15 (Graves, Willoughby, Crocker tries; Graves 3 goals.) Referee: Tom McMahon. Crowd: 60,160.

THE SECOND TEST
GREAT BRITAIN v AUSTRALIA
at Station Road, Swinton
November 9, 1963

THE scenes of sheer joy which engulfed the Australian camp after their historic 50-12 win over Great Britain might on the surface seem hard to understand.

But such was the class of this side that they were hailed, by the British, as the greatest Australian team ever seen.

The praise owed much to the style and grace of the victory rather than the overwhelming score.

Great Britain held Australia for 13 minutes before the floodgates opened. In 11 minutes Australia scored four tries and had another three by halftime. In the second half they added another five.

Making of a hero ... Ron Roberts slides over in the SCG corner to seal the Ashes for Australia for the first time in 30 years

1916: Australians vote 'no' against Government proposal to conscript Australian men to serve in the Great War. Six o'clock closing for hotels in Sydney and Melbourne. Talented middleweight boxer **Les Darcy**, 20, easily outpoints American George 'KO' Brown in a fierce 20 rounder in Sydney. In just 27 hours of fighting on the Somme the AIF 5th Division loses 5533 men.

1917: Nationalists sweep back to power, headed by Bill Hughes. Boxer Les Darcy dies in America of blood poisoning. The fighter is later given a hero's send-off in Maitland, where over 100,000 people view his body in a local chapel. Australia's greatest railway undertaking completed, linking Melbourne to Fremantle. A crowd of over 10,000 people stage a noisy protest outside Federal Parliament against the high cost of living.

Glory dive ... Noel Kelly dives over for one of Australia's 12 tries at Swinton

With this victory, Australia erased the highest score in Anglo-Australia Tests, the 40-17 win to Britain in Sydney in 1958.

Man of the match was John Raper who had what many believe was his finest game in a stellar career – he had a hand in nine of the 12 tries but did not score himself.

AUSTRALIA: Ken Thornett, Peter Dimond, Reg Gasnier, Graeme Langlands, Ken Irvine, Earl Harrison, Barry Muir, Johnny Raper, Dick Thornett, Ken Day, Noel Kelly, Ian Walsh (c), Paul Quinn.
GREAT BRITAIN: Ken Gowers, Mike Sullivan, Eric Ashton (c), Neil Fox, John Stopford, Frank Myler, Alex Murphy, Vince Karalius, Ron Morgan, Jim Measures, Cliff Watson, Len McIntyre, Bill Robinson.
AUSTRALIA 50 (Irvine 3, Dimond 2, Langlands 2, Gasnier 2, Harrison, Kelly, R Thornett tries; Langlands 7 goals.) **GREAT BRITAIN 12** (Measures, Stopford tries; Fox 3 goals). Referee: D Davies. Crowd: 30,843.

THE FIRST TEST
AUSTRALIA v GREAT BRITAIN
at Lang Park
Brisbane, June 6, 1970

GREAT Britain were overwhelming favourites but, when the dust cleared from the Battle of Brisbane II, Australia had won a handsome victory.

The British pack was formidable but a calculated gamble by Australian coach Arthur Summons to take them on proved a masterstroke.

Victory came at a cost. Jim Morgan had his face split open by a head butt. Ron Lynch had his jaw broken and John Wittenberg's face was badly cut.

The Australian forwards dominated the match and, combined with a plan to pepper the English fullback Terry Price with high balls, achieved for Australia a win against the odds.

The forwards were the heroes that day, but the backs paid for their keep, too, after an all-in brawl.

Arthur Beetson in the forwards and Phil Hawthorne in the backs carved up the British team.

Head butting and high tackles took a heavy price on the Australians but from a 13-5 halftime lead they were in command 23-5 early in the second half. Australia scored five tries in a 37-15 victory.

'We seem to have lost the fight but won the match,' Beetson said later, surveying the wreckage in the dressing room.

AUSTRALIA: Graeme Langlands (c), Johnny King, John McDonald, John Brass, John Cootes, Phil Hawthorne, Billy Smith, Ron Coote, Arthur Beetson, Ron Lynch, John Wittenberg, Elwyn Walters, Jim Morgan. Col Weiss replaced Lynch.
GREAT BRITAIN: Terry Price, Clive Sullivan, Frank Myler (c), Mike Shoebottom, John Atkinson, Alan Hardisty, Keith Hepworth, Mal Reilly, Doug Laughton, Dave Robinson, Cliff Watson, Peter Flanagan, Dave Chisnall. Bob Irving replaced Robinson.

1910-19

AUGUST 9, 1913: Eastern Suburbs secure their third consecutive premiership title when they beat Souths 14-7 at the Sydney Cricket Ground. By virtue of their third straight victory, the Tricolours are awarded the Agricultural Shield.

AUGUST 23, 1913: Dally Messenger, the champion player of the game's early years, announces his retirement from the game. Eastern Suburbs present Dally with the ornate Agricultural Shield as a testamant to his contribution to the club and the game since 1908.

JULY 4, 1914: A 10-man England side scores an epic 14-6 victory over Australia at the Sydney Cricket Ground in a Test which is dubbed 'Rorke's Drift' *(see story page 35).*

AUGUST 15, 1914: England and New South Wales clash in an exhibition match at the Melbourne Cricket Ground. But in a poor introduction to the people of Victoria, the game degenerates into a series of running brawls. Leggo, the NSW winger, has his jaw smashed by a stiff arm. British frontrower Chilcott's head is split open by a flying boot and Longstaff of Britain is sent off following a fiery brawl.

APRIL 25, 1915: Sergeant Edward Rennix Larkin, the first paid secretary of the New South Wales Rugby League, is killed at Gallipoli.

JUNE 7, 1915: Wonder winger Harold Horder crosses for his 10th try in the space of three days in the interstate series against Queensland. Horder scores five times in the Blues' 53-9 win on the Saturday and a further five on the holiday Monday when NSW win 39-6.

The way we were...

1918: Ernest Fisk of AWA receives first direct wireless message transmitted from England. Melbourne successfully trials electric train. Writer and illustrator May Gibbs publishes *Snugglepot and Cuddlepie*, destined to become a children's classic. At 11am, on the 11th day, of the 11th month of 1918, Germany admits defeat and signs an armistice. Australian casualties of war: 59,432 dead and 166,819 wounded. The British Empire's highest award for gallantry, the Victoria Cross, is awarded to 64 Australians.

1919: Germany signs Peace Treaty, the formal conclusion to WWI. Artilleryman wins Melbourne Cup. Former PM Alfred Deakin dies. One in every 10 Australians works in the public service. Thousands of Australians die from deadly 'flu epidemic, believed to have come from Europe with returned servicemen.

Surrounded ... Australian secondrower Arthur Beetson outnumbered in Brisbane in 1970

AUSTRALIA 37 (Morgan 2, King 2, McDonald tries; Langlands 9 goals, Hawthorne 2 field goals). **GREAT BRITAIN 15** (Flanagan, Watson, Laughton tries; Price 3 goals). Referee: Don Lancashire. Crowd: 42,807.

THE FIRST TEST
AUSTRALIA v NEW ZEALAND
at Lang Park
Brisbane, June 18, 1985

THIS match would be remembered for all the wrong reasons as crowd trouble and fighting players overshadowed a magnificent game of rugby league.

New Zealand fielded their most competitive side for years, fuelled by players who had cut their teeth in the Australian competition.

The Australians were not a harmonious team, with interstate rivalries from the State of Origin series still simmering after the national team was announced.

New Zealand lost their skipper Mark Graham after a crunching tackle from Steve Roach and Noel Cleal and the scores were 14-all at halftime.

The Kiwis looked to have won the match when Dean Bell ran in a try to give them a 20-14 lead but Australian skipper Wally Lewis continued with an expansive game plan.

The Australians ran in two late tries with John Ribot diving across the tryline for the winner just minutes from fulltime. He converted his own try from the sideline to give Australia a 26-20 victory.

The French referee, Julian Rascagneres, was out of his depth in a match played on a Tuesday night.

Births (and Deaths) of clubs...

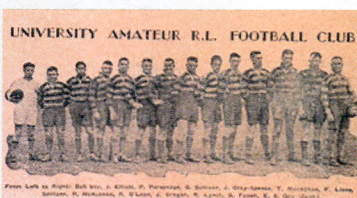

SYDNEY UNIVERSITY
JOINED competition in 1920 and remained for 18 years before voluntarily withdrawing after 1937. In their first year the side had one win against Annandale, avoiding the wooden spoon.
COLOURS: Blue and gold.
NICKNAME: The Students.

GLEBE
GLEBE was Australia's first rugby league club and was formed at what was described as a well attended meeting at Glebe Town Hall on January 9, 1908. The club played their first game against Newcastle at Wentworth Park on April 20 that year, winning 8-5.

The sin-binning of Kevin Tamati and Greg Dowling resulted in a sideline fight between the pair spilling into the crowd.

AUSTRALIA: Garry Jack, John Ribot, Chris Close, Mal Meninga, John Ferguson, Wally Lewis (c), Mark Murray, Wayne Pearce, Peter Wynn, Noel Cleal, Steve Roach, Greg Conescu, Greg Dowling. Replacements: Steve Ella, Peter Tunks.
NEW ZEALAND: Gary Kemble, Dean Bell, Gary Prohm, James Leuluai, Dane O'Hara, Olsen Filipaina, Clayton Friend, Hugh McGahan, Kurt Sorensen, Mark Graham (c), Kevin Tamati, Howie Tamati, Owen Wright. Replacements: Ricky Cowan, Mark Elia.
AUSTRALIA 26 (Ribot 2, Close, Cleal, Roach tries; Meninga 2, Ribot goals.)
NEW ZEALAND 20 (McGahan, Filipaina, Bell tries; Filipaina 4 goals.) Referee: Julian Rascagneres (France). Crowd: 22,000.

THE SECOND TEST
GREAT BRITAIN v AUSTRALIA
at Old Trafford
November 10, 1990

ACE Australian halfback Ricky Stuart went from villain to hero within minutes as Australia stunned Great Britain to win in injury time.

Although Australia were significantly the better team, the dogged British could not be overcome until the last seconds of the game as Stuart combined with his captain Mal Meninga to achieve a thrilling 14-10 victory.

An intense first half saw Australia lead 4-2 and then only after Cliff Lyons laid on an individual piece of trickery to create for Dale Shearer a classic try.

The Kangaroos were struggling to retain the Ashes after a first Test loss when Paul Dixon blasted through Australian tacklers after a scheming effort by Garry Schofield.

The Australians seemed destined to win when a magnificent team try was scored by Lyons. But the

Winners ... Ricky Stuart and Mal Meninga

Aussies were unable to shake Britain. Pressing too hard to seal the match, Stuart passed too close to Paul Loughlin who intercepted and ran 50 metres to score.

With the scores tied at 10-all in injury time, Stuart dummied and ran from his own '22' and managed to avoid pursuers for 50 metres.

As he died on his run Meninga bullocked through pursuing British tacklers to receive Stuart's despairing pass and pull the Test out of the fire, and ultimately the series.

AUSTRALIA: Gary Belcher, Andrew Ettingshausen, Mal Meninga (c), Laurie Daley, Dale Shearer, Cliff Lyons, Ricky Stuart, Steve Roach, Ben Elias, Glenn Lazarus, Paul Sironen, Bob Lindner, Brad Mackay.
GREAT BRITAIN: Steve Hampson, Paul Eastwood, Daryl Powell, Carl Gibson, Martin Offiah, Garry Schofield, Andy Gregory, Karl Harrison, Lee Jackson, Andy Platt, Denis Betts, Paul Dixon, Ellery Hanley (c). Paul Loughlin replaced Offiah, Kevin Ward replaced Harrison.
AUSTRALIA 14 (Shearer, Lyons, Meninga tries; Meninga goal).
GREAT BRITAIN 10 (Dixon, Loughlin tries; Eastwood goal). Referee: Alain Sablayrolles (France). Crowd: 46,615.

1910-19

JUNE 28, 1915: One of the game's founding fathers, cricketing legend **Victor Trumper**, dies in Sydney of Bright's Disease, aged 37.
AUGUST 21, 1915: Balmain become the first team to go through a season undefeated and the first club to win all three grades in the same year. The Tigers are captained by New Zealand-born Bill Kelly and win 12 and draw two of their 14 premiership matches. A crowd of 15,000 watch the Tigers in their final match of the season against South Sydney.
JULY 26, 1916: Balmain win all three grades for the second successive season. In first grade, Balmain defeat Souths 5-3 in a tense, midweek final at the Sydney Cricket Ground.
MAY 12, 1917: Dan 'Laddo' Davies, a player not residentially qualified to play for Glebe, turns out for the club against Annandale. Glebe win the match 26-5, but later have their two competition points stripped and Davies is suspended for life.
JULY 14, 1917: Balmain secure their third consecutive first grade title with an 18-0 defeat of Eastern Suburbs at the Sydney Cricket Ground. In three seasons, the Tigers have lost only four matches.

The club left the competition in 1929.
COLOUR: Red, the same as their rugby union counterparts.
NICKNAME: The Dirty Reds.

ANNANDALE
JOINED the competition in 1910, playing 14 games, winning five and drawing one.

On October 13, 1920, the NSW Rugby League general committee voted to cut Annandale from the competition.
COLOURS: Maroon and gold.

NICKNAME: The team was known as The Dales.

CUMBERLAND
HAD the shortest run of any club in premiership history, joining the competition after the second round in 1908.

They were beaten in their first premiership game by Souths 23-2.

On July 25 Norths beat them 45-0. They were two players short at kick-off and co-opted two Norths officials to play. Next season they were gone.
COLOURS: The club played in blue and gold.
NICKNAME: The Fruitpickers.

1910-19

GLEBE'S FAMOUS BURGE BROTHERS

JULY 21, 1917: The Glebe side stages rugby league's first player strike. The club's entire first grade side refuses to play a match against Balmain in protest at the way they believe they have been treated by the NSWRL. After a lengthy inquiry, the League suspends the players until the start of the 1919 season – effectively a one-year ban. The players are subsequently reinstated early in 1918.

AUGUST 25, 1917: Dally Messenger emerges from retirement to play in a patriotic match, Kangaroos v The Rest.

AUGUST 21, 1919: An Australian side under the captaincy of Arthur 'Pony' Halloway sets sail for its first tour of New Zealand. Australia win the four-Test series 3-1 and score massive victories in many of the tour matches.

WHAT A GAME!
ST GEORGE v BALMAIN 1928

The Earl Park riot

IMPECCABLE crowd behaviour has been one characteristic of rugby league that has set it apart from other major football codes around the world. But the one most notable exception to this rule came on a bitterly cold winter's day in August, 1928.

A vicious match between St George and Balmain resulted in fans storming the ground and attacking players. It was a black day for rugby league and an infamous match that has gone down in history as the Earl Park Riot.

Some 9000 fans turned up at the Arncliffe ground, then the home base of the Dragons, blissfully unaware of the drama that was to unfold.

The first hint of trouble came early in the second half when Saints' international centre George Carstairs felled Balmain halfback Mick Roberts.

Carstairs, a giant of a man, did considerable damage, splitting Roberts' eye and leaving him badly dazed. Balmain skipper Whip Latta told Tony Russell *(pictured)* to move out into the centres, from second row, to mark Carstairs.

Russell took to the challenge and the pair waged war for the rest of the game.

After a scrum flared up, Russell dropped Carstairs, allegedly stamping on his head. The incident inflamed the partisan St George crowd, who believed Russell had kicked their centre star.

St George ended up winning the game 21-3, but as the players left the field, several began trading blows. To the crowd, that was the signal to get involved.

Hundreds of fans invaded the field, several arming themselves with fence palings.

The players managed to get to the safety of the dressing rooms, barricading the doors and listening to the ugly sounds of the riot as police reinforcements arrived.

Russell and Carstairs were both so seriously injured by their on-field feud they were taken to hospital. But stunned medicos had to separate the pair as they threatened to carry on the battle in the back of the ambulance.

I was there...

*Australia v Great Britain
third Test, 1950*

'Ron Roberts only played two Tests for Australia but the second one earned him a place in football folklore. Some 14 minutes from the end of the third Test, Australia created an overlap for Roberts, who wasn't a noted ball handler. He caught it superbly and dashed over for the winner. Would you believe it, Ronny had another great chance two minutes later but dropped it with the line wide open!'

Bernie Purcell
(who played second row in the 1950 third Test)

I was there...

*Australia v New Zealand,
first Test, Lang Park, 1985*

'Tamati and I were sin-binned and there was plenty of heated chat as we made our way off the field. I didn't fancy walking through the tunnel ahead of him and gestured for him to go first. Tamati didn't take kindly and elbowed me. I just let fly.'

Greg Dowling
on the infamous sideline brawl with Kevin Tamati

Team of the Decade...
1910-1919

A TEAM that contains some of the greatest names from one of league's golden eras. Horder and Blinkhorn, Fraser, Burge and Hallett rank among the all-time greats. Halfback is Chris McKivat, an under-rated figure in the game's history and the man who masterminded Australia's first Ashes victory over England in 1911-12.

Fullback: Howard HALLETT (Souths).
Wingers: Harold HORDER (Souths), Cec BLINKHORN (Norths, Souths).

Centres: Herb GILBERT (Easts, Wests, Souths), Charles 'Chook' FRASER (Balmain).
Five-eighth: Viv FARNSWORTH (Newtown).
Halfback: Chris McKIVAT (Glebe).
Lock: Frank BURGE (Glebe).
Secondrowers: Robert CRAIG (Balmain), Jack WATKINS (Easts).
Frontrowers: Paddy McCUE (Newtown), Con SULLIVAN (Norths).
Hooker: Sandy PEARCE (Easts).

Howard Hallett

Cec Blinkhorn

Man on Man
Clive Churchill vs David Peachey

CLIVE Churchill was a tiny player with a big heart – an outstanding attacking fullback with innate timing. Physically, David Peachey is a giant by comparison. His long, loping strides enable him to launch his team's counter-attacks when the opposition kick to him and he uses his 186cm when the ball is in the air. The physique of the two fullbacks says a lot about the changing game. Height is a big advantage to the modern-day fullbacks, who are regularly tested under the high ball. Tryscoring fullbacks were a rarity in Churchill's day. 'My job was to set up tries, not score them,' he would say.

Timing his run into the backline to create the extra man in attack and set up his wingers became Churchill's trademark.

Clive CHURCHILL
Born: Jan 21, 1927 **Died:** Aug 9, 1985.
Played: 1946-61.
Club: South Sydney.
(also Central Newcastle, Brisbane Norths .and Moree).
Position: Fullback.
Playing weight: 74kg (11st 10).
Height: 171cm (5ft 7½ins).
Tests: 34.
Career games: 298.
Career points: 402 (tries 26).

David PEACHEY
Born: April 21, 1974.
Played: From 1994.
Club: Cronulla.
Position: Fullback.
Playing weight: 78kg (12st 4).
Height: 186cm (6ft 1ins).
Career games: 106.
Career points: 192 (tries 48).

Steve ROACH
Born: 1962

90 STEVE 'Blocker' Roach was a cornerstone of the Australian front row during the mid-to-late 1980s. A product of Wollongong, Roach loved the physical confrontation of the front row and was one of the game's last great characters. Made his first grade debut for Balmain in 1982 and stayed with the club for over a decade. Played in the 1989 grand final, appeared in 17 State of Origin games for NSW and made his Test debut against New Zealand in 1985. 19 Tests (1985-91), Kangaroo 1986, 1990.

Garry JACK
Born: 1961

89 IN 1987 an international panel of judges rated Jack the No 1 player in the world. Unchallenged as leading player in his position for five years during mid-1980s. Wonderful last line of defence, Jack was pacy and penetrative and safe under the high ball in an era when the 'bomb' became an accepted hazard for fullbacks. Began career at Wollongong and played a season at Wests in 1981 before enjoying great success with Balmain. 20 Tests (1984-88), Kangaroo 1986.

Jack BEATON
1914 - 1996

86 RETIRED at 24 to work in a brewery but in a short career proved his status in the top echelon. Member of the champion Easts sides of the 1930s, Beaton played in four grand finals (three premierships) and 10 Tests. Equally at home at wing, centre and fullback. Beaton rose from the St Josephs First XV to first grade with Easts within two seasons. A player of speed, clever change of pace and sidestep. Also a fine long-distance goalkicker. 10 Tests (1936-38), Kangaroo 1937-38.

THE Daily Telegraph

WE SELECT THE BEST OF THE CENTURY

Dick THORNETT
Born: 1940

84 A VERSATILE sportsman, Dick Thornett represented Australia in three sports. Played 11 rugby union Tests, represented Australia in water polo at the 1960 Olympics and appeared in 11 league Tests. Joined Parramatta from Randwick union club in 1963 and rapidly established himself as a secondrower of immense power and class. Weighed around 108kg (17st) but for a big man had outstanding hands and was a noted ball distributor. Key member of Australia's 1963 Ashes triumph. 11 Tests (1963-66), Kangaroo 1963-64.

Albert ROSENFELD
1885-1970

83 ROSENFELD, like Brian Bevan, is still revered in the north of England, even though the career of the one-time Easts winger ended 75 years ago. The first of the game's great tryscorers, Rosenfeld found fame in Britain after touring with the First Kangaroos. Played just two seasons with Easts, mainly at five-eighth, but on Huddersfield's wing he set records that have never been broken. Eighty tries in 1913-14 remains unchallenged. 4 Tests (1908-09), Kangaroo 1908-09.

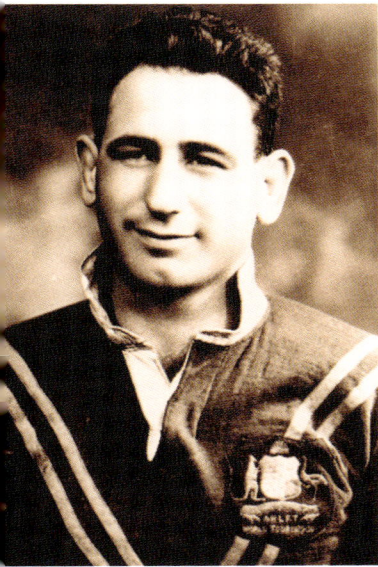

Vic ARMBRUSTER
1902 - 1984

88 A RESPECTED critic of the late 1920s rated Armbruster the greatest forward since Frank Burge – high praise since Burge continues to hold a position among Australia's all-time greats. Armbruster grew up at Mullumbimby and represented the State before moving to Toowoomba in 1924. There he honed his talents as a member of the renowned 'Galloping Clydesdales'. Was a great handler, able to offload in heavy traffic and ran like a three-quarter. 8 Tests (1924-30), Kangaroo 1929-30.

Kevin SCHUBERT
Born: 1927

87 DESCRIBED as 'the prince of hookers', Schubert emerged from Wollongong to play the first of his 19 Tests for Australia in 1948. Joined Manly in 1950, where he helped the fledgling club gain credibility in the Sydney premiership. Career highlight came in the Ashes-winning series against Great Britain in 1950 after his starring role opposite legendary rake Joe Egan. Could have played second row at the highest level if he had not made it as a hooker. 19 Tests (1948-52), Kangaroo 1948-49, 1952-53.

Peter DIMOND
Born: 1938

85 AN aggressive winger, Dimond played Test football in his first season in Sydney. Was just 19 when he represented Australia against Great Britain in 1958. A star of the 1963-64 Kangaroo tour when the side became the first all-Australian team to bring home the Ashes. Scored a record 84 first grade tries for Western Suburbs in a career spanning 1958-67. Learned his football on the South Coast at Dapto and played in four grand finals for the Magpies. 10 Tests (1958-66), Kangaroo 1963-64.

The Great 100

Andrew JOHNS
Born: 1974

82 JOHNS is headed for a higher position in a future list of Australia's top 100 players but already, at 25, the Newcastle halfback commands a place among the game's greats. Joined the Knights in 1992 and played his first top grade game in '94. Debuted in rep football the following season and is now among the first chosen for NSW and Australia. Highly skilled, mentally tough and a powerful defender, Johns was a central figure in Newcastle's remarkable grand final victory in 1997. 11 Tests (1995-99).

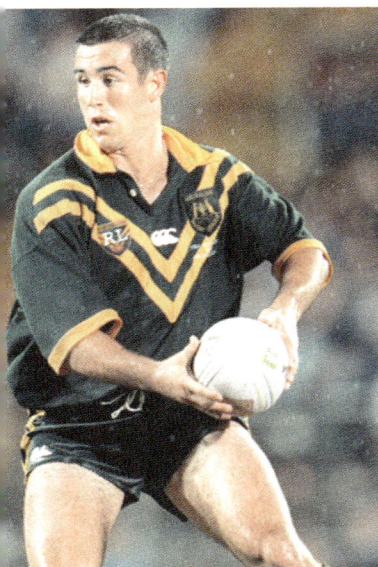

Steve WALTERS
Born: 1965

81 HAS been described as one of the finest hooker-forwards of the modern era. Emerged from the domestic competition in Brisbane to play with Canberra in 1986. Took time to establish himself on representative scene but in early 1990s was a permanent fixture in Queensland Origin and Australian Test teams. Man of the match in World Cup final at Wembley in 1992, Walters also played in premiership-winning sides for Canberra in 1989, '90 and '94. 15 Tests (1991-94), Kangaroo 1994.

Matters of State

BY IAN HEADS

The way we were...

I was there...

'It was 'Turvey' Mortimer's first rep game and we trailed Queensland by 11 points. Time was running out and I had Tommy (Raudonikis) on the sideline frothing at the mouth because Mortimer had taken his spot.

I sent him out and he immediately put on a stink with Greg Oliphant, changing the course of the game. Tommy took control up the middle, Mick Cronin landed a goal to win it.'

Terry Fearnley, NSW coach for the controversial 1977 interstate clash at Lang Park.

Matters

INTERSTATE football arrived with the dawn of Australian rugby league, the chants of 'Blue, Blue, Blue' and 'Red, Red, Red' signalling the highlight of many seasons from the very first, back in 1908.

The yearly showpiece featuring the game's foundation States went close to running out of legs in the 1960s and 70s thanks to the raids of the poker machine-backed Sydney clubs on Queensland players – before its miraculous 1980 transformation via the State of Origin concept.

The fierce and passionate across-the-border rivalry of recent (Origin) years is nothing new.

Progressively from the 1920's, State football, featuring the champion players of the various eras, drew huge crowds and ignited vast and deep loyalties – especially so during the 20s with the arrival of the first period of Queensland dominance.

The annual battles – STATE against STATE – represent a great pillar of the game.

Only for two brief periods – during the World Wars – was annual interstate football not played, and both times its resumption was greeted with enormous enthusiasm – even when the teams trotted out in strange colours on Peace Day, July 21, 1919 due to wartime shortages: NSW in dark blue jerseys breasted with a kangaroo and Queensland in red, white and blue.

Outgunned for 14 years and 22 straight matches from 1908, Queensland came of age with their great side of the 20s, winning 10 of 11 games between 1922 and 1925.

An early editorial in the *Rugby League News* cuts pretty much to the heart of what modern day fans have seen so regularly in the team from up north: 'The superiority of the southerners remained most pronounced for many years but the determined

True blue ... the first NSW team to take on Queensland in 1908
Photo: David Middleton

manner in which the northerners took their lacings and came back full of grit, marked a fighting spirit that would never cry "enough".'

The Queensland dominance of the 1920s was based in the city of the Darling Downs, Toowoomba, a centre of league inspiration.

In successive matches in 1926 a team built on big, powerful forwards and dashing backs beat NSW 38-0 and 37-19.

In 1925, when NSW managed a rare win, so great was the rejoicing that the crowd swept up winger Benny Wearing (*pictured opposite*) and carried him from the field on their shoulders.

Wearing had scored 21 of the Blues' 27 points. Wonderful stories dot the early days:

■ Dally Messenger's absolute domination of the 1911 series (he scored 72 points).

■ The famous tackle made by Queensland's Billy Paten in front of the old Sheridan Stand at the SCG to stop NSW's Wearing as he was launching himself for a match-winning try in 1926.

■ The debut of the game's 'wonder man' of the 1930s, Dave Brown, in 1931 – a performance described by the *Brisbane Courier Mail* as 'glorious'.

■ A Queensland decision to send the Toowoomba team *en masse* to play the first game of the 1933 series. NSW whipped them 24-0.

■ The astonishing turnaround of 1939 when the Blues won the first two games 50-15 and 54-13 – yet Queensland came back to square the series.

'They were stung by some of the things said and written in Sydney,' explained coach Herb Steinohrt.

In the 54-13 game, Blues winger Sid Goodwin scored six tries.

The post-war years can be judged the beginning of a new era in the STATE against STATE story.

For the first time, in 1947, the two sides travelled to matches by plane, a TAA Skymaster.

After the series the NSWRL launched an

# of State

investigation into the behaviour of the Blues players at their hotel base in Brisbane – eventually deciding that damage done could not be sheeted home to any individual.

Crowd support for interstate football swelled in the 50s; the first game of 1952 drew 55,467 – then the second best on record.

During the NSW domination of the 1964 series (28-12, 41-3, 31-5, 22-11) ex-Kangaroo and Brisbane-based journalist Jack Reardon aired a fascinating idea: 'While the NSW score was mounting at the SCG last dismal Tuesday, someone in the press seats suggested that Queensland should be allowed to call on their former players now with Sydney clubs.'

It was an idea for its time.

Gloom abounded in Queensland with the steady flow of players to increasingly wealthy leagues club-backed Sydney clubs.

Mick Veivers and Ken Day had gone to Manly, Arch Brown to Parramatta – part of an increasing exodus which was to include the likes of Arthur Beetson, John Rhodes, Elton Rasmussen and John Wittenberg.

When in 1967 Queensland broke a run of 18 matches without a win, the *Brisbane Telegraph* celebrated with the headline 'WE DID IT!' on its front page.

Other Queensland wins in 1968 and 1970 were greeted with similar enthusiasm.

But the truth of it was that NSW was hugely in the ascendancy – and with the sense of true contest often lacking, the annual State series slipped into the doldrums.

In 1971 when only 6487 people watched a match at the SCG, there was a call to do away with interstate football altogether.

In 1973, the Queenslanders failed to score a point for the first time in 65 years – going down 16-0, 10-0 and 26-0.

Now and then the spark was still there – and especially so for Queensland under the coaching of firebrand Barry Muir – the man who placed the 'Cockroaches' tag on NSW ('I thought we went pretty well for a team of cockroaches,' said NSW coach Graeme Langlands after a 33-9 win in 1976).

In 1975 Muir declared that his Maroons would 'knock the stuffing' out of NSW in the second game at Lang Park – and they did, winning 14-8 against a line-up which included such players as Beetson, Ron Coote and Bob Fulton.

So, even in its dying years the 'old' State concept could now and then produce huge drama – such as in 1977 when NSW coach Terry Fearnley famously sent Tom Raudonikis out to replace the youthful Steve Mortimer at Lang Park.

At 13-2 to Queensland, Raudonikis promptly sparked a wild brawl which changed the nature of the game. The Blues won 14-13.

From the 1978 series the Maroons found a new hero in teenage wing sensation Kerry Boustead.

When Boustead switched to Sydney (Eastern Suburbs) it was just about the last straw – and especially so with the growing enthusiasm in the north around two young stars who had arrived on the scene – Wally Lewis and Mal Meninga.

When NSW won a lacklustre series of 1979 in a hand canter (30-5, 31-17), the old STATE against STATE tradition was just about dead – crying out now for something different.

'A major suggestion now is a State of Origin series,' wrote Lawrie Kavanagh in *The Courier Mail* in the wake of the two games, declaring that Queensland fans were sick of rolling up to a 'stacked deck'.

After long years and famous days, the old way had run its course in interstate football. Salvation lay just around the corner ...

1920-29

MAY 8, 1920: A team of amateurs from Sydney University play their first match in the NSWRL premiership competition. Wearing jerseys of blue and gold, the Students are beaten 36-12 by Norths at North Sydney Oval.

JUNE 5, 1920: England play Sydney in the opening match of their Australian tour before a capacity crowd of 67,739 at the **Sydney Cricket Ground**. Police are forced to keep sections of the huge crowd back from the touchlines.

JUNE 19, 1920: Glebe forward **Frank Burge** scores eight tries (a record that still stands) and four goals in a match against University at Sydney's Agricultural Ground. Glebe win the match 41-0 and Burge contributes 32 points.

JULY 3, 1920: A Sydney Cricket Ground crowd of 40,000 watches Australia win the Ashes in Australia for the first time. Captained by **Herb Gilbert**, the Australians win the second Test 21-8 after claiming the first 8-4.

OCTOBER 13, 1920: A momentous meeting of the NSWRL votes to eliminate Annandale from the competition after 11 uneventful seasons and admit a team from St George.

The way we were...

1922: Teenaged swimmer Michael Coghlan punches and kicks a shark which attacks him during a surf carnival at Coogee on February 4. Lifesaver **Jack Chalmers** and Olympic medallist **Frank Beaurepaire** rescue Coghlan who later dies in hospital.

1923: General Motors signs agreement with Holden for manufacture of car bodies at Woodville, South Australia. Billy Hughes forced to retire as PM and is succeeded by NCP leader **Stanley Bruce**. Hoadley's Chocolates makes first Violet Crumble Bar.

Birth of a club...

LOCAL issues appear to have influenced North Sydney's participation in the rugby split of 1907. 'There are some suggestions that discontent with the district rugby union competition was strongest in North Sydney,' said Andrew Moore in his fascinating history of North Sydney, *The Mighty Bears*! The first meeting of the North Sydney RLFC was held at the North Sydney School of Arts in Mount Street on February 7, 1908. The club could find no local ground as a base and was forced to use Birchgrove Oval for home games. In their first premiership game Norths were beaten 11-7 by Souths. Norths' first captain, Dinny Lutge, was also captain of the First Kangaroos in 1908.

COLOURS: Red and black.

NICKNAME: The Shoremen. The club became known as the Bears in 1959 after a deal was struck with FJ Palmer Holdings, which operated the new Big Bear Supermarket at Neutral Bay.

NSW 43, QUEENSLAND 0
July 11, 1908
Royal Agricultural Ground (Sydney Showground)

THE first NSW versus Queensland match was a peculiar, one-sided affair, dominated by the Blues and featuring a referee who couldn't keep time.

Played on a rain-slicked Sydney Showground the match ran for 53 minutes in the first half when the ref, Mr Fred Henlen, lost track of the passing minutes.

The elongated half was not good news for the out-gunned Maroons who found themselves down 20-nil at the break.

The Blues ran in five more tries in the second half, with a forward pack which included such famous figures of the early game as Billy Cann and Arthur Hennessy, in complete control.

One newspaper described the Queensland performance – they were beaten 43-0 – as 'lamentable'.

The match completed a sensational double for foundation South Sydney winger Tommy Anderson.

It was Anderson who scored the first ever try in interstate football – adding to his feat in scoring Souths' historic first try on the opening day of the first premiership earlier the same year.

Anderson tormented his Queensland wing opponent O'Brien as evidenced in a newspaper report the next day: 'O'Brien's play on the wing excited much laughter and the crowd began to advise him seriously as to the methods he should adopt to stop the NSW rushes.'

Underpinning NSW teamwork, described as 'magnificent', was the goalkicking of nonpareil Herbert Henry 'Dally' Messenger.

He landed eight with the muddy ball.

In two more matches that week, NSW won 37-8 and 12-3.

The tradition had begun, and so too a pattern of NSW domination unbroken for years.

NEW SOUTH WALES: Charlie Hedley, Frank Cheadle, Dally Messenger, Andy Morton, Tommy Anderson, Sid Deane, Arthur Butler, Bill Cann, Tom McCabe, Lou Jones, Larry O'Malley, Arthur Hennessy, Robert Graves.
QUEENSLAND: Eddie Baird, W Abrahams, Bill Heidke, Mick Bolewski, Alf O'Brien, O Olsen, Mick Dore, J Thompson, Eddie Cartmill, Bob Tubman, Vic Anderson, Jack Fihelly, Bill Hardcastle.
NSW 43 (Anderson 4, McCabe 2, Cann, Butler, Deane tries; Messenger 8 goals)
QUEENSLAND 0. Referee: Fred Henlen. Crowd: 5000.

QUEENSLAND 25, NSW 9
September 23, 1922
Sydney Sports Ground

AFTER 22 successive defeats since 1908, the Maroons finally broke through for a famous victory in 1922.

With a team built around a nucleus of outstanding players – Tom Gorman (later to captain the 1929-30 Kangaroos), Eric Frauenfelder, E 'Nigger' Brown, Cec Aynsley and Norm Potter, their skipper – the Maroons of 1922 signalled that the balance of power had swung.

The sporting newspaper of the time, *The Referee*, called the 25-9 win, 'a decisive whipping'.

The historic victory was the beginning of a golden era for Queensland football, beginning an unprecedented period of interstate domination.

Built around players from the city on the Downs, Toowoomba (the team there known famously as 'the Galloping Clydesdales'), Queensland were to win nine of the next 10 games played between 1922-25.

QUEENSLAND: Eric Frauenfelder, Bill Paten, Tom Gorman, J McBrien, Bill Spencer, Edwin Brown, Cyril Connell, J Johnston, Norm Potter, E Stanley, A Brown, Claude O'Donnell, Jim Bennett.
NEW SOUTH WALES: Frank McMillan, Jim Flattery, Les Steel, Oscar Quinlivan, Cec Blinkhorn, Dallas Hodgins, Duncan Thompson, Jack Watkins, Vic Armbruster, Ted McGrath, Arthur Oxford, Clive Evatt, Felix Ryan.
QUEENSLAND 25 (Gorman, Spencer, Brown, Stanley, Paten tries; Paten 5 goals) **NSW 9** (Flattery 2, Oxford tries). Referee: Tom McMahon.
Crowd: 8000.

NSW 14, QUEENSLAND 10
June 27, 1927
Sydney Cricket Ground

SO high was the status of interstate football by the later 1920s that the annual series was sometimes referred to in the press as 'The Ashes'.

The opening game of the 1927 series is regarded as one of the most famous in the entire canon of NSW-Queensland football.

Controversially refereed by the former Souths and Australian fullback Webby Neill, it provided huge drama before a then-record 56,487 crowd at the SCG.

On the same day an Australia v Czechoslovakia soccer match at the Sydney Showground drew 60,000 fans – some league followers, unable to get into the

Great to be a Queenslander ... Herb Steinohrt, a hard man in his playing days and later coach of Queensland

The great Dally Messenger lines up a kick in 1908

SCG, paid to stand on the Showground steps and look across to the neighbouring ground.

'Redcap', writing in the *Brisbane Courier* called the match: 'A titanic struggle, full of fiery tackling, bewildering pace and sustained thrills', and wrote how it had 'intoxicated' the fans.

The game was rated the most gruelling and remarkable seen on the SCG to that time.

NSW, captained by Souths icon Alf 'Smacker' Blair, won it 14-10 with a last gasp try to tough Souths secondrower Eddie Root.

Wrote Brisbane-based 'Redcap': 'Queensland was the better side, beaten by wholesale shepherding and penalties, the cause of which left them completely mystified.'

NEW SOUTH WALES: Alan Righton, Benny Wearing, Vic Lawrence, Frank O'Rourke, Harry Finch, Alf Blair, Harry Owen, Aub Kelly, Jim Parsons, George Treweek, Harry Cavanough, Arthur Justice, Eddie Root.
QUEENSLAND: Harry Caples, R King, Tom Gorman, Jeff Moores, Cecil Aynsley, K Hughes, Jim Craig, Vic Armbruster, Harry Leibke, Jim Purcell, Herb Steinohrt, Arthur Henderson, Norm Potter.
NSW 14 (Wearing, Root tries; O'Rourke 2, Blair goals) **QUEENSLAND 10** (Craig, Leibke tries; Craig 2 goals). Referee: Webby Neill. Crowd: 56,487.

NSW 30, QUEENSLAND 2
May 29, 1971
Lang Park

A S Australia's Test halfback (1950-58), Keith Holman competed in some of the toughest games ever played. But 'Yappy' Holman never had a wilder match on his hands than the one he refereed at Lang Park, on Saturday, May 29, 1971.

Following a torrid opening game on the Tuesday night which christened the new Lang Park lights (won 12-3 by NSW), feelings were running high between the two sides.

Caught in the middle of it in the Saturday game, referee Holman triggered a near riot when he sent off three Queenslanders (Ray Laird, Rod Tolhurst and Russell Hughes) plus NSW and Test prop Bob O'Reilly.

As he left the field after the Blues' 30-2 victory – surrounded by NSW players and police – beer cans, bottles and rubbish rained down as the Lang Park crowd vented their fury on Holman.

Near the end of the game a spectator ran on, hell bent on getting to Holman – but was hustled away by police as the players shielded the referee.

The games of that season in which a 'gun' NSW side built around the likes of Langlands, Fulton, McCarthy, O'Neill and O'Reilly was clearly superior, helped build Lang Park's reputation as the most atmospheric and volatile ground in football.

NEW SOUTH WALES: Graeme Langlands (c), Ray Branighan, Bob Fulton, Des Kimmorley, Lionel Williamson, Tony Branson, Bob Grant, Paul Sait, Bob McCarthy, Ron Costello, John O'Neill, Dick Jeffrey, Bob O'Reilly. Mark Harris replaced Kimmorley, Keith Campbell replaced Sait.
QUEENSLAND: Ray Laird (c), Wayne Bennett, Glen Harrison, Ron Beauchamp, Bob Peut, Marty Scanlan, Johnny Brown, Col Weiss, Russell Hughes, Rod Tolhurst, Len Dittmar, Hugh O'Doherty, Jim Murphy.
NSW 30 (Fulton 2, Langlands 2, Harris 2, Grant, Sait tries; Campbell 2, Langlands goals)
QUEENSLAND 2 (Bennett goal). Referee: Keith Holman. Crowd: 19,308. Sent off: Laird (Qld, 25 min), O'Reilly (NSW, 46 min), Tolhurst (Qld, 52 min), Hughes (Qld, 76 min).

Scrumbase action ... NSW five-eighth Alf Blair chips over the top in 1927

1920-29

APRIL 23, 1921: St George play Glebe in their first premiership match – coincidentally on St George's Day – at the Sydney Sports Ground and lose 4-3.

MAY 25, 1921: The biggest crowd ever seen at a club match in NSW (48,476) witnesses a classic contest between North Sydney and Eastern Suburbs at the SCG. The game finishes 8-all after Norths draw level in the last minute of play.

JUNE 18, 1921: North Sydney beat Wests 12-7 at Pratten Park to secure their first premiership. The competition is reduced to eight rounds because of the departure of the game's leading players on the Kangaroo tour.

JULY 28, 1921: The third Kangaroo team sails for England aboard the RMS *Tahiti*. The team just fails to win the Ashes but the tour is regarded an outstanding success with **Cec Blinkhorn** (39 tries), **Harold Horder** (35 tries) and Frank Burge (33 tries) setting marks that stand the test of time.

AUGUST 17, 1921: The first Maher Cup competition is staged in the NSW Riverina with Gundagai beating Tumut 11-4. Author Ian Heads describes the Maher Cup 'as the centrepiece in countless wrangles, brawls, sensations, betting disputes and protests as towns squabbled for possession of the modest trophy'.

SEPTEMBER 22, 1922: Queensland break one of sport's longest droughts when they score their first interstate victory over NSW. The Maroons had lost 22 successive matches since 1908.

The way we were...

1924: New tennis courts open at Kooyong, Melbourne. The **Ford Motor Company** announces it will establish assembly and body building plants in Australia. Opera star **Dame Nellie Melba** makes her 'last farewell' at Melbourne's Her Majesty's Theatre.

1925: Federal Conference launches the slogan: 'Buy Australia-made Goods'. Benito Mussolini and PM Bruce exchange telegrams when Italian airman Major di Pendo arrives at Broome on world flight from Rome.

Birth of a club...

PADDINGTON Town Hall was the venue for the first meeting of the club on January 24, 1908. Harry 'Jersey' Flegg had the distinction of being appointed Easts' first captain, secretary, a foundation selector as well as delegate to the NSW Rugby League. 'The fact that a local butcher was unanimously chosen president suggests the new body is out for gore,' reported *The Bulletin*. Easts' first game against Newtown was played at Wentworth Park. 'A capital display considering that the contestants have as yet only a fair acquaintance with the rules,' reported *The Daily Telegraph*. Easts won the game 32-16, with their winger Johnno Stuntz the standout performer. The club's big star, however, was rugby union recruit Dally Messenger.

COLOURS: The club's colours of red, white and blue were inspired by Rev Mullineux's 1899 British Rugby Union touring team.

NICKNAME: The Tricolours. They became the Roosters in the 1950s.

Mate against Mate

ONE journalist (Jack Reardon) mentioned it in print as far back as 1964; another (Lawrie Kavanagh) wrote this in *The Courier Mail* in 1979: 'A major suggestion now is a State of Origin series.'

A third scribe, Hugh Lunn, has related the story of a conversation he had with Queensland Rugby League chairman Ron McAuliffe on a plane trip to Canberra in 1979 during which, Lunn says, he pushed hard to the senator the idea of an 'Origin' series for rugby league.

And there is absolutely no doubt that ex-VFL president Dr Alan Aylett, another Brisbane journo, Kev Keliher, and the former state manager of Rothmans, Queensland, Des Hancock, all had some hand in it too.

The queue forms on the right.

So when the envelope is opened just who is the winner – the man behind the greatest success story in modern football? Our vote goes to the wily Ron McAuliffe, driving force in Queensland football for many years up to his death in 1988. A man who once declared: 'All things considered, it is awfully hard to be humble when you're a Queenslander.'

If James Joseph Giltinan can be said to have been the father of rugby league in Australia, then Ron McAuliffe can claim eternal, paternal rights to State of Origin football.

McAuliffe's close pal Hancock and ex-ARL boss Kevin Humphreys concur – that the credit for State of Origin football belongs most of all to him ... with his timely push to 'give it a go' in 1980, just when the traditional NSW-Queensland annual series was on its last legs.

These were the stats when McAuliffe convinced NSW bigwigs such as Humphreys and Bob Abbott to give the concept a try: from 1961 to 1981 when the last of the traditional games were conducted (players playing for State of residence) NSW won 57 of 67 matches, four were drawn – and Queensland won just six.

NSW scored 1499 points to Queensland's 625.

State of Origin football can be viewed as McAuliffe's legacy to the game he loved.

Without question, the concept has been the great triumph of Australian football in the post-war years in any code; the VFL's (now AFL) Origin contest, kicking off in 1977, has never matched the passion or the power generated by MATE against MATE in rugby league.

The images the annual matches have imprinted, the sights and sounds of Origin nights since the experiment of 1980, are among the most searing in Australian sport:

■ Above all of them 'King' Wally Lewis, relentlessly stalking the Blues in his domain – a mighty player who did for Origin football on the field what McAuliffe had done off it, a combination of god and arch-villain.

■ The roar of the crowd at 'The Cauldron', Lang Park (Suncorp Stadium) – the most chilling and primitive sound in sport.

■ Chris Close ripping Eric Grothe away from the ruck via a savage backhander in 1981 as the never-say-die Queenslanders came back from 15-nil down to win.

■ Greg Dowling scoring a miraculous try in the mud at the SCG after a kick ricocheted off the goalposts.

■ Lewis and Mark Geyer chest bumping and snarling at the SFS in 1991 – with referee David Manson bravely trying to put the lid on World War III.

■ Mark Coyne scoring The Try That Fell From Heaven to win the 1994 series.

■ The full moon beaming over an astonishing 87,000 crowd in 1994 – in Melbourne!

■ Barry Gomersall – 'The Grasshopper' – a referee pulled from the Queensland north who became a celebrity, hero or the devil in disguise, depending on where you hailed from.

Clockwise from above ... The Cauldron, Lang Park; the Origin 'King', Wally Lewis and (opposite page) three Queensland powerbrokers, Lewis, Ron McAuliffe and Arthur Beetson

Photos: *Rugby League Week*

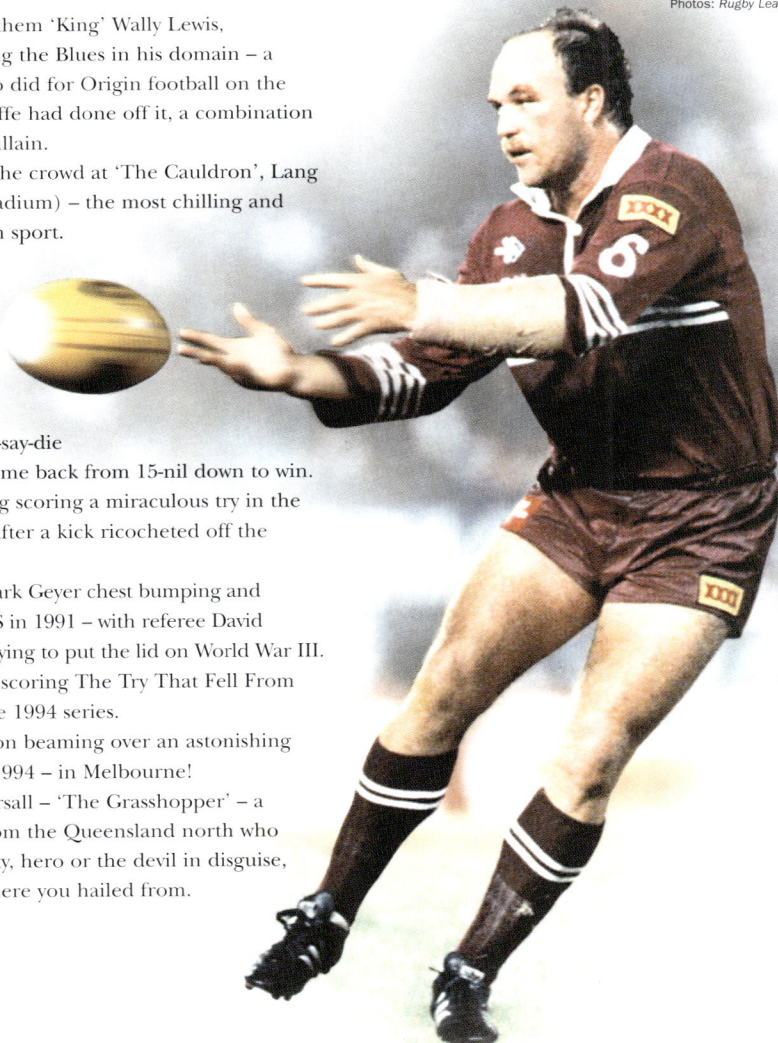

1920-29

AUGUST 13, 1923: Legendary North Sydney halfback **Duncan Thompson** is involved in an incident at the Sydney Cricket Ground which leads to him turning his back on Sydney football. Thompson, who maintains his innocence, is sent from the field on a touch judge's report, charged with kicking a Glebe opponent. He is suspended for the remainder of the season but on appeal the sentence is reduced to three matches.

JULY 29, 1924: League enters the radio age when the final of the 1924 competition is broadcast on 2SB (later 2BL). Balmain secretary Bob Savage's call of the match between Balmain and Souths is the first football broadcast on radio in Australia. Balmain win a hard-fought game 3-0.

DECEMBER 4, 1924: The Australian Board of Control, the forerunner to the Australian Rugby League, is formed in Sydney. It is set up with the specific intention to foster the game on an international level.

JUNE 24, 1924: Pioneer player Tedda Courtney is joined in Western Suburbs pack by his son, Ed junior, in a match against Glebe at Pratten Park.

The way we were...

1926: The first underground section of railway line is opened between Central Station and St James in Sydney. The Sydney Council is asked to ban 'barbaric and sensual' dance the Charleston.

1927: Final sitting of Federal Parliament in Melbourne before the move to Canberra. Cenotaph in Sydney's Martin Place is dedicated by Premier Jack Lang. Widespread Australian outrage over the Queensland Government's declaration of open season for killing koalas.

Melbourne underworld boss **Les 'Squizzy' Taylor** is shot dead by rival gangster. Victorian batsman William Ponsford blazes 427 against Queensland in Melbourne.

1928: Air Force Cross awarded to

Bert Hinkler for completing first solo flight from England to Australia. Local aviation heroes Charles Kingsford Smith and Charles Ulm form their own passenger airline, Australian National Airways Ltd.

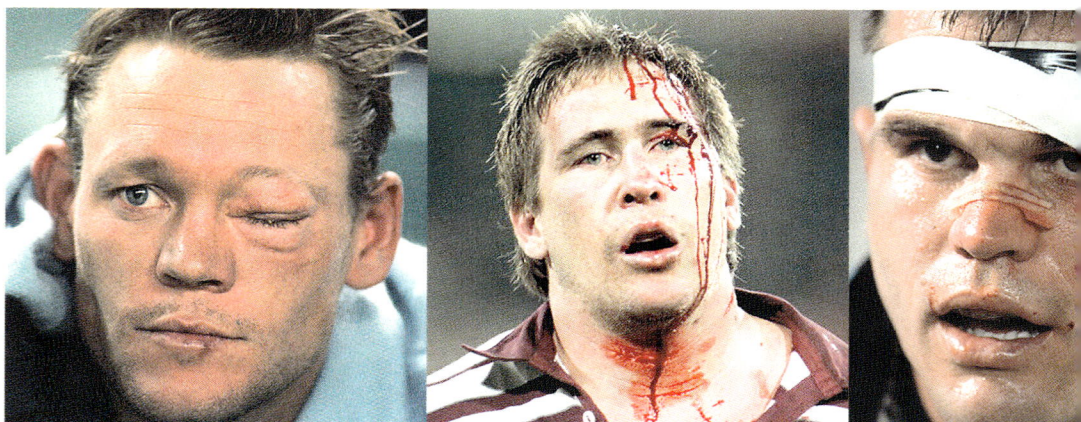

■ Michael O'Connor booting a sideline goal through the rain and mist at the SFS to win for NSW in 1991.

■ Benny Elias, bleeding for his State in 1992 – his mum rushing from the crowd to attend to her son.

■ Arthur Beetson, 35 and larger than life, his chest swelling with pride as he led Queensland to victory in State of Origin I in 1980.

■ Steve Mortimer on his hands and knees, the tears welling in his eyes when the Blues won their first series in 1985.

■ Referee Mick Stone sin-binning Wally Lewis at Lang Park in 1988 – triggering a barrage of cans and fruit.

■ Stone again – his magnificent decision as he peered through the flying bodies to award Mark McGaw a match-winning try in Brisbane, 1987.

■ Queensland's audacious win (24-23) in Origin I, 1998, via Tonie Carroll's last-gasp try.

It was called the greatest Origin match ever played.

These are just part of the story ...

By June 8, 1999, when a record 88,336 fans braved Sydney's soaking rain to watch NSW beat Queensland 12-8 in Match II at the mighty Stadium Australia, rugby league State of Origin football had long since taken its place in the sporting pantheon.

Before a vast TV audience totalling in the millions, the gladiators played for their lives and the old colours they wear in a typically climactic struggle – MATE against MATE.

The spectacle was brutal, brilliant ... captivating.

Ron McAuliffe, wherever he may be, would have been very proud ... 🏉

MATCH I, JULY 8, 1980
at Lang Park

WHETHER or not Arthur Beetson did actually thump Parramatta teammate and close pal Mick Cronin in the match that kicked off the State of Origin phenomenon is purely academic. It's long since gone down in league folklore as fact. And much more than that – as the signpost that this was fair dinkum all right, despite the doubters.

Origin I will live forever as Big Artie's night, even

Footbrawl ... the MCG erupts in 1995 and (top) the scars of battle show on Rod Wishart, Gavin Allen, Paul Harragon and Mark Coyne

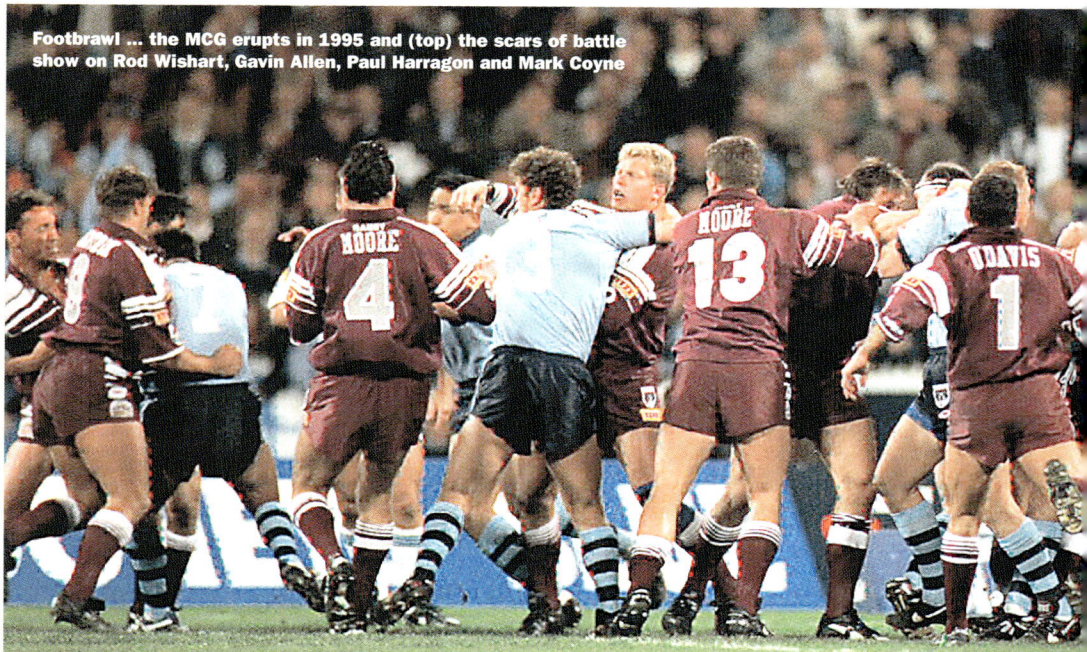

though Chris 'Choppy' Close got man of the match – and even NSW coach Ted Glossop admitted to being moved by the passion of the Lang Park crowd's chant as they urged the 35-year-old front row legend on.

Beetson wore the Maroon jersey for the first of only three times that July night and played wonderfully well. For him it was a night of special pride – after years of travelling north to help the Blues whip the socks off his home State.

And did Artie really belt The Crow? Well, no, actually. The story is a fallacy says Beetson, and Cronin agrees.

'I came over the top a couple of times to smother the ball but I didn't throw any punches,' says Beetson.

But if Beetson didn't throw any blows (at Cronin), plenty of others did in a fire-breathing match in which the Queenslanders caught NSW thoroughly on the hop. The match was played as the third in the series – with the first two non-Origin games won clearly by NSW (35-3) and (17-7).

The match had a little of everything – with a

furious first half brawl ramming home to everyone involved just how serious this new idea was. Doubters in Sydney had floated the suggestion that there was no way teammates would go in full bore against each other.

They were wrong – as has been proven every year since.

Brilliant goalkicking by the youthful Mal Meninga (seven from seven) provided Queensland with their wide winning margin. But the killer thrust in the game came from Close – a dynamic try from a standing start in the second half which ranks still as one of Origin football's finest moments.

Above all it will be remembered as Beetson's night, and the headline the next morning shouted the right message – THANKS A MILLION, ARTIE!

Although officialdom was a little slower to embrace the concept than the fans, Origin football was here to stay on the strength of the fury and drama of 1980's kickoff match.

Artie Beetson *(pictured above)* only ever played for Queensland twice more (in 1981) – and it was left to the young man who played lock that first night, Wally Lewis, to step up in the seasons that followed, as the new 'King'.

QUEENSLAND: Colin Scott, Kerry Boustead, Mal Meninga, Chris Close, Brad Backer, Alan Smith, Greg Oliphant, Wally Lewis, Rod Reddy, Rohan Hancock, Arthur Beetson (c), Johnny Lang, Rod Morris. Replacements: Norm Carr, Bruce Astill. Coach: John McDonald.
NEW SOUTH WALES: Graham Eadie, Chris Anderson, Steve Rogers, Mick Cronin, Greg Brentnall, Alan Thompson, Tom Raudonikis (c), Jim Leis, Graeme Wynn, Bob Cooper, Craig Young, Steve Edge, Gary Hambly. Replacements: Steve Martin, Robert Stone. Coach: Ted Glossop.
QUEENSLAND 20 (Boustead, Close tries, Meninga 7 goals) **NSW 10** (Raudonikis, Brentnall tries, Cronin 2 goals). Referee: Billy Thompson (Great Britain). Crowd: 33,210.
Man of the match: Chris Close (Qld).

1920-29

AUGUST 8, 1925: South Sydney complete an undefeated season in first grade and claim premierships in all three grades. The Rabbitohs' dominance is so commanding – they win the minor premiership by 10 points – that the league cuts short the premiership and brings forward the knockout City Cup.

AUGUST 14, 1926: A 12-man Newtown stage one of the greatest recoveries in premiership history when they come from 18-0 behind against the champion South Sydney side to win 25-24.

SEPTEMBER 4, 1926: A new four-team finals series comes into effect. The first-past-the-post system had killed off interest when dominant teams (such as Souths in 1925) had the competition sewn up several weeks out. Under the new system, if the minor premiers are beaten in their semi-final they have the right to challenge the winner of the final in a grand final.

JUNE 25, 1927: A crowd of 56,487 watch an interstate match between NSW and Queensland at the SCG. The crowd remains a record for interstate football for 67 years.

JUNE 23, 1928: Australia adopt colours of green and gold for the first time in a Test. Captained by Queensland centre Tom Gorman, the Australians are beaten 15-12 by Jonathan Parkin's touring English side.

Birth of a club...

There is some confusion about when Newtown started. There were suggestions the club's first meeting was held on January 8, 1908, but newspapers of the time clearly state the inaugural meeting was held on January 14 at Newtown Town Hall. The King Street premises of local tailor N H Scott became the club's first headquarters. The formation of the club caused great bitterness from the local Newtown Rugby Union Club which ceased to exist in 1912. Newtown was excluded from the 1984 competition and played its final NSWRL premiership game against Canberra in 1983.

COLOURS: Newtown played in royal blue with white knickers, the same as the local union team.

NICKNAME: The Blues, which later became the Bluebags. In their final few years they became the Jets.

I was there...

'When Guru (Eric Grothe) tackled Colin Scott near the line, I was the first Queenslander to arrive. The Blues only had Steve Rogers back in defence and I fancied my chances of scoring.

I yelled at Grothe to let him go but he kept clinging. I grabbed him by his long hair and pulled his head back but he still hung on. I then hit him with the biggest backhander I could muster, got the ball, and scored.'

Queensland centre **Chris 'Choppy' Close** on his infamous moment with Eric Grothe in 1981.

MATCH II, JUNE 14, 1989
at Sydney Football Stadium

QUEENSLAND'S unforgettable performance against all odds stands as State of Origin's 'Rorke's Drift'.

It was also the jewel in the crown among 'King' Wally Lewis's many dominating displays in Origin football.

At the end of it, there was no booing.

The silence of the capacity NSW crowd was its own profound tribute to the raw courage that marked the match.

Thumping 36-3 winners in the first game at Lang Park, the Queenslanders were seemingly on the ropes by halftime in the second.

Three of their stars – Mal Meninga, Allan 'Alfie' Langer and Paul Vautin – were gone from the game with serious injuries.

The sound of 'Alfie' Langer's leg snapping was enough to put any side off its game.

Midway through the second half winger Michael Hancock joined the injured.

Then, as the minutes ticked away, lock Bob Lindner was stretchered off with a serious leg injury.

Down to 12 the Maroons somehow hung on.

Lewis was both their skipper and their champion that night.

It was his second half 30m sprint for the tryline, past Laurie Daley and Chris Mortimer, then surviving his confrontation with fullback Garry Jack on the line that wrapped up the match for Queensland.

Lewis had all the answers that night, kicking superbly, plugging up the defence at key moments, exhorting his team to lift in the face of adversity.

Even the Sydney fans who hated him could not begrudge him his man of the match medal.

QUEENSLAND: Gary Belcher, Michael Hancock, Tony Currie, Mal Meninga, Alan McIndoe, Wally Lewis (c), Allan Langer, Martin Bella, Kerrod Walters, Sam Backo, Paul Vautin, Gene Miles, Bob Lindner. Replacements: Michael Hagan, Dale Shearer, Trevor Gillmeister, Gary Coyne. Coach: Arthur Beetson.

NEW SOUTH WALES: Garry Jack, Chris Johns, Andrew Ettingshausen, Laurie Daley, John Ferguson, Chris Mortimer, Greg Alexander, Peter Kelly, Mario Fenech, Paul Dunn, Bruce McGuire, Gavin Miller (c), Bradley Clyde. Replacements: Des Hasler, John Cartwright, Brad Mackay, Alan Wilson. Coach: Jack Gibson.

QUEENSLAND 16 (Hancock, Walters, Lewis tries; Meninga, Belcher goals)

NSW 12 (Daley, Johns tries; Alexander 2 goals). Referee: David Manson. Crowd: 40,000. Man of the match: Wally Lewis (Qld).

Don't argue ... NSW halfback Andrew Johns fends off Queensland's Dale Shearer

MATCH II, MAY 29, 1991
at Sydney Football Stadium

WHAT to talk about after such a game? The rain that had pelted down all night, doing its best to soak and to spoil?

The chest-bumping duel between Mark Geyer and Wally Lewis with its potential for an unprecedented explosion of halftime fisticuffs? Or Michael O'Connor's brilliant sideline conversion through the murk to steal the game in the last gasp for NSW?

This was epic Origin football ... epic sport.

The Blues came to the SFS one down – scoring the only try in Match I in Brisbane (Laurie Daley) but falling to Mal Meninga's three goals.

The foul weather that greeted the teams, and the fans, on May 29 only added to the sense of drama.

On the paddock it was both brilliant ... and brutal, with the Blues' 'Towering Inferno' Mark Geyer in the thick of it.

Referee David Manson's intervention was just enough to prevent the Lewis-Geyer confrontation breaking into furious warfare as the teams left the field at halftime.

In the second half Geyer felled Queensland fullback Paul Hauff with a dubious tackle – an incident that was to bring him a five-week suspension. With Geyer in the sin-bin, Dale Shearer scored to nudge Queensland ahead.

But with four minutes to go two fine plays by NSW sent replacement centre Mark McGaw spinning across in the corner.

Through the mist and rain as millions held their breath, O'Connor kicked his unforgettable goal.

NSW had won 14-12.

NEW SOUTH WALES: Andrew Ettingshausen, Chris Johns, Laurie Daley, Michael O'Connor, Rod Wishart, Cliff Lyons, Ricky Stuart, David Gillespie, Ben Elias (c), Steve Roach, Mark Geyer, Ian Roberts, Bradley Clyde. Interchange: Des Hasler, Mark McGaw, Brad Mackay, John Cartwright. Coach: Tim Sheens.
QUEENSLAND: Paul Hauff, Michael Hancock, Peter Jackson, Mal Meninga, Willie Carne, Wally Lewis (c), Allan Langer, Steve Jackson, Steve Walters, Martin Bella, Mike McLean, Andrew Gee, Gary Larson. Interchange: Kevin Walters, Dale Shearer, Gary Coyne, Gavin Allen. Coach: Graham Lowe.
NSW 14 (Johns, McGaw tries; O'Connor 3 goals) **QUEENSLAND 12** (Carne, Shearer tries; Meninga 2 goals). Referee: David Manson. Crowd: 41,520. Man of the match: Steve Walters (Qld).

Controversial referee, Barry 'The Grasshopper' Gomersall

MATCH I, MAY 23, 1994
at Sydney Football Stadium

ORIGIN football has produced many breathtaking finishes since 1980.

Never has there been one to match Queensland's snatch-and-grab raid in the first match of the 1994 series.

With five minutes to play in a match which ran NSW's way for almost all the journey, it was 12-4 and the home crowd was settling back to enjoy the kill.

With the Maroons, however, there is only one truth – it ain't over till it's over. Suddenly, from nowhere they pulled back a try – Willie Carne darting through near the posts – and Mal Meninga knocked over the conversion. 12-10.

Hearts were racing again – coaches Wally Lewis (Queensland) and Phil Gould (NSW) lived out their own small versions of hell.

With less than a minute to play, and Queensland seemingly pinned deep in their own territory, the match still looked over.

Suddenly, a break down the left. Allan Langer, Kevin Walters, Carne – then Steve Renouf was into open ground.

Trapped by the cover, Renouf turned it back inside to Hancock, Smith, Langer, Meninga ... and finally to centre Mark Coyne.

With a big step off the right foot, Coyne came back inside Brad Fittler and Ricky Stuart ... and planted the ball over the line.

In the Channel 9 box high above, Ray Warren called it brilliantly – 'That's not a try, that's a miracle!'

Something pretty close to the try of the century had knocked NSW stone cold.

QUEENSLAND: Julian O'Neill, Michael Hancock, Mal Meninga (c), Steve Renouf, Willie Carne, Kevin Walters, Allan Langer, Andrew Gee, Steve Walters, Martin Bella, Trevor Gillmeister, Gary Larson, Billy Moore. Interchange: Mark Coyne, Darren Smith, Mark Hohn, Darren Fritz. Coach: Wally Lewis.
NEW SOUTH WALES: Tim Brasher, Graham Mackay, Brad Fittler, Paul McGregor, Rod Wishart, Laurie Daley (c), Ricky Stuart, Glenn Lazarus, Ben Elias, Ian Roberts, Paul Sironen, Paul Harragon, Brad Mackay. Interchange: Andrew Ettingshausen, Chris Johns, David Gillespie, David Barnhill. Coach: Phil Gould.
QUEENSLAND 16 (O'Neill, Carne, Coyne tries; Meninga 2 goals).
NSW 12 (B Mackay, Harragon tries, Wishart, G Mackay goals). Referee: Bill Harrigan. Crowd: 41,859. Man of the match: Willie Carne (Qld).

1920-29

JULY 21, 1928: After losing the first two Tests and the Ashes, Australia regain some prestige with a 21-14 third Test victory at the SCG. South Sydney winger **Benny Wearing**, in his one and only Test match, scores a record 12 points from two tries (one a spectacular kick-and-chase effort) and three goals.

AUGUST 11, 1928: Fans riot after a St George-Balmain match at **Earl Park**, Arncliffe. One newspaper describes the incident as 'the most serious outbreak of violence on a sports ground in recent years'. Sections of the crowd of 6000 jump the fence, ripping off palings in the process. Police battle the rioters with batons and handcuffs to restore order.

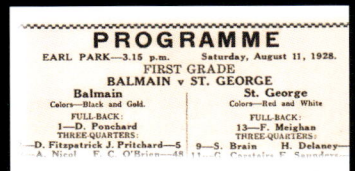

PROGRAMME
EARL PARK—3.15 p.m.   Saturday, August 11, 1928.
FIRST GRADE
BALMAIN v ST. GEORGE

DECEMBER 22, 1928: The first **night rugby league** match is played when Easts and Souths do battle in a nine-a-side exhibition match at Sydney Showground.

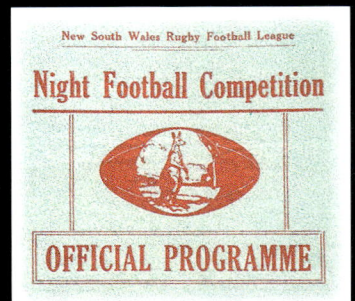

New South Wales Rugby Football League
Night Football Competition
OFFICIAL PROGRAMME

The way we were...

1929: Hoyts convert 20 suburban theatres from 'silent' to 'talkie'. Future PM **Robert James Lee Hawke** is born. Australian singer Florence Austral is banned from performing in a London festival because of her involvement in divorce proceedings years earlier.

Man on Man
George Treweek vs Bryan Fletcher

GEORGE Treweek was one of the game's giants in a career that spanned the years 1926 to 1934. He measured 188cm (6ft 2ins) and was extremely tall for a player of his day. Treweek ran with a characteristic high-striding and arms-flailing action. When he arrived at Souths from the Tumut district, via Mascot third grade in the mid-1920s, Rabbitoh fans were quick to christen him 'Arms and Legs'. Treweek specialised in running wide and trampling opponents. Sydney City's Bryan Fletcher is taller than Treweek, but is not regarded as a player of unusual height in an age when most top grade backrowers hover over the 180cm mark. Fletcher was a late developer, coming into first grade at 23, whereas Treweek was playing regular first grade at 21. Fletcher's forte is his ability to offload the ball in heavy traffic.

I was there...

'The feeling after we won the first Origin game was a mixture of elation and relief. NSW, containing plenty of Queenslanders, had given us heaps over the years and it was terrific getting one back. I was 35 and it was a huge thrill to be selected. Wally Lewis spoke emotionally to the players about my recall and I'll never forget that.

Later we had one big party and I reckon that beer has never tasted so good.'

Arthur Beetson, Queensland's first Origin skipper.

George TREWEEK
Born: March 31, 1905.
Died: October 28, 1991.
Played: 1926-34. **Club**: South Sydney.
Position: Second row.
Weight: 90kg (14st2).
Height: 188cm (6ft2). **Tests**: 7.
Career games: 172.
Career points: 177.

Bryan FLETCHER
Born: April 12, 1974.
Played: From 1997.
Club: Sydney City.
Position: Second row.
Weight: 106kg (16st9).
Height: 190cm (6ft3).
Tests: 3 **Career games:** 63.
Career points: 32.

Team of the Decade...
1920-1929

QUEENSLAND enjoyed their greatest period of dominance over NSW during the 1920s and that is reflected in the selection of seven Queenslanders in the team of the decade. The greatest club side of the period was Souths and they supply winger Wearing and secondrower Treweek. Five Test captains appear in this all-star 13 – Fraser, Craig, Gorman, Johnston and Steinohrt. **Fullback:** Charles 'Chook' FRASER (Balmain). **Wingers:** Bill PATEN (Ipswich, Mackay), Benny WEARING (Souths). **Centres:** Tom GORMAN (Toowoomba, Brisbane Brothers), Jimmy CRAIG (Balmain, University, Ipswich, Wests). **Five-eighth:** Albert 'Ricketty' JOHNSTON (Newtown, St George). **Halfback:** Duncan THOMPSON (Norths, Toowoomba Valleys). **Lock:** Jack 'Bluey' WATKINS (Easts). **Secondrowers:** George TREWEEK (Souths), Vic ARMBRUSTER (Mullumbimby, Toowoomba Valleys, Brisbane Grammar, Brisbane Valleys). **Frontrowers:** Norm POTTER (Ipswich, Brisbane Wests), Herb STEINOHRT (Toowoomba Valleys). **Hooker:** Arthur 'Snowy' JUSTICE (St George).

Duncan Thompson

WHAT A GAME!
NEWTOWN v SOUTHS
1926

NEWTOWN's amazing comeback from an 18-0 deficit against South Sydney at the SCG in 1926 rates among the most epic fightbacks in league history.

Souths, the strongest team in the land in that era, led 13-0 at halftime and when a try soon after the resumption extended their lead to 18-0, Newtown's fate looked to be sealed.

Unbeaten since the start of 1925, Souths were an awesome unit including the likes of Benny Wearing, Alf 'Smacker' Blair, Ernie Lapham, Alf O'Connor, George Treweek and Eddie Root.

Newtown, on the other hand, were a team of mere battlers who looked set to become the latest in the Rabbitohs' long line of victims.

To add to the Bluebags' problems, they lost frontrower Charlie 'Bull' Prendergast with a bad ankle injury early in the match. No replacements were allowed and they had to battle on with 12 men.

When Root, the game's outstanding backrower of the day, scored just after halftime, it became a question of by just how much Souths would win.

As the Bluebags waited behind the tryline for the conversion attempt, captain Keith Ellis said to his players: 'Let's get stuck into them and let the ball run like they are. Give it a try.'

The result was both immediate and spectacular. Newtown were transformed from a team of hard tacklers into a devastating attacking machine. A series of quick tries saw them reduce Souths' lead to 18-15, and eventually hit the lead to outlast a stunned Souths 25-24.

1920-29

MARCH, 1929: H 'Jersey' Flegg is elected fifth president of the NSWRL, succeeding Sir James Joynton Smith, who had held the post since 1910. Smith is named the game's new patron following the death of Fred Flowers.

SEPTEMBER 14, 1929: Souths win their fifth straight premiership when they account for Newtown 30-10 in the final. It is a win of considerable merit for Souths after five of their star players depart with the Kangaroos in late July.

NOVEMBER 11, 1929: Foundation club Glebe is axed from the premiership after a 13-12 vote by the NSW Rugby League. Glebe was the first club formed in 1908 but with disappointing results in their final three seasons and the loss of their home ground Wentworth Park to soccer, the club's demise was not unexpected. A petition of 3000 signatures and an appeal to the NSWRL general committee fails to reverse the decision.

Viv FARNSWORTH
1891-1953

80 DESCRIBED as a 'dream centre, with speed, attacking prowess and deadly, determined tackling', Farnsworth formed half of a celebrated centre pairing with Herb Gilbert, which helped Australia to Ashes victories in 1911-12 and 1920. He played union with Newtown before switching codes, along with his older brother Bill, in 1909. In 1911, the pair became the first brothers to play Test football for Australia. After the 1911-12 tour, Farnsworth returned to England to play with Oldham and served in World War One before resuming his career in Australia. 6 Tests (1911-20), Kangaroo tourist 1911-12.

Herb GILBERT
1888-1972

76 STRONG defensive centre of the game's early years, Gilbert was regarded as one player capable of keeping 'The Master' in check. Duels between Gilbert's Souths and Dally Messenger's Easts were among the most keenly anticipated contests in club football and rarely did Messenger get the better of his opposite. Gilbert enjoyed great success in Australia with Souths, Easts, Wests and St George (he was Saints' first captain) and in three seasons with Hull. Played in two Ashes winning sides for Australia (1911-12 and 1920). 7 Tests (1911-20), Kangaroo tourist 1911-12.

Herb STEINOHRT
1900-1985

74 DEPENDING on the circumstances, Herb Steinohrt could play lock, second row or front row. A member of the great Toowoomba sides of the 1920s, Steinohrt was as tough as any player who has worn the green and gold. His tackling technique – he perfected the spear tackle – would invite censure from today's authorities, but in his time, it was well within the rules. Most memorable display came in the Battle of Brisbane Test in 1932, when he led a battered Australian side to a famous victory over the old foe. 9 Tests (1928-32), Kangaroo tourist 1929-30.

Peter 'Mick' MADSEN
1900 - 1979

79 THREE years after his death in 1979, Madsen, a granite-tough frontrower of the Depression years, was named in Australia's greatest ever team. It was a testament to the impact the Toowoomba forward had on the game during one of its toughest eras. Stories of Madsen's courage are legion. In England in 1929, he 'collected a smash in the face that would have hospitalised an ordinary man ...' Madsen merely spat out a tooth and played on. Later tests revealed he had broken his jaw in two places. 9 Tests (1929-36), Kangaroo tourist 1929-30, 1933-34.

THE Daily Telegraph

WE SELECT
THE BEST
OF THE CENTURY

Jack RAYNER
Born: 1921

73 JACK Rayner was 'discovered' as a footballer playing in the mud of Papua New Guinea during World War II. Former international Eric Lewis persuaded the young forward to join Souths and in 1946, Rayner began an association with the club which lasted until his retirement in 1957. Rayner quickly rose to the South Sydney captaincy and in the next decade he led the club to five premierships. A gentle giant, Rayner was a stickler for fair play and was never sent from the field in more than 250 career games. 5 Tests (1948-49), Kangaroo tourist 1948-49.

The Great 100

Steve MORTIMER
Born: 1956

78 STATE of Origin was the ideal theatre for Steve Mortimer, who played the game with a rare passion. A brilliant, will-o'-the-wisp halfback, Mortimer achieved his crowning moment in the game in 1985 when he led NSW to their maiden series victory in Origin football. At club level, Mortimer played a pivotal role in four Canterbury premiership wins in the 1980s and helped lift the Bulldogs to a pre-eminent position in the competition. Arrived at Canterbury in 1976 from Wagga's Turvey Park club. 8 Tests (1981-84), Kangaroo tourist 1982.

Bob O'REILLY
Born: 1949

77 A GIFTED, ball-playing frontrower, O'Reilly became Parramatta's first home-bred international when he made a meteoric rise to Australia's Test team in 1971 at the age of 21. After period in the wilderness, his career was rejuvenated under the coaching of Jack Gibson at Easts in 1978 and he was rated unlucky to miss Kangaroo tour that year. Wanting to end his career where it began, O'Reilly returned to Parramatta, and in 1981 finished on a high when he played in the Eels' maiden premiership victory. 9 Tests (1971-74), Kangaroo tourist 1973.

Brian HAMBLY
Born: 1936

75 EMERGED from South Sydney in 1956 to forge a career as a forward of outstanding ability over the next 12 seasons. Started out as a backrower with good hands and clever offloading skills, and after transferring to Wagga, won a place with the Kangaroos of 1959-60. Australia narrowly failed to win the Ashes, but Hambly would earn another trip four years later while playing for Parramatta. The tourists of 1963-64 claimed the prized trophy for the first time in more than 50 years on British soil. 18 Tests (1959-65), Kangaroo tourist 1959-60, 1963-64.

Eddie LUMSDEN
Born: 1936

72 ALTHOUGH better known these days as a representative selector, Lumsden was once one of the game's most powerful wingers. On one end of a breathtaking St George backline (Johnny King the other), Lumsden became a tryscoring phenomenon, finishing with 136 tries in 158 games for the Dragons. He played in 10 winning grand final sides after joining Saints from Kurri Kurri in 1957. Teammate King described him as 'a devastating runner who was almost impossible to stop once he got a sniff of the tryline'. 15 Tests (1959-63), Kangaroo tourist 1959-60.

Arthur 'Pony' HALLOWAY
1885-1961

71 THE succession of brilliant Australian halfbacks traces back to Halloway, the first half to join league's breakaway movement in 1907. Tough and resourceful, he is said to have played a game for Balmain just hours after chopping off a finger in a lathe. Played in seven premiership-winning sides for Easts and Balmain between 1913 and 1920 after beginning his league career with Glebe. The first player to make four overseas tours (two to England and two to New Zealand), Halloway holds a special place in the game's history. 10 Tests (1908-19), Kangaroo tourist 1908-09, 1911-12.

CHAPTER FOUR

Dynasty Makers

BY IAN HEADS

Dynasty

1930-39

JANUARY 4, 1930: One of the most controversial incidents in the history of Anglo-Australian football is played out at Swinton's Station Road ground. Australian halfback Joe 'Chimpy' Busch is denied a fair try after a touch judge rules he has taken the corner post. Referee Bob Robinson is reported to have said: 'Fair try, Australia, but I am over-ruled.' The Test finishes in a nil-all draw and England go on to retain the Ashes after an unprecedented fourth Test.

AUGUST 16, 1930: Western Suburbs captain-coach **Jim Craig** lays claim to being the game's most versatile player by playing five-eighth, lock, hooker and fullback all in the one game against Eastern Suburbs. Despite Craig's amazing utility value, Wests are beaten 23-18.

OCTOBER 4, 1930: Wests win their maiden premiership title after beating St George 27-2 in the game's first official grand final. The NSWRL admit the season has finished too late after a meagre crowd of 12,178 turns out for the decider.

NOVEMBER 14, 1930: Death of pioneer hooker Sandy Pearce. An all-time great of the game, Pearce played 14 Tests for Australia, the last at the age of 41. He toured with the Kangaroos in 1908-09 and 1921-22.

THE teams that can truly wear the tag 'champions' in rugby league's passing parade can be identified at a glance. They are the ones that have been able to win premierships ... then win again ... and again and again. Punctuating the game's 91 years, such teams have emerged in almost every decade – rising up like tsunamis to sweep all before them.

Sometimes it has seemed that these special ones would never be beaten; in the 1950s and 60s the certainty of St George winning the competition was akin to the daily rising and setting of the sun. For 11

Pride of the league ... Souths' 1950 premiership-winning side

straight years the other sides tilted at the windmill ... and failed. When Saints finally fell in 1967, there was jaw-gaping disbelief. Was there really to be a grand final without the mighty Saints?

The word dynasty (any sequence of powerful leaders of the same family) suits such teams perfectly. The rise and fall of the great teams highlights the game's graph in the 20th century. In the beginning came Dally Messenger-inspired Eastern Suburbs, winners in 1911-12-13 and gaining permanent possession of the Agricultural Shield because of their triple strike. The trophy, which is the bounty of the game's first dynasty, remains in the possession of the Messenger family to this day. Close on the Tricolours' heels came Balmain (1915-16-17-19-20), setting their own record-breaking standards. From 1915 to 1917 the Tigers won all three grades of the premiership. At the end of that run the first grade record was: played 43, won 37, drawn 2, lost 4.

Then came the others in steady procession – their collective story telling of the finest club teams the game ever saw: Souths – winners seven out of eight years in the 1920s and early 30s; Easts, unbeaten for almost three full years in the 1930s; Souths again, winners five times in six years at the start of the 1950s; St George – impossibly – winning 11 seasons straight (1956-66); Souths, yet again, winners four out of five years from 1967-71; Manly, four-time winners in the 1970s after a wait of 25 years to break through; Canterbury and Parramatta sharing the pedestal as they traded premierships in the 1980s – winning four times each.

No club since has quite scaled those heights, although Canberra threatened (premiers 1990-91 and again in 1994) while the undoubted quality of Brisbane's effort in the 1990s of winning four titles (1992-93-97-98) is checked only by the fact that one of those crowns (Super League, 1997) was gained in half a competition – and so is inevitably devalued to an extent in the bigger picture.

The dominant teams of the years since 1908 share a lot more than their success. The presence in each of them of powerful individuals, men who rose way above the common herd, is the linking thread – whether player, coach or administrator. These were some of them:

Easts (1911-12-13): Dally Messenger, rugby league's 'Master'.

Balmain (1915-16-17-19-20): Champion players such as 'Chook' Fraser and 'Pony' Halloway and an outstanding leader in captain-coach Bill Kelly.

Souths (1925-26-27-28-29-31-32): A groundbreaking coach who laid down the formula (Arthur Hennessy), a great captain to start the run ('Smacker' Blair) and many great players.

Easts (1935-36-37): Simply a dream team of every hoped-for talent with Dave Brown, in the centres, their dazzling points machine when the run kicked off in 1935. A shrewd, plain-speaking coach in Pony Halloway.

Souths (1950-51-53-54-55): Jack Rayner, a wonderful leader, Clive Churchill ('The Little Master'), the greatest fullback of them all, countless star players. Unstoppable Souths spirit.

St George (1956-66): On-field innovators (Ken Kearney, Harry Bath), great captains (Norm Provan, Ken Kearney, Ian Walsh), dazzling players far too

Makers

Top shelf ... two halfbacks who dominated a decade, Canterbury's Steve Mortimer (left) and Parramatta's Peter Sterling

Photo: *Rugby League Week*

1930-39

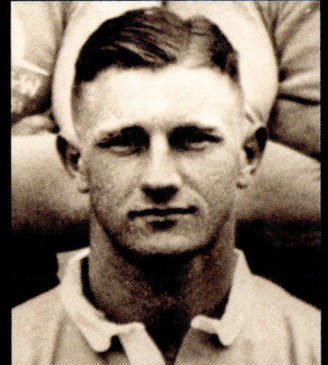

JUNE 6, 1931: Champion centre **Dave Brown** makes a memorable debut for NSW – at the age of 18 – in the first interstate match for the year against Queensland. NSW win the game 39-17 before a crowd of 20,010 at the Sydney Sports Ground.

JUNE 6, 1932: A rugby league world record crowd of 70,204 turns out for the first Test between Australia and Jim Sullivan's English tourists at the **Sydney Cricket Ground**. The visitors claim first blood in the Ashes series with an 8-6 victory.

JUNE 18, 1932: An epic Test is played at the Brisbane Cricket Ground where a heroic Australian side levels the series against England. *The Referee* newspaper graphically describes the dramatic finale to the match, which became known as the Battle of Brisbane: 'It became the most desperate and rugged game imaginable. Players were strewn like dead men on the field, or were carried off to the touch lines to recover. They were chiefly Australians.' The home side won 15-6.

〈 65 〉

1930-39

SEPTEMBER 24, 1932: Souths win their seventh first grade title in eight years. The Rabbitohs down Wests 19-12 in a closely fought grand final.

JUNE 3, 1933: Queensland selectors send the entire Toowoomba 13 to Sydney to represent Queensland in the first interstate match of the season against New South Wales. The move backfires badly when the Maroons are beaten 24-0.

AUGUST, 1933: A plan to pursue amalgamation talks with Aussie rules authorities is defeated by a (15-10) vote of the NSW Rugby League. One prominent writer noted: 'To paraphrase Kipling, "league is league and rules is rules and never the twain shall meet".'

AUGUST 10, 1933: A pall is cast over the tour of the fifth Kangaroos when popular University centre **Ray Morris** dies of an ear infection in Malta.

DECEMBER 31, 1933: The Kangaroos play England in the first rugby league match in France. Just two weeks after England complete a 3-0 whitewash in the Ashes series, they are stunned by a 63-13 defeat at Paris's Stade Pershing. Dave Brown is the hero for Australia with 27 points from three tries and nine goals.

JANUARY 1934: The Country Rugby League of NSW is established. The first Country team to play under the CRL banner later defeats City 13-11.

APRIL 1934: A match between the returned Kangaroos and The Rest is staged as a testimonial to one of the game's founders, James J Giltinan. Giltinan is paid 50 per cent of the game's proceeds.

numerous to list (Gasnier, Raper, Clay, Langlands, etc), an administration ahead of its time, led by Frank 'Fearless' Facer.

Souths (1967-68-70-71): A great captain (John Sattler), wonderful home-grown players (Coote, McCarthy, Simms etc) and shrewd importations from outside the club.

Manly (1972-73-76-78): A brilliant buying program (with secretary Ken Arthurson ahead of the game), the best players of their era (such as Bob Fulton, Mal Reilly), shrewd, hard-nosed coaches (Ron Willey and Frank Stanton).

Canterbury (1980-84-85-88): Mortimers (several), Hughes's (several), a cutting-edge coach, Warren Ryan, a streetwise administration headed by Peter 'Bullfrog' Moore, a never-say-die Bulldog spirit.

Parramatta (1981-82-83-86): A supercoach, Jack Gibson, and an abundance of fabulous, free-spirited players: Price, Sterling, Kenny, Ella, Cronin and co. A great captain (Steve Edge).

St George, arguably the greatest of them all in their beyond-belief achievement of winning 11 times in a row, have been summed up this way: 'Saints had great players, great administration, pride, a desire to keep winning and an infusion of bold new ideas (courtesy of English-schooled players such as Ken Kearney and Harry Bath).'

These would seem universal qualities underpinning all the clubs that have managed to build dynasties down the years. St George were the model for all who followed, relentless in their player recruiting whenever they saw a potential crack in the armament – even if it was fleetingly glimpsed a couple of years down the track.

Saints added to their ranks selectively (but brilliantly), much preferring to 'grow their own'. Matches were played on Saturdays in those days and on Sundays a small battalion of shrewd Saints men would head out into the NSW (or sometimes Queensland) country districts or to watch an afternoon of junior football – relentlessly identifying, monitoring, searching.

St George wouldn't buy a player unless three of their men had given the thumbs-up. By their achievements through the years the great clubs like Souths and Saints built an expectation of success, making them tougher still to beat – whenever and wherever they played.

It is the quality that the new clubs of recent years cannot (yet) match or manufacture. It comes only after a long, slow cook, developed over many years and many victories. Brief words from Frank Facer, jotted down by a pressman long ago, said a lot about dynasties and sustained achievement in the game. 'Look at the record books,' the Saints secretary said to fellow St George officials one afternoon. 'You'll see that South Sydney won five competitions in a row and seven in eight years. That will be on the books for all time. Even if people read of it in 100 years time, they will say, 'That must have been a very great team'. Our aim should be for St George to make a similar mark on the record book.'

For Saints it was always a case of setting the bar high ... and never flinching. Very likely, when the champion teams of rugby league – The Dynasty Makers – are under consideration, this quality is the secret. Or one of them at least.

Elevenses ... captain-coach Ian Walsh is chaired from the field after St George's 1966 grand final win over Balmain

Souths
Pride of the League

1925-26-27-28-29-31-32
1950-51-53-54-55
1967-68-70-71

SOUTH Sydney's record in the premiership years 1923-1932 reads this way: second, second, premiers, premiers, premiers, premiers, premiers, third, premiers, premiers. Only St George (1956-66) have ever bettered such a run ... or are ever likely to in rugby league's ongoing story.

When Souths trekked to Brisbane in 1930 the posters plastered around town read: WONDER TEAM OF AUSTRALIA.

And so they were ... but for the Rabbitohs, the achievements of the 1920s and 1930s were to be only a beginning when it came to the business of building formidable empires in rugby league.

In the 1950s, under the leadership of Jack Rayner, a mighty Souths team won five times in six years. In the late 1960s and early 1970s, under the captaincy of hardman John Sattler, Souths won four more times – in just five years.

It can fairly be said that when it comes to the word dynasty in the rugby league story the men in cardinal and myrtle have set the pace.

It was during the first Golden Era, in the 1920s, that distinguished league journalist Claude Corbett labelled Souths 'The Pride of the League' – the name that has stuck for evermore.

League pioneer Arthur 'Ash' Hennessy was the man who laid down the famous Souths' 'no kick, run-at-all-costs' style which featured so spectacularly during the 1920s and never really left the club – although the rule changes of modern times eventually shaped league into a very different game. Hennessy's philosophy was to keep the ball moving, to run it from anywhere on the paddock.

Hennessy and skipper Alf 'Smacker' Blair were giant figures of Souths' brilliant run of the 1920s. Blair played as one of two five-eighths in a revolutionary team configuration that the Rabbitohs used for much of the period, featuring only five forwards.

Souths dominated not just as a team but as a club. The Rabbitohs' reserve grade side won the competition eight times in the 10 years from 1923-32, adding lustre to those long and often golden seasons.

In the late 1940s and again in the mid-1960s, Souths experienced similar serendipity to the 1920s. Great players were magically drawn to the club in numbers, or grew locally; each time a team emerged which stood far above all others in the competition.

The run of five premierships gathered from 1950 (1950-51-53-54-55) was checked only by the controversial loss to Wests in 1952 from which referee George Bishop emerged as a villain for the club's folktales.

In 1969, after two straight premierships (with two more to follow), Souths started 1/3 favourites but were thwarted by stubborn Balmain, beaten 11-2.

The three great Rabbitoh eras produced scores of champion players – and wonderful and famous victories beyond counting – all of which live on in the storytelling traditions of the club.

SOUTHS 1967-71 Ultimates

Eric Simms, Ray Branighan, Paul Sait, Bob Honan, Mike Cleary, Denis Pittard, Bob Grant, Ron Coote, Gary Stevens, Bob McCarthy, John O'Neill, Elwyn Walters, John Sattler (c).

1930-39

JUNE 7, 1934: The first interstate match is played under lights. A disappointing crowd of 9000 fails to warm to the night fixture at Sydney's Agricultural Ground, won 14-10 by Queensland. The *Truth* newspaper headlines a short-sighted reaction: 'We've Seen Last of Night Football ... Dead as Caesar'.

SEPTEMBER 1, 1934: Bad weather forces the NSWRL to delay the grand final for a week. Seven days later **Western Suburbs** claim their second premiership with a 15-12 win over an emerging **Eastern Suburbs**.

APRIL 25, 1935: Competition newcomers Canterbury-Bankstown play their first competition match, falling 20-5 to Norths at North Sydney Oval. Forward Jack Hartwell scores the club's first try.

MAY 11, 1935: St George take advantage of Canterbury's inexperience at first grade level by inflicting a 91-6 hiding at Earl Park. Saints cross for 19 tries and land 17 goals in the 85-point massacre. The score and the winning margin remain records for the premiership competition.

MAY 18, 1935: The legendary Dave Brown scores a premiership record 45 points in one match at the Sydney Sports Ground. Brown's effort in crossing for five tries and kicking 15 goals has never been beaten. The victims again are hapless newcomers Canterbury-Bankstown.

1930-39

SEPTEMBER 28, 1935: At 22 and 177 days, Dave Brown becomes Australia's youngest Test captain when he plays against New Zealand in the first Test at Auckland's Carlaw Park.

JULY 18, 1936: Rugged Australian frontrower **Ray Stehr** earns a place in the history books when he is sent off for the second time in the Ashes series against England. Stehr receives his marching orders from referee Lal Deane in the first Test, won 24-8 by Australia, and again by Deane in the Ashes-deciding third Test, won 12-7 by England.

JUNE 19, 1937: Eastern Suburbs complete their third consecutive premiership victory, with a 23-5 romp over Wests at the Sports Ground. With the Kangaroos to tour England and France (for the first time), the competition lasts just one full round. It is the last first-past-the-post premiership. After 18 seasons, the University club plays its last match in the premiership competition.

JANUARY 2, 1938: Australia account for France 35-6 at Stade Buffalo in Paris in the first Test match between the two countries.

APRIL 25, 1938: The champion Eastern Suburbs side loses its first match in almost three years when beaten 21-14 by South Sydney at the SCG.

SEPTEMBER 3, 1938: In only their fourth year in the competition, **Canterbury** win their first premiership with a 19-6 victory over **Eastern Suburbs**.

JUNE 10, 1939: Balmain winger Sid Goodwin scores a record six tries as NSW whip Queensland 54-13 in Sydney.

St George

Never before, never again

1956-57-58-59-60-61-62-63-64-65-66

TO win a single premiership is a momentous feat. To win 11 in succession is a sporting miracle, something almost extra-terrestrial in nature, defying belief and logic.

But the achievement of the St George juggernaut, 1956-66, is stamped indelibly in the record books and imprinted on the game's psyche.

We shall never see its like again.

The St George feat is unchallenged as the most remarkable team accomplishment in Australian, if not world, sport.

And it remains a world record for

St George icon Norm Provan stretches out to score a try against Parramatta

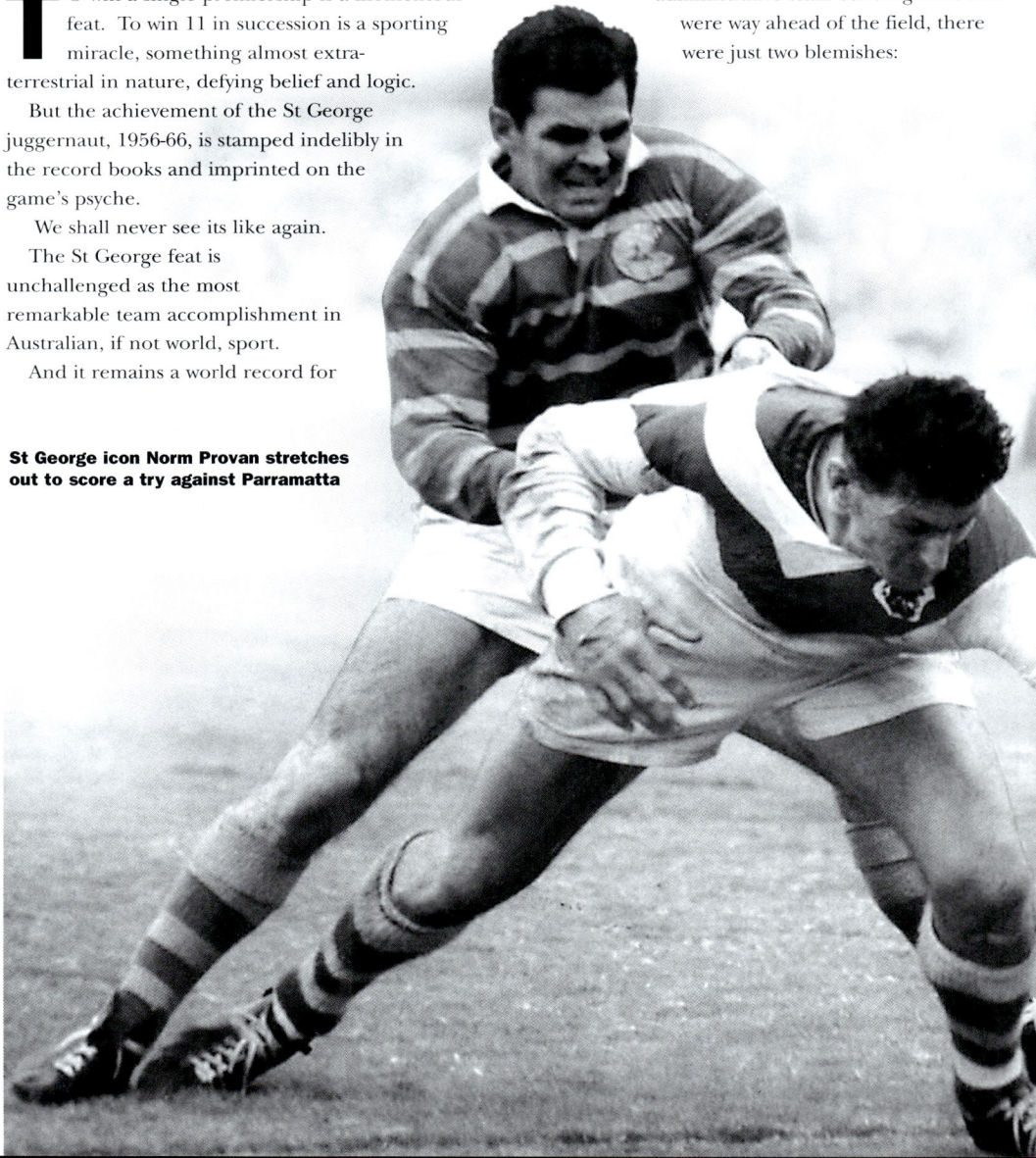

major football – bettering the 10-straight premierships achieved by Fremantle in the WA Australian Rules competition (1887-1896) and the nine straight titles won by Bulgarian soccer club CDNA Sofia.

The facts are these: from the September day in 1956 that the Saints played a man short for 67 of the 80 minutes to beat Balmain in the grand final (18-12), the men in red and white bowled over one grand final opponent after another, sometimes easily, sometimes closely – always finding that extra edge when it was needed.

They played 222 games in the 11 years for 183 wins, five draws and 34 defeats, scoring 5109 points against 2153. When finally it ended on September 9, 1967, with Saints falling 12-11 in a cliffhanger to Canterbury in the final, tears flowed like a summer shower in the Dragons dressing-room.

In 11 years of wonderful football marked by a glittering galaxy of stars (Reg Gasnier, Norm Provan, John Raper, Graeme Langlands et al) and administrative team-building skills that were way ahead of the field, there were just two blemishes:

Provan leaves the field a hero after his final match, the 1965 grand final

The way we were...

1930: L H B Lasseter leaves Alice Springs for ill-fated expedition to a rich gold reef he claims to have found. First soccer World Cup won by Uruguay in Montevideo. International acclaim for **Marx Brothers**' new movie, *Animal Crackers*. Birth of Rolf Harris, entertainer, Richie Benaud (cricket) and astronaut Neil Armstrong. **Phar Lap** wins the Melbourne Cup.

1931: First NSW State lottery drawn.

■ In a midweek match in 1962 the touring Great Britain side thrashed Saints 33-5 before a huge SCG crowd. There were excuses – players missing and injured – but it was quite an uncharacteristic beating for all that.

■ Growing claims from star Wests players in recent years that the muddy grand final of 1963 was 'hot'. Respected Magpies forwards Jack Gibson and Noel Kelly have gone strongly on the record with their beliefs that referee Darcy Lawler backed St George – and robbed Wests of victory (Saints won 8-3 amidst controversy).

Any search for reasons behind the Saints' Miracle of 1956-66 gives clear-cut answers: very great players with the gaps filled as stars grew old; brilliant administration, headed by the hard-nosed secretary Frank 'Fearless' Facer; the new ideas and methods that two great football men, Ken Kearney and Harry Bath, brought back from English football.

It added up to a simply irresistible package, bringing success that no other team, surely, can ever hope to match.

ST GEORGE 1956-66 Ultimates

Brian Graham, Eddie Lumsden, Reg Gasnier, Graeme Langlands, Johnny King, Brian Clay, Billy Smith, Johnny Raper, Norm Provan (c), Elton Rasmussen, Harry Bath, Ian Walsh, Kevin Ryan.

'Puff the Magic Dragon', Reg Gasnier, in full flight at the SCG

‹ **69** ›

The way we were...

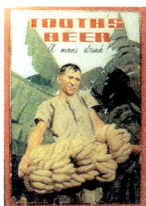

Parramatta
1981-82-83-86

A Decade of Dominance

Canterbury
1980-84-85-88

CANTERBURY Bulldogs and the Parramatta Eels were rugby league's superpowers of the 1980s – trading punch and counterpunch throughout the decade.

Theirs was a shared dynasty, the balance of power shifting first this way, then that.

In the seasons 1980-88 only once (1987) did one of the two not win the premiership.

Canterbury won in 1980, 1984, 1985, 1988; Parramatta won in 1981, 1982, 1983, 1986.

It was an extraordinary, unprecedented struggle between two ambitious outfits underwritten by the cascading profits of their wealthy leagues clubs and with fortunes guided by shrewd men prepared to do whatever it took in the quest for ongoing domination.

In the fierceness of their personal duel in the mid-80s, the clubs inch by inch dragged rugby league into one of the grimmest periods in its history.

Try time ... Steve Mortimer scores against Parramatta

In the Canterbury win of 1980 and the Jack Gibson-inspired Parramatta triumphs of 1981-82-83, there was much dazzling football.

The Bulldogs under coach Ted Glossop were 'The Entertainers' and in the 18-4 grand final win over Easts in 1980 the wonderful try scored by Steve Gearin was an everlasting reminder for the game of the style of football they played.

Gibson's wondrous Eels machine of the early 1980s produced much magic, too, as the coach let loose the rare talents of Sterling, Kenny, Cronin, Ella, Grothe and company.

Eric Grothe's miraculous try against Canterbury in the semi-final of 1983 (Parramatta 30-22) was, perhaps, the greatest individual moment.

The arrival at Canterbury of Warren Ryan, the coach who had run Parramatta close with his unsung Newtown side of 1981, changed the balance – and the style.

With their precision power play, based on a take-no-prisoners pack of forwards, Canterbury became the most feared team in league. They won in 1984 (6-4 over the Eels) and 1985 (7-6 over St George). It sure wasn't pretty, but it worked.

A trademark of the Ryan era was the ability of coach and team to continue to operate with brutal efficiency – even when things were fraying badly within the club.

The 1986 grand final could be rated the high, or low, point of the new-style league, depending on your point of view. It was the only tryless grand final in league history – won 4-2 by John Monie's Eels to provide a magical farewell for Parramatta warriors Ray Price and Mick Cronin.

At the hooter, Canterbury hooker Mark Bugden was a metre from the Parramatta line.

Effectively it was the end of an era. Their stars gone, or ageing, Parramatta were back in the pack.

And amid much bickering Ryan left Canterbury in 1987, bound for Balmain.

In 1988 there came a postscript to this story of two-club domination.

Ryan's Tigers unleashed a withering late-season run, taking six sudden-death matches in a row with England's Ellery Hanley their star.

But in the grand final Canterbury, under first-term coach Phil Gould, were ready for them and won convincingly 24-12.

In the story of the Eels, the Bulldogs and the furiously fought 80s, it was the final chapter.

PARRAMATTA 1981-86 Ultimates

Paul Taylor, Eric Grothe, Mick Cronin, Steve Ella, Neil Hunt, Brett Kenny, Peter Sterling, Ray Price, Peter Wynn, John Muggleton, Ron Hilditch, Steve Edge (c), Bob O'Reilly.

CANTERBURY 1980-88 Ultimates

Greg Brentnall, Peter Mortimer, Chris Mortimer, Andrew Farrar, Chris Anderson, Terry Lamb, Steve Mortimer, Paul Langmack, Steve Folkes, David Gillespie, Peter Tunks, George Peponis (c), Peter Kelly.

Parramatta captain Steve Edge is chaired from the field in 1981

I was there...

'Saints were more respected than hated during that incredible run. We had heaps of great players and played in front of the biggest crowds the game had known. We won all those grand finals but got knocked off every now and then during the premiership rounds. Our opponents rose several levels every time they played us but when we lost, it was mainly because of complacency.'

Norm Provan who, as a player or captain-coach, figured in 10 of mighty St George's record 11 titles.

I was there...

'Everyone called Canterbury the 'Family Club' in the 1980s and we were like one big, happy family. The players got on extremely well, they shared each other's good and back luck and generally had a lot of fun. On the field, the Bulldogs played a terrific brand of football. We had plenty of pace and flair but when the need arose for the tough stuff, we had players who never took a backward step.'

Peter Moore, godfather to the Canterbury Bulldogs.

Man on Man
Sandy Pearce vs Jason Hetherington

Born: May 31, 1883.
Died: November 14, 1930.
Played: 1907-21.
Club: Easts.
Position: Hooker.
Weight: 87kg (13st 8lb).
Height: 178 (5ft 10in).
Tests: 14. **Career games:** 249.
Career points: 13.

Born: August 23, 1969.
Played: Since 1991.
Club: Canterbury (also Ipswich and Gold Coast).
Position: Hooker.
Weight: 90kg (14st 2lb).
Height: 175cm (5ft 9in).
Career games: 122.
Career points: 64.

NO playing position has undergone a greater transformation down the years than that of hooker. In Sandy Pearce's day the hooker worked feverishly in as many as 40 scrums per match. That was when the scrum was a genuine contest, where the ability of a hooker to get the better of his opponent both physically and mentally often meant the difference between his team winning and losing. Pearce toured with the first two Kangaroo outfits of 1908-09 and 1921-22. Such was his strength and stamina he invariably wore down his opposite number and guaranteed his team a steady flow of possession. The hooker's role today has changed from scrummager to specialist dummy-half and to that of a defender around the rucks. It is interesting to note that the physical attributes of old-time hookers and today's rakes have changed very little. Hetherington is slightly heavier than Pearce but Pearce was around an inch (2.5cm) taller.

WHAT A GAME!
CANTERBURY v PARRAMATTA
1998

CANTERBURY produced the most stunning fightback ever seen in finals football to win through to the grand final in 1998.

Trailling a committed Parramatta 18-2 only 11 minutes from time, the Bulldogs looked to be heading to an inglorious exit from the premiership. But Steve Folkes' men piled on three late tries to level the scores at 18-all at the end of regulation time, sending the game into an extra 20 minutes.

With the momentum clearly going their way, the Bulldogs then stormed home to win 32-20 in extra time.

Parramatta dominated most of the game and appeared headed for a grand final showdown with hot favourites Brisbane. When they sped to 18-2, the Eels seemed to lose focus and that was all Canterbury needed. Craig Polla-Mounter *(left)* gave the Bulldogs a glimmer of hope with a determined try, then fullback Rod Silva scored one of his runaway specials five minutes from the finish to narrow the gap to 18-12.

Just 90 seconds later, Kiwi rookie Willie Talau finished a backline move in the corner, leaving Daryl Halligan with possibly the most important conversion of his career.

Ice-cool Halligan calmly sent the ball spiralling between the posts to level the scores and send the game into overtime.

One minute later, Polla-Mounter, one of the Bulldogs' stars, landed a field goal to put his team ahead for the first time.

'Polly' then barged over for a determined try and booted another field goal, with a late Travis Norton try sealing a memorable win.

Canterbury couldn't repeat the feat the following week against Brisbane, proving no match for the Broncos in the premiership decider.

The way we were...

1936: Ampol Petroleum established. The last **Tasmanian Tiger** in Hobart Zoo dies. Australian Cricket Board wants to ban barracking at Test matches. Eastern Suburbs win their sixth premiership with Balmain runners-up.

1937: South African rugby union touring team, the Springboks, complete triumphant first visit to Australia, winning two Tests, both in Sydney. Walter Burley Griffin dies of peritonitis in Lucknow, India. Hubert Opperman completes a record 13-day bicycle ride from Perth to Sydney. Swimmer Dawn Fraser is born.

1938: Australians celebrate 150 years of settlement. Five die when freak waves overwhelm swimmers at Bondi beach. **Melbourne Cup** is stolen from the Athenaeum Club in Melbourne. C J Dennis, famous Australian writer, dies aged 61.

1939: Temperature in Adelaide reaches 117.7 degrees farenheit (47.6 degrees centigrade) on January 12, the highest recorded in an Australian capital city. Bushfires rage in NSW and Victoria. **Robert Menzies** becomes Prime Minister. Australia declares war on Germany immediately following Britain's declaration of war.

Easts
The Nonpareils
1935-36-37

THE great Eastern Suburbs team of the 1930s went for 1036 days without losing a match – an achievement that ranks as one of the most remarkable in the game's history. This was a true red, white and blue dynasty – manifested in absolute domination of all they surveyed by a team of all the talents.

Between June 22, 1935, and April 25, 1938, Easts did not lose a single game.

Their record in its entirety for seasons 1935-36-37 – years in which they imposed an iron hand on the premiership – was this: played 41, won 36, drew 4, lost 1 (11-18 v Souths at the SCG, June 22, 1935).

The final link with this extraordinary side was broken only in May 1999 with the death of Andy Norval at 87.

Norval, a punishing lock forward who played on the wing for Australia, was the last of the Easts' Nonpareils.

What a team it was – great enough for the renowned *Daily* and *Sunday Telegraph* league scribe George Crawford to call it, in 1975: "Probably the greatest club side in Australian rugby league history."

The recently departed Norval, a demon tackler, was just one of many Tricolour stars.

Radio legend Frank Hyde recalls Norval driving Newtown's powerful wing man Sid Goodwin on to the bike track at Sydney Sports Ground one afternoon in 1938 with the most powerful cover defending tackle he ever saw.

'The most punishing defender I've ever seen," his successor at lock, Dick Dunn, said of Norval.

With hardmen like Ray Stehr and Joe Pearce up front, outstanding halves in Viv Thicknesse and

Ernie Norman and dazzling speed and brilliance in the three-quarter line, Easts had all the answers.

Undoubted jewel in the crown in such a team was the bald-headed, head-geared 'Wonder Man' of 1930s football – centre Dave Brown.

Brown, one of the great gentlemen of the Australian game, re-wrote the record books with his flashing opportunistic play and goalkicking talent.

Season 1935 was his great year in football; he scored 38 tries for Easts, a season's record 244 points (beating Dally Messenger's mark) and 385 points in all games.

Against the premiership's newest team, Canterbury, on May 18, 1935, he scored 45 points – five tries and 15 goals (Easts won 87-7).

When Brown left to play with Warrington in 1936, Easts promptly discovered a dazzling new centre out of the GPS rugby competition, Jack Beaton from St Joseph's College, whose career was short (1936-38) but brilliant.

When Beaton retired to become a publican in 1939, J C Davis, editor of the sporting newspaper *The Referee*, wrote of him: 'In all his football he displays the chivalry of a Knight.'

Coached by a hero of league's early days, Arthur 'Pony' Halloway, Eastern Suburbs 1935-36-37 was a team of football aristocrats – a champion side which soared impossibly high above the pack.

EASTS 1935-37 Ultimates

Tom Dowling, Fred Tottey, Dave Brown (c), Jack Beaton, Rod O'Loan, Ernie Norman, Viv Thicknesse, Andy Norval, Harry Pierce, Joe Pearce, Max Nixon, Tommy McLachlan, Ray Stehr.

On the fly ... Easts' Jack Beaton takes on the Newcastle defence in a 1930s State Cup match and (above) Eastern Suburbs' premiership-winning side of 1937

I was there...

'We had a well balanced team from fullback right through to the front row and played attractive, open football. Our wingers Ian Moir and Johnny Graves saw plenty of ball and scored dozens of tries. We dominated the premiership from 1950 to 1955. The only year we didn't win it was 1952 when we were robbed by a referee.'

Jack Rayner, Souths secondrower and captain-coach of the 1950s.

Birth of a club...

In June, 1934, the NSWRL set up a special committee to investigate increasing the number of teams in the competition. A newspaper report at the time said everything was shaping towards a new team in the Canterbury-Bankstown area. The move was opposed by Western Suburbs, who would lose players and junior area. Those protests proved unsuccessful and the club was formed in October that year. The team entered the competition the next year and trained on a cow pasture in Burwood Road, Belmore.

The first coach was Tedda Courtenay, who did it tough in his first season. The side won only two games that first year and at one stage were beaten by St George 91-6 and Easts 87-7 the following week.

COLOURS: Blue and white.
NICKNAME: Originally the Berries or the See-Bees. They became the Bulldogs in 1977.

Wally Prigg

Team of the Decade...
1930-1939

IT was the era of the great Eastern Suburbs sides and six players from that period are included in this team. The Tricolours lost only one game in three seasons (1935-37) and a production line of talent spawned some legendary league figures. Beaton, Brown, Norman, Pearce and Stehr formed the nucleus of one of the game's greatest dynasties.

Fullback: Frank McMILLAN (Wests).
Wingers: Alan RIDLEY (Queanbeyan Blues, Wests), Jack BEATON (Lismore, Easts).
Centres: Dave BROWN (Easts, Warrington), Ernie NORMAN (Easts).
Five-eighth: Vic HEY (Wests, Toowoomba, Leeds).
Halfback: Joe 'Chimpy' BUSCH (Easts, Leeds, Balmain).
Lock: Wally PRIGG (Central Newcastle).
Secondrowers: Joe PEARCE (Easts), Jim GIBBS (South Newcastle).
Frontrowers: Ray STEHR (Easts, Mudgee), Mick MADSEN (Past Brothers Toowoomba).
Hooker: Arthur FOLWELL (Newtown).

Joe Pearce

Manly

Making up for lost time

1972-73-76-78

Action man ... Manly's dynamic five-eighth Bob Fulton in determined mood for the Sea Eagles and (right) enforcer John O'Neill

THE club that had been carved from North Sydney territory in 1947, Manly Warringah, ached for a premiership in 1972. Manly had been to the 'edge' five times by then – beaten in the grand finals of 1951-57-59-68-70.

After an excellent 1971 season in which they were pipped 15-12 by St George in the final, the club, via shrewd secretary Ken Arthurson, added the final two cogs to the machine – signing champion Souths pair Ray Branighan and John 'Lurch' O'Neill, adding them to the likes of Malcolm Reilly (from England), Ken Irvine (from Norths) and the brilliant young fullback Graham Eadie.

In *The Daily Telegraph* Mike Gibson wrote: 'Now, for Manly, there can be no more excuses.'

As it turned out the team from the northern peninsula had no need for excuses – then, or for the rest of the decade. When Manly beat Easts 19-14 in 1972 there were, as Arthurson recalls, 'blokes crying everywhere'.

In 1973 Manly won again – in a grand final never forgotten.

Referee Keith Page's loose rein on a potentially explosive Manly-Cronulla decider helped turn the first half into a street brawl, tagging the game as the 'most savage grand final ever played'.

Two virtuoso Bob Fulton tries in the thick of the mayhem took Manly all the way home.

The addition of quality players, sometimes controversially at the expense of 'fibro' clubs, enabled Manly to stay as league's frontrunners for much of the 1970s.

In later years Arthurson has talked about how 'driven' he was to make up for all the lost years once Manly finally started winning premierships.

Coached by Frank 'Biscuits' Stanton, the Sea Eagles won again in 1976, pipping Parramatta 13-10 in a splendid grand final highlighted by the Eels pulling an unexpected 'Flying Wedge' move out of the hat.

Then in 1978 came an admirable fourth premiership toughed out through a minefield of injuries, replayed matches, dramas and unstoppable controversy – much of it centred on referee Greg 'Hollywood' Hartley.

The ongoing Hartley row devalued a simply magnificent Manly performance: six finals matches, five of them sudden death, including two replays in 24 days, culminating in the grand final (replay) win over Cronulla (16-0).

The Eagles had won four 1970s premierships in seven years – after winning none in their first 25 – and they had done it via their trademark brand of adventurous attack and defensive muscle.

Hated by many for their perceived pillage of other clubs and the 'Hollywood' Hartley row of 1978 they were, for all that, very special.

MANLY 1972-78 Ultimates

Graham Eadie, Tom Mooney, Bob Fulton (c), Ray Branighan, Ken Irvine, Alan Thompson, Dennis Ward, Mal Reilly, Phil Lowe, Terry Randall, John O'Neill, Max Krilich, John Harvey. 🏉

DROUGHTS & FAMINES

DOWN through the years, the golden runs enjoyed by clubs such as Easts, Souths and St George have been well documented but for some, there have been times of extreme football famine.

The defunct **University** club lost 42 consecutive matches between 1934 and 1936 while **Annandale**, another club that was disbanded, twice failed to win a single match in a season.

Whitewashes were not confined to pioneer teams in rugby league's infant years in Australia.

The **South Sydney** Rabbitohs of 1946 did not win a game, nor did the **Eastern Suburbs** outfit of 1966 (as a point of

interest, ex-Rooster Jack Gibson took over Easts as coach in 1967 and guided them to the finals).

North Sydney won premierships in 1921 and 1922 but celebrations for a third title success have been on hold now for 77 years.

Cronulla fans, however, have yet to taste grand final victory champagne after entering the league in 1967.

History shows that **Parramatta** took 34 years to win their first title and the fans were so excited on that joyous night of September 1981, they burnt down the old Cumberland Oval grandstand.

The **wooden spoon** – rugby league's fictitious 'prize' for running last – has been won by Wests on 17 occasions but the Parramatta Eels were rock bottom from 1956-61.

Droughts have not only occurred at club level. In interstate football, **Queensland** lost the first 22 games played against NSW before achieving the breakthrough.

And, on the international scene, **Great Britain** hasn't won an Ashes series in England since 1959 nor in Australia since 1970.

Birth of a club...

St George were founded on February 22, 1908, at a meeting at Rockdale Town Hall but they were not in the inaugural 1908 first grade competition. St George third grade League Football Club played its first game on April 30, 1910, against Newtown at Sans Souci, winning 36-0. From 1911-15 they played in the third grade competition as 'Wests III'. In 1920, the NSWRL voted 10-9 to add St George to the first grade competition in place of Annandale. The St George District Rugby League Club was born at a meeting held at the Kogarah School of Arts on November 8, 1920. In their debut season in 1921 the club won three games.

COLOURS: Red and white with six inch bars. During the war, when material was in short supply, the club bought white jumpers and a supporter sewed on a red V.

NICKNAME: Blood and Bandages, then Dragonslayers. In the 1950s they became the Dragons.

Kel O'SHEA
Born: 1933

70 FORMED half of one of Australia's most revered second-row partnerships. His cohort was St George's towering backrower Norm Provan. Together, the pair played nine Tests during the 1950s. O'Shea emerged from Ayr in North Queensland, representing his State in 1953 and earning the first of his 15 Test jerseys against Great Britain in 1954. Joined Wests in 1956 and his confrontations with Provan at club level provided some momentous battles. 15 Tests (1954-58), Kangaroo tourist 1956-57.

Arthur CLUES
1924-1998

69 PLAYED first grade rugby for Parramatta before being graded by Western Suburbs league side in 1943 at 17. Powerfully built, Clues was a dynamic attacking secondrower, whose career on Australian fields was limited to just four seasons. Rose to Test selection against touring English side of 1946 before accepting offer from Leeds. Played for more than a decade in England, where he scored more than 100 tries. Represented Other Nationalities 14 times. 3 Tests (1946).

Ray STEHR
1913-1983

66 ONE of the game's most colourful characters in a career which spanned 18 seasons from 1929 to 1946. At 16, the youngest player ever to have played premiership football. A frontrower from the 'old school', Stehr mixed it with the toughest opponents during an era when only the most resourceful survived. Regularly at loggerheads with officialdom, but remained one of the first players chosen at representative level. Grew up at Warialda and overcame a crippling blood clot at the base of his spine to forge a highly successful career. 11 Tests (1933-37), Kangaroo tourist 1933-34, 1937-38.

THE Daily Telegraph

WE SELECT THE BEST OF THE CENTURY

Ken KEARNEY
Born: 1924

64 KEARNEY'S tactics and ruthless approach to defence set the trend for St George's record winning run from 1956-66. A squat, unathletic looking hooker, Kearney was captain of Saints when their run began in 1956 and captain-coach from 1957 until retirement in 1961. A dual rugby international, Kearney switched codes in 1948, joining English club Leeds. He transferred to St George in 1952 and played the first of his 25 Tests the same year. 25 Tests (1952-58), Kangaroo tourist 1952-53, 1956-57.

Roy BULL
Born: 1929

63 THE first Manly player to represent Australia, Bull was one of the toughest frontrowers to play the game. Expert onside scrummager and a polished dummy-half, he had a workrate that was unmatched by his contemporaries. Made five overseas trips for Australia and played in Manly's first three grand finals. Retired after the loss to St George in the 1959 decider. A fitness fanatic, he rowed for Freshwater Lifesaving Club to increase his strength. 22 Tests (1949-57), Kangaroo tourist 1952-53, 1956-57.

Kerry BOUSTEAD
Born: 1959

68 BURST on to the scene as an exciting 18-year-old flyer from Innisfail during the 1978 interstate series. Determined efforts against powerful Souths winger Terry Fahey earned him a place in the Australian Test side the same year. With sizzling pace and sound defence, 'Bowie' became an automatic Test selection for the next seven years. Lured to Sydney in 1979, played with Easts before transferring to Manly in 1982 and then finished his career with Norths. Scored 15 Test tries. 25 Tests (1978-84), Kangaroo tourist 1978, 1982.

Brian CLAY
1934-1987

67 IN his only season of Test football, Clay earned rave reviews from the British press for his toughness and courage, attributes that were typical of his performances for St George in 11 seasons with the club. Nicknamed 'Poppa', Clay was a father-figure for young Dragons such as Johnny Raper and Reg Gasnier. Played in eight of Saints' 11 grand final victories. A five-eighth with granite-like defence, Clay provided immaculate service to Saints' all-star backline. 5 Tests (1959-60), Kangaroo tourist 1959-60.

The Great 100

Terry LAMB
Born: 1961

65 CAREER for Australia was limited to seven Tests in one season (1986), but Lamb holds a special place in the game's history on the strength of his resilience and uncanny tryscoring ability. Holds the record for most premiership games (349, for Wests and Canterbury) and is second on the list of premiership tryscorers (164). A tough and gritty competitor, Lamb was a magnificent support player, who helped Canterbury rise to pre-eminence in the 1980s. The only player to appear in every match on a Kangaroo tour (1986). 7 Tests (1986), Kangaroo tourist 1986.

Lionel COOPER
1923-1987

62 PLAYED only three Tests, but gained fame in England, where he developed into one of the game's greatest tryscorers. A powerful winger, Cooper was discovered playing for the army during World War II. Made immediate impact after joining Easts in 1945 and was in Australia's Test side within a year. Scored 70-metre try on Test debut against England. Joined Huddersfield in 1946-47 and went on to score 420 tries for the club. Represented Other Nationalities in 14 internationals. 3 Tests (1946).

Eric GROTHE
Born: 1960

61 DEVASTATING winger who brought crowds to their feet with blockbusting efforts for Parramatta, NSW and Australia during the 1980s. Scored some of the most memorable tries of the modern era, including his effort in 1983 semi-final against Canterbury, where he beat six defenders in a 60-metre surge. Scored at least one try in every Test he played. Fearsome play belied his gentle nature away from the field, where he was known as 'The Guru'. 8 Tests (1982-84), Kangaroo tourist 1982.

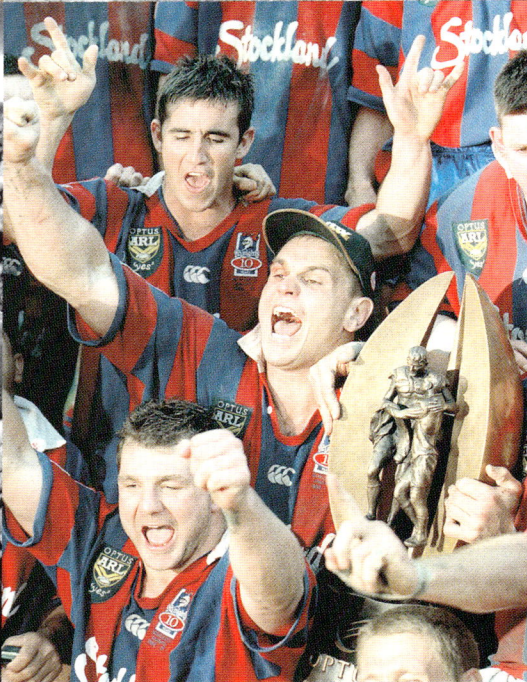

CHAPTER FIVE

A Date with Destiny

BY PETER FRILINGOS

A Date with

The way we were...

1940: First contingent of the AIF (6th Division) sails from Sydney for the Middle East to take on German forces of **Adolf Hitler**. Norman Thomas Gilroy becomes Catholic Archbishop of Sydney. War Savings certificates go on sale. Petrol rationing begins.

1941: Australia put on total war footing. Diggers triumph at **Tobruk**, forcing the surrender of 40,000 Italians. Private Evelyn Owen, from Wollongong, designs new machine gun (Owen gun) which is capable of firing 800 rounds per minute. It is tipped to replace the Tommy gun. Payroll tax introduced. Lamb chops four pence each. War formally declared on Japan (December 9).

I T is the most important day in a player's career, its significance can surpass playing for your country and to the select few who experience it in any given season, a grand final will always hold a special place in their lives.

The majority of players, including many seasoned internationals, never make a grand final to either live the ultimate exhilaration of taking a premiership or plumb the depths of despair in defeat.

Even for the St George players of the 1950s and 1960s, when the club won a world record 11 straight grand finals, the event never became commonplace.

Legendary forward Norm Provan played in 10 of those grand finals (1956-65) and said that each one was unforgettable in its own way.

Controversy and heroism have always been uncomfortable bedfellows in the history of grand finals.

South Sydney's John Sattler played through most of the 1970 grand final against Manly with a broken jaw.

Although grand finals were not mandatory until 1954, the Rabbitohs won their second premiership decider on a forfeit in 1909 when Balmain failed to turn up at the Agricultural Ground following a dispute about the game being staged as a curtain-raiser to a Wallabies versus Kangaroos representative match.

In front of 4000 spectators, Souths kicked off with no opposition and were declared premiers, a result that perpetuated enmity between the two clubs as late as the 1970s.

Mateship ... Souths' Ron Coote commiserates with Saints' Graeme Langlands in 1971

The first 'true' grand final – under a revised format where the minor premiers could challenge the winners if beaten in the final – was played in 1930 between Wests and St George. It was fought in October and a crowd of little more than 12,000 reflected the lack of interest in such a late finish. Wests won the grand final easily, 27-2, to claim their first title.

Three decades later the 1963 season saw St George take on Wests for the third successive year in the grand final – it was also the year that photographer John O'Gready snapped the game's most enduring image – the Gladiators – of rival captains Provan and Arthur Summons in their mud-caked embrace after another St George triumph.

The years 1977 and 1978 saw drawn grand finals between St George and Parramatta then Manly and Cronulla, with Saints and Manly becoming decisive winners through replays.

Grand finals are played for keeps, the entire season comes down to a final showdown in which players can become part of league folklore by winning or, for that matter, losing.

Canberra's first premiership in 1989 provided the perfect illustration of that analogy as they came back from the dead at 12-2 down against Balmain to snatch victory in extra time.

The utter devastation of Balmain skipper Wayne Pearce, who experienced his second successive grand final loss, compared with the tearful ecstasy of Raiders skipper Mal Meninga *(pictured top right)* said it all.

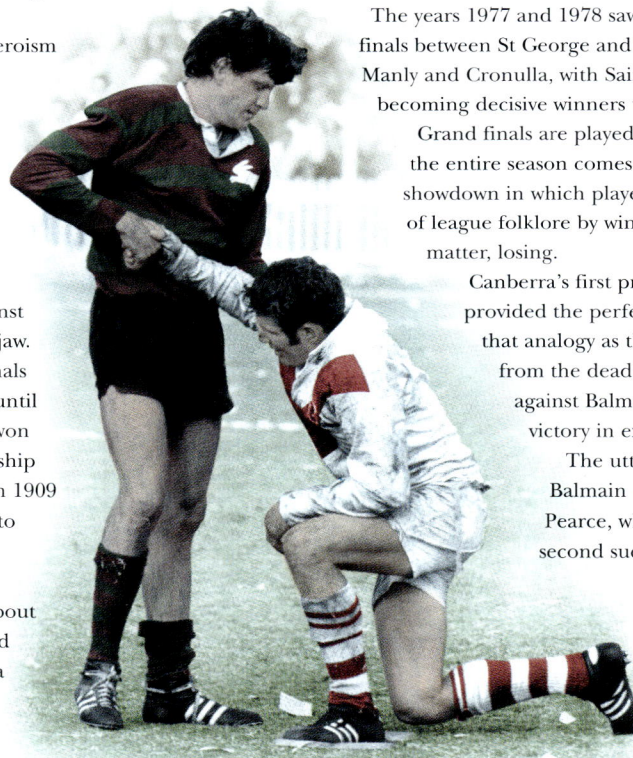

Referees have never been far removed from the eye of grand final storms with the 1952, 1963 and 1969 deciders the most controversial.

Destiny

In 1952 Souths went into the game long odds-on to make it three in a row against a Western Suburbs team coached by former Test referee Tom McMahon.

Wests won 22-12 but the victory was soured by the performance of referee George Bishop whose leniency towards the Magpies came in for widespread criticism.

The 1952 season was the one and only year McMahon coached at first grade level and to this day Souths say his association with Bishop went way beyond their bond as referees.

Before the match there were widespread stories about betting, including one where a South Sydney player keen to back his side was told to keep his money in his pocket by a friendly bookmaker.

Bishop made a series of decisions that cost Souths tries, Wests won the penalty count 15-4, Bishop retired after the game and the following year the Magpies finished with the wooden spoon while Souths won the next three premierships.

In muddy, rain-swept 1963 referee Darcy Lawler twice ruled in favour of Saints in hotly disputed decisions that had Wests and their fans complaining for years.

The first decision involved Saints winger Johnny King regaining his feet to score after a tackle Wests claimed had fairly grounded him and the ball should have been played.

Then came a kick from Summons where Wests' Peter Dimond won the race for the ball over the goal line against Saints' Eddie Lumsden, but Lawler ruled Dimond had not grounded the ball cleanly in the swamp-like conditions.

There were no television or video replays in those days so Saints went marching on to another title, leaving the Magpies spitting chips and black Bulli mud.

Referee Keith Page had to bear the brunt of criticism after Balmain beat Souths 11-2 in 1969 to spring a grand final upset probably even greater than the 1952 Wests-Souths result.

Page was powerless to do anything about Balmain's exploitation of the game's injury rules which called for stoppages in play if a player was on the ground seeking medical attention.

The game became known as the 'lay-down grand final' and although Page could do nothing to prevent the Tigers from feigning injuries Souths claimed he was part of the Balmain plot.

Turning point ... Newcastle fullback Robbie O'Davis scores the try that gave the Knights hope in the 1997 decider

1940-49

MAY 4, 1941: The game loses a legendary figure with the death of former halfback, **Chris McKivat**, aged 61. McKivat made a major contribution to the rugby codes, captaining Australia in both.

JUNE 7, 1941: History is made when brothers Lin Johnson (Canterbury) and Dick Johnson (Cessnock) are the opposing fullbacks in the annual City-Country match.

AUGUST 30, 1941: St George score five second-half tries in a 31-14 defeat of Easts in the premiership final to claim their maiden title. Almost 40,000 fans turn out for a bruising encounter in which referee **Tom McMahon** sends off opposing forwards Bill Tyquin (St George) and Jack Arnold (Easts).

The way we were...

1942: Darwin bombed by massive Japanese air raids. Australian cruiser HMAS *Perth* is hit by four torpedoes and sunk off Java. Heroic US general **Douglas MacArthur** arrives in Melbourne to take over as supreme commander of allied forces in the south-west Pacific. Fierce battles between Australian and Japanese troops in New Guinea. Swimmer Jon Konrads and tennis player Margaret Court born.

1943: Japanese plane sighted over Sydney (February 19). City blacked out and anti-aircraft guns on full alert. Jack Lang expelled from ALP after criticising the party in the *Century* newspaper. Australian hospital ship, *Centaur*, sunk by Japanese submarine near Brisbane: 268 dead.

I was there...

'St George were the favourites but we really fancied our chances that day. We had beaten the Dragons in both premiership rounds and again in the semi-final and thought we could control their speed men on the heavy SCG ground. A few things went against us, the boys are still talking about them, but in the end Saints were a touch too good.'

Wests captain, **Arthur Summons**, on the muddy and controversial 1963 grand final.

Mass eruption ... the 1973 grand final between Manly and Cronulla turns ugly

So intense was the debate over Balmain's tactics that the league changed the rules to ensure games were never stopped again to cater for minor injuries.

Page also had to control, if that's the right word, the 1973 Manly-Cronulla grand final which produced the very best and worst aspects of rugby league.

The first half was little more than a series of violent brawls, including a mass eruption involving most players, which saw Page hand out cautions to all players.

But when the fighting died down champion Manly centre Bob Fulton scored two memorable tries to steer Manly home 10-7 and secure their second straight title.

On both occasions Fulton scored from apparently impossible situations. It was said at the time that no other player in the game could have scored those tries and there was no argument from the Sharks.

Saints' Johnny King scored tries in six straight grand finals, 1960-65, but the grand final try that still holds pride of place was Bob McCarthy's 75-metre intercept that won the 1967 decider against Canterbury.

That year the league introduced four-tackle football to open up the game and not, as was often said at the time, because a rule had to be devised to stop St George's dominance of the game.

After losing that grand final to Souths the Canterbury Bulldogs, or Berries as they were known back then, had to wait until 1980 before taking another title. They sealed victory against Eastern Suburbs with a try to winger Steve Gearin that exemplified their tag as 'The Entertainers'.

Gearin dashed 30m to catch a towering kick from fullback Greg Brentnall over his shoulder to touch down and wrap up his side's 18-4 win over the Bob Fulton-coached Roosters.

Master coach Jack Gibson became the grand final king by taking Parramatta to three straight titles in 1981-83.

Gibson had earlier won back-to-back premierships with Easts in 1974-75 and the 1983 Parramatta win meant he had won five of the last 10 titles contested as a coach.

After Parramatta's bitter disappointment at losing grand finals in 1976-77, Gibson's one-liner after the Eels' 1981 triumph – 'ding, dong the witch is dead' – summed up the feeling of fans in Sydney's outer western suburbs who had waited decades for premiership spoils.

There are no doubt compelling reasons why every grand final deserves recognition, but we've come up with 10 of the best in 100 years of rugby league. Read on...

1955
SOUTHS 12, NEWTOWN 11

IN 1955 they called it a once-in-a-lifetime performance and Souths still regard it as their crowning glory.

At the halfway mark of the premiership Souths were in last place and given no hope of retaining their title.

To take out the grand final they would have to win 11 straight games and on form alone that prospect appeared to be as unlikely as the players spending their annual holidays on the moon.

Captain-coach Jack Rayner held a meeting with

Rising to the challenge ... captain-coach Jack Rayner inspired his troops in 1955

Mudheap ... Wests and St George players are hardly recognisable at game's end, 1963

his players in the Redfern Oval grandstand after the side was beaten 17-16 by Newtown in the first game of the second half of the minor premiership.

There is no official record of what was said that day but, whatever it was, the Rabbitohs rose to the challenge and won 10 sudden-death games to make the grand final.

On four occasions in the run to the premiership decider Souths left it until the dying minutes to snatch victory and that tradition was to get them home against Newtown in the big one.

Newtown winger Kevin Considine had put his side in front late in the game when Rayner kicked the ball clear in a play-the-ball, then toed it over the Newtown goal line.

Rabbitoh halfback Col Donohoe beat Newtown fullback Gordon Clifford to the ball over the line for the try and a Bernie Purcell conversion put Souths ahead 12-11 with only three minutes left on the clock.

Newtown had one last chance to win when Souths' Norm Nilson was penalised for punching but Clifford's 45m shot at goal fell under the crossbar.

Souths had become the first team to win the premiership from fourth place in the semi-finals

and no side matched that feat until Canberra beat Balmain in the 1989 grand final.

SOUTHS: Don Murdoch, Ian Moir, Martin Gallagher, Malcolm Spencer, Dale Puren, Johnny Dougherty, Col Donohoe, Les Cowie, Jack Rayner (c), Bernie Purcell, Denis Donoghue, Ernie Hammerton, Norm Nilson. Coach: Jack Rayner.

NEWTOWN: Gordon Clifford, Kevin Considine, Dick Poole (c), Brian Clay, Ray Preston, Ray Kelly, Bobby Whitton, Peter Ryan, Frank Narvo, Henry Holloway, Les Hampson, Greg Ellis, Don Stait.
Coach: Dick Poole.

Souths 12 (Moir, Donohoe tries; Purcell 3 goals).
Newtown 11 (Considine try; Clifford 3 goals, field goal). At Sydney Cricket Ground, September 17, 1955. Referee: Col Pearce. Crowd: 44,466.

1963
ST GEORGE 8, WESTS 3

AFTER losing to St George in the 1961 and 1962 grand finals, Wests had every reason to believe 1963 would be their year.

They had beaten Saints in both premiership rounds and completed the treble by beating them 10-8 in the major semi-final. Torrential rain turned

The way we were...

the SCG into a mudheap but that didn't deter a record 69,860 fans turning out for the premiership decider and the possible end of St George's seven-year winning streak.

Magpies skipper Arthur Summons had simple tactics for the game.

'Our plan was to kick and chase, to keep the ball away from the wings,' Summons said.

Wests also planned to kick specifically for big winger Peter Dimond and it was to be a controversial decision by referee Darcy Lawler involving Dimond that helped decide the outcome.

Lawler had earlier allowed a try to Saints winger Johnny King, who regained his feet after being tackled when Wests claimed he should have played the ball.

Then came a Summons kick over the St George line with Dimond and Saints' Eddie Lumsden racing for the ball.

Dimond got there first but Lawler ruled he had not grounded the ball cleanly and Wests' last chance at levelling the scores was lost.

ST GEORGE: Graeme Langlands, Eddie Lumsden, Reg Gasnier, Billy Smith, Johnny King, Bruce Pollard, George Evans, Johnny Raper, Elton Rasmussen, Norm Provan (c), Kevin Ryan, Ian Walsh, Monty Porter. Coach: Norm Provan.

WESTS: Don Parish, John Mowbray, Bob McGuiness, Gil MacDougall, Peter Dimond, Arthur Summons (c), Don Malone, Kevin Smyth, John 'Chow' Hayes, Kel O'Shea, Denis Meaney, Noel Kelly, Jack Gibson. Coach: Jack Fitzgerald.
St George 8 (Evans, King tries; Gasnier goal).
Wests 3 (MacDougall try). At Sydney Cricket Ground, August 24, 1963. Referee: Darcy Lawler. Crowd: 69,860.

1965
ST GEORGE 12, SOUTHS 8

I T was the classical confrontation of the champions against the young Turks – St George with nine successive titles challenged by a Souths side with potential but little big-match experience.

Rabbitoh coach Bernie Purcell had moulded a young side featuring names like Sattler, McCarthy, O'Neill, Coote, Lisle, Cleary and Morgan into a potent attacking force.

Souths' glory ... captain John Sattler is swamped by teammates and coach Clive Churchill after beating Canterbury in 1967

Souths had good reason to be confident about their chances despite St George's awesome grand final record under captain-coach Norm Provan.

In the first round they overcame Saints 14-4 then repeated the dose 17-8 in round two and, while they went into the decider as underdogs, the league public sensed the red-and-white domination of the premiership might be terminated.

The fans turned out in droves to post a then Australian rugby league record 78,056 crowd at the SCG. At least that was the official crowd figure. There were rumours the attendance was much closer to 100,000.

With hundreds if not thousands of fans perched on grandstand roofs both at the SCG and the neighbouring Showground, and children allowed around the perimeter of the ground, police placed a 70,000 safety limit on the SCG after the game.

At 34, Provan announced his intention to retire after the match no matter what the result and his imminent departure motivated his teammates to ensure 'the boss' was sent out a winner.

Souths gave their supporters the thrill of a lifetime when a long-range goal by fullback Kevin Longbottom saw the Rabbitohs take an early 2-0 lead.

That advantage was shortlived when Johnny Raper and Reg Gasnier combined to set up a try for Billy Smith and while Souths threw everything at the Dragons in attack they were met with a brick-wall defence.

Coote established his reputation as a Raper clone by mowing down Gasnier and Smith with cover-defending tackles when tries appeared certain.

With Saints leading 9-6 late in the game, winger Johnny King scored from an Elton Rasmussen pass to wrap up the game and earn the distinction of notching tries in six straight grand finals.

Saints won and went on to make it a world record 11 successive titles the following year but the game signalled the imminent changing of the guard.

ST GEORGE: Graeme Langlands, Eddie Lumsden, Reg Gasnier, Billy Smith, John King, Brian Clay, George Evans, John Raper, Norm Provan (c), Elton Rasmussen, Kevin Ryan, Ian Walsh, Robin Gourley. Coach: Norm Provan.
SOUTHS: Kevin Longbottom, Eric Simms, Arthur Branighan, Bob Moses, Mike Cleary, Jim Lisle (c), Ivan Jones, Ron Coote, John Sattler, Bob McCarthy, John O'Neill, Fred Anderson, Jim Morgan. Coach: Bernie Purcell.
St George 12 (Smith, King tries; Langlands 3 goals)
Souths 8 (Longbottom 3, Simms goals). At Sydney Cricket Ground, September 18, 1965. Referee: Col Pearce. Crowd: 78,056.

1967
SOUTHS 12, CANTERBURY 10

IMAGES of Bob McCarthy bolting 75 metres to score his intercept try for Souths will haunt Canterbury players and fans for the rest of their lives.

With Canterbury attacking late in the first half, McCarthy gambled by going for the intercept of hooker Col Brown's lofted pass out wide. Had he missed the ball the Berries would have scored and probably won the game.

Instead, it was McCarthy who scored up the other end of the SCG to give Souths a 10-8 lead and ultimately the grand final.

It was a dramatic year for rugby league: Canterbury had ended St George's 11 straight years of premiership domination by beating them 12-11 in the preliminary final in the game's first season of limited-tackle (four-tackle) football.

Secondrower George Taylforth kicked four goals and lock Ron Raper a 45m field goal for Canterbury, but with the scores locked at 10-all late in the second half Souths' fullback Kevin Longbottom lined up a shot at goal from halfway.

As the ball hit an upright before being caught behind the crossbar by Canterbury fullback Les Johns, referee Col Pearce was left with one touch judge with his flag in the air and the other signalling no goal. Pearce stopped the game to confer with both touch judges before disallowing the goal.

Fortunately for Souths, their young centre that day was goalkicking prodigy Eric Simms, who potted the winning goal just four minutes from time.

Canterbury captain-coach Kevin Ryan and Taylforth went into the referees room after the game to congratulate Pearce on his handling of the game and, while there, confirmed Longbottom had scored a legitimate goal.

Under the four-tackle rule, rugby league took on a new dimension of attacking football ... just as another golden era for Souths started.

SOUTHS: Kevin Longbottom, Mike Cleary, Bob Moses, Eric Simms, Brian James, Jim Lisle, Ivan Jones, Ron Coote, Alan Scott, Bob McCarthy, John O'Neill, Elwyn Walters, John Sattler (c). (Greg Norgard replaced Cleary, injured). Coach: Clive Churchill.
CANTERBURY: Les Johns, Barry Reynolds, Bob Hagan, John Greaves, Clive Gartner, Bob Doyle, Ross Kidd, Ron Raper, George Taylforth, Kevin Goldspink, Kevin Ryan (c), Col Brown, Merv Hicks. Coach: Kevin Ryan.
Souths 12 (McCarthy, O'Neill tries; Simms 3 goals)
Canterbury 10 (Taylforth 4 goals, Raper field goal). At Sydney Cricket Ground, September 16, 1967. Referee: Col Pearce. Crowd: 56,358.

1940-49

JULY 28, 1945: St George prop Bill McRitchie spends 22 weeks in hospital after part of his right ear is bitten off in a scrum during his team's clash with Newtown at Henson Park. McRitchie accuses Newtown prop **Frank 'Bumper' Farrell** of biting him, but more than six months later, the League's general committee clears Farrell of all charges, by 15 votes to 13.

SEPTEMBER 1, 1945: Easts lock Dick Dunn enjoys the finest day of his career when he scores 19 points (three tries and five goals) in his team's 22-18 win over Balmain in the premiership final. Dunn's effort remains the record individual score by a player in a premiership decider.

MAY 22, 1946: The first post-World War II tour by an international team gets under way, when **Gus Risman**'s English side defeat Southern Division 36-4 before a crowd of 6135 in Junee.

JUNE 17, 1946: War-weary fans turn out in their droves to watch the Englishmen, who are dubbed 'The Indomitables' after the aircraft carrier that brought them to Australia. A crowd of 64,527 watch the first Test at the SCG which finishes in an 8-all draw.

The way we were...

Handstands ... the Tigers celebrate as the hooter sounds in 1969 and (below) retiring skipper Peter Provan is chaired from the field

1969
BALMAIN 11, SOUTHS 2.

Souths, the 1967-68 premiers, went into the 1969 grand final against Balmain the shortest-priced favourites in the history of title deciders.

Souths were sent out 1/3 shots against a Balmain side that had scraped into the grand final on the back of a miraculous try by former rugby star George Ruebner in the preliminary final against Manly.

The cocky premiers got much more than they bargained for from the Tigers right from the start of the game and Balmain led 6-0 at halftime.

Rabbitoh hardman John O'Neill was later to reveal he had told skipper John Sattler during the first half that the Tigers had them beaten.

Four of the six first-half points came from South African goalkicking freak Len Killeen while former Great Britain star Dave Bolton landed a field goal.

When Ruebner went off injured, replacement winger Sid Williams scored the only try of the game in the 55th minute to virtually seal the match.

Leading 9-0 the Tigers resorted to delaying tactics with players constantly feigning injury to halt the game, especially when Souths built momentum.

Referee Keith Page was powerless to thwart the tactics under the injury rules as they stood and, while the Tigers were the better side on the day, their 'flop' tactics embittered Souths.

The stunning victory came a year too late for Tigers icon Keith Barnes, who retired at the end of the 1968 season without winning a premiership. Champion forward Arthur Beetson also missed the game – through suspension – and had to wait until 1974 with Easts to take his first grand final.

BALMAIN: Bob Smithies, George Ruebner, Allan Fitzgibbon, Terry Parker, Len Killeen, Keith Outten, Dave Bolton, Peter Provan (c), Joe Walsh, John Spencer, Barry McTaggart, Peter Boulton, Garry Leo. (Sid Williams replaced Ruebner for second half). Coach: Leo Nosworthy.
SOUTHS: Eric Simms, Mike Cleary, Bob Honan, Kerry Burke, Brian James, Denis Pittard, Bob Grant, Ron Coote, Bob Moses, Bob McCarthy, John O'Neill, Elwyn Walters, John Sattler (c). (Paul Sait replaced Moses for second half). Coach: Clive Churchill.

Balmain 11 (Williams try; Killeen 2 goals, Bolton 2 field goals).
Souths 2 (Simms goal). At Sydney Cricket Ground, September 20, 1969. Referee: Keith Page. Crowd: 58,825.

1971
SOUTHS 16, ST GEORGE 10

SOUTHS can thank nuggety hooker George Piggins for keeping them alive in the grand final after Jack Gibson's Dragons almost pulled off an upset to rival Balmain's 1969 victory.

It was Piggins with his lightning-fast boots continually raking the ball back in the play-the-ball that gave the Rabbitohs the breathing space they needed to hold the fast-finishing Dragons.

Souths had qualified for their fifth straight grand final and the Clive Churchill-coached side was expected to win easily in the game's first six-tackle grand final. An Eric Simms field goal was the only score of the first half but straight after the break Ray Branighan notched the first try. When Ron Coote added a second, Souths led 9-0.

When Simms took the score to 11-0 with a goal, it appeared Souths would cruise to their fourth title in five years but Saints, with Test stars Graeme Langlands and Billy Smith calling the shots, had other ideas.

The duo sparked a red-and-white revival that led to tries by Barry Beath and Teddy Walton, accompanied by sideline conversions from Langlands.

Leading only 11-10 Souths needed something special and Piggins answered the call.

St George hooker Col Rasmussen won what was to be the final scrum of the match and from the first couple of rucks Souths were in desperate trouble until Piggins raked the ball back from Russell Cox in a play-the-ball. With Saints now on the back foot and tiring, Ron Coote broke the line and sent an inside pass to Bob McCarthy, who ran 20m to score under the posts and seal the game. It was the end of another golden era for Souths.

They have remained anchored on 20 premierships ever since and have failed to make another grand final.

SOUTHS: Eric Simms, Keith Edwards, Paul Sait, Bob Honan, Ray Branighan, Denis Pittard, Bob Grant, Ron Coote, Gary Stevens, Bob McCarthy, John O'Neill, George Piggins, John Sattler (c). Coach: Clive Churchill.
ST GEORGE: Graeme Langlands (c), Ken Batty, Bob Clapham, Ken Maddison, Geoff Carr, Tony Branson, Billy Smith, Ted Walton, Barry Beath, Peter Fitzgerald, Grahame Bowen, Col Rasmussen, Harry Eden. (Russell Cox replaced Bowen for second half, Mick Dryden replaced Fitzgerald after 35 mins). Coach: Jack Gibson.

Souths 16 (Branighan, Coote, McCarthy tries; Simms 3 goals, field goal).
St George 10 (Beath, Walton tries; Langlands 2 goals). At Sydney Cricket Ground, September 18, 1971. Referee: Keith Holman. Crowd: 62,838.

1973
MANLY 10, CRONULLA 7

RUGBY League's image, along with the Manly and Cronulla players, took a severe battering at the SCG on grand final day 1973.

To this day, Manly and Cronulla blame each other for the vicious brawling that broke out sporadically for much of the game despite referee Keith Page's desperate attempts to restore order.

If it had not been for the stunning brilliance of Manly centre Bob Fulton the game would be remembered only for its thuggery during a series of no-holds-barred incidents.

The Sharks were making their first grand final appearance since elevation to first grade in 1967 and captain-coach Tommy Bishop wanted to make the most of the club's opportunity to take the J J Giltinan Shield.

The former Great Britain Test halfback decided the only way to beat the reigning premiers was to unsettle them with niggling tactics and is said to have instructed his players to 'turn it on' from the kickoff.

The players took their boss at his word and Manly playmaker Mal Reilly was taken out when kicked in the back.

While the Sharks were later to claim the kick from hooker Ron Turner was accidental, it was actually a square-up after an incident between the pair in the brawling 1970 World Cup final.

Reilly left the field to have three pain-killing needles but was no more than a passenger and lasted only until the 25th minute.

Manly prop John O'Neill felled Cronulla lock Chris Wellman in a ruck sparking an all-in brawl and, with Bishop niggling Manly forwards Peter Peters and Terry Randall, the game was little better than a series of running skirmishes.

A solo try to Fulton from a Freddy Jones flick pass saw Manly lead 5-0 after 29 minutes and, when referee Page read the riot act after another brawl early in the second half, both sides started to play football.

Fulton beat replacement fullback Rick Bourke and rookie centre Steve Rogers to score his second try but Bourke squared accounts late in the game to cut Manly's 8-2 lead to 8-7.

But, with three minutes to go, Graham Eadie kicked a goal for a 10-7 lead and the Eagles defended stoutly to win back-to-back titles.

I was there...

'With the scores locked 16-all with a minute to go, extra time seemed inevitable. But nobody told 'Joey' Johns when he took off on a blindside run. He caught Manly off guard and passed to Darren Albert. When he planted the ball over the line, it was the sweetest sight we've ever seen. It's still hard to believe it really happened ... but I'm glad it did for a great bunch of blokes and the people of Newcastle.'

Former Knights captain, **Paul Harragon**, on Newcastle's amazing, last-gasp win in 1997's brilliant decider.

Birth of a club...

THE embryo for the birth of the Parramatta Rugby League Football Club occurred in 1936 with the formation of 'a district club committee'.

The club was the brainchild of Jack Scullin and Jack Argent, who recognised the need for another club in western Sydney and so approached the NSWRL with their plans.

But the formation of Parramatta was delayed by World War II.

Finally, in 1946 the club was granted permission to join the competition and the team played their first game on April 12, 1947, against Newtown at Cumberland Oval going down 34-12.

COLOURS: Blue and Gold, the same as Parramatta City Council.

NICKNAME: They were known as the Fruitpickers because the area was surrounded by orchards. They became the Eels in 1965 after a discussion between Argent and journalist Peter Frilingos. Parramatta is the Aboriginal word for 'the place where the eels lie down'.

MANLY: Graham Eadie, Ken Irvine, Ray Branighan, Bob Fulton, Max Brown, Ian Martin, John Mayes, Malcolm Reilly, Terry Randall, Peter Peters, John O'Neill, Fred Jones (c), Bill Hamilton. (John Bucknall replaced Reilly, injured). Coach: Ron Willey.

CRONULLA: Warren Fisher, Ray Corcoran, Steve Rogers, Eric Archer, Bob Wear, Chris Wellman, Tommy Bishop (c), Greg Pierce, John Maguire, Ken Maddison, Grahame Bowen, Ron Turner, Cliff Watson. (Rick Bourke replaced Fisher at halftime). Coach: Tom Bishop.

Manly 10 (Fulton 2 tries; Eadie 2 goals)
Cronulla 7 (Bourke try; Rogers 2 goals). At Sydney Cricket Ground, September 15, 1973. Referee: Keith Page. Crowd: 52,044.

1977
ST GEORGE 9, PARRAMATTA 9
Replay
ST GEORGE 22, PARRAMATTA 0

AFTER 100 minutes of football St George and Parramatta were locked at 9-all in the game's first drawn grand final. Saints had led 9-0 at halftime after a spectacular kick-and-chase try by fullback Ted Goodwin and looked to be the better side.

The Dragons were also winning the fight with their forwards, headed by Rod Reddy and Robert Stone, goading the Parramatta pack with Ray Price and Ray Higgs their major targets.

In the second half centre Mick Cronin kicked three goals to reel in Saints, but with three minutes left in regular time Parramatta's hopes of a first premiership appeared to be gone.

With the Eels camped near the St George line for what might have been the last time, Cronin passed to Price and the international lock went on a diagonal run before passing inside to centre Ed Sulkowicz who scored.

Cronin's difficult conversion kick to win the game was waved away.

In the ensuing 20 minutes of extra time both sides missed field goal attempts and St George winger John Chapman's penalty shot at goal was wide of the posts.

The replay set down for the following Saturday was expected to be just as tight as the grand final – it wasn't and 48,000 fans were stunned by both the ferocity of the St George players and the 22-0 scoreline in St George's favour.

Referee Gary Cook cautioned Saints secondrower Rod Reddy seven times for foul play as he set about subduing the Parramatta pack.

Cook left Reddy on the field and it was later revealed Parramatta captain Ray Higgs and coach Terry Fearnley fell out at halftime because the coach would not permit Higgs to take the law into his own hands.

St George led 7-0 at the break and, when Stone scored a controversial try from a scrum after Parramatta pivot John Peard was impeded by referee Cook, the game was over.

For the second straight year the Eels had been denied their first title and would have to wait until 1981 under coach Jack Gibson to perform their first lap of honour.

ST GEORGE: Ted Goodwin, Steve Butler, Graham Quinn, Robert Finch, John Chapman, Rod McGregor, Mark Shulman, Rod Reddy, John Jansen, Robert Stone, Craig Young, Steve Edge (c), Bruce Starkey. (John Bailey replaced Shulman, Tony Quirk replaced Goodwin). Coach: Harry Bath.

PARRAMATTA: Phil Mann, Jim Porter, Ed Sulkowicz, Michael Cronin, Graeme Atkins, Mark Levy, John Kolc, Ray Price, Ray Higgs (c), Geoff Gerard, John Baker, Ron Hilditch, Graham Olling. (Denis Fitzgerald replaced Baker, John Peard replaced Mann). Coach: Terry Fearnley.

Tie time ... the Parramatta try that levelled the scores in the 1977 draw against St George

Wasteland ... the total devastation of losing a grand final in extra time is etched on the face of Balmain skipper Wayne Pearce in 1989

St George 9 (Goodwin try; Goodwin 2, Chapman goals) **Parramatta 9** (Sulkowicz try; Cronin 3 goals). At Sydney Cricket Ground, September 17, 1977. Referee: Gary Cook. Crowd: 65,959.

1977 REPLAY

ST GEORGE: Ted Goodwin, Steve Butler, Graham Quinn, Robert Finch, John Chapman, Rod McGregor, John Bailey, Rod Reddy, John Jansen, Robert Stone, Craig Young, Steve Edge (c), Bruce Starkey. (Barry Beath replaced Reddy). Coach: Harry Bath.

PARRAMATTA: Mark Levy, Jim Porter, Michael Cronin, Ed Sulkowicz, Graeme Atkins, John Peard, John Kolc, Ray Price, Geoff Gerard, Ray Higgs (c), John Baker, Ron Hilditch, Graham Olling. (Denis Fitzgerald replaced Baker). Coach: Terry Fearnley.

St George 22 (Jansen, Stone, Bailey (penalty) tries; Goodwin 6 goals, field goal)

Parramatta 0. At Sydney Cricket Ground, September 24, 1977. Referee: Gary Cook. Crowd: 47,828.

1989
CANBERRA 19, BALMAIN 14

U NDER normal circumstances it would take a lot to make Mal Meninga cry. The Queensland and Australian centre had tasted State of Origin and Test victory without shedding a tear and even managed to stay dry-eyed after playing in the losing Canberra grand final side against Manly in 1987.

But the 1989 grand final was something completely different – some say it was the greatest grand final ever played – and Mal blubbered like a baby when the final hooter sounded.

The Tigers lived up to their tag as title favourites by leading 12-2 at halftime after tries by James Grant and Paul Sironen. Yet, despite that commanding lead, there was a feeling the Raiders had plenty left in reserve.

After all, they had qualified for the grand final from fourth place in the top five and, while no side

had won the title from the sudden-death position, the Raiders had demolished Cronulla, Penrith and Souths along the way.

Fullback Gary Belcher scored Canberra's first try after passes from Ricky Stuart and John Ferguson, but at 12-8 Balmain missed two opportunities to put the game out of reach.

Halfback Mick Neil was ankle-tapped by Meninga when he appeared certain to score under the posts and Wayne Pearce dropped the ball with Tim Brasher unmarked outside him.

As the clock wound down Balmain coach Warren Ryan replaced Steve Roach with Kevin Hardwick and Sironen with Michael Pobjie, claiming the Test stars were tiring and the replacements were sound defensive players.

With 90 seconds left, a kick from Chris O'Sullivan bounced off Garry Jack to Laurie Daley whose high pass to Ferguson saw the winger dart inside to score. Meninga converted for 14-all sending the game into extra time and with the Raiders on a roll and heartened by the absence of Sironen and Roach, the scent of Tiger blood was in their nostrils.

The Canberra kill came in the shape of an O'Sullivan field goal then a legendary try by unknown replacement forward Steve Jackson who carried Neil, Hardwick, Shaun Edwards and Gary Freeman over the line to score.

Meninga had recovered from breaking his arm a fourth time to lead the Raiders to victory. He was entitled to cry tears of joy and he wasn't alone.

CANBERRA: Gary Belcher, Matthew Wood, Mal Meninga (c), Laurie Daley, John Ferguson, Chris O'Sullivan, Ricky Stuart, Bradley Clyde, Dean Lance, Gary Coyne, Brent Todd, Steve Walters, Glenn Lazarus. (Paul Martin replaced Wood, Steve Jackson replaced Todd, Kevin Walters replaced Daley (head bin), Daley replaced Coyne). Coach: Tim Sheens.

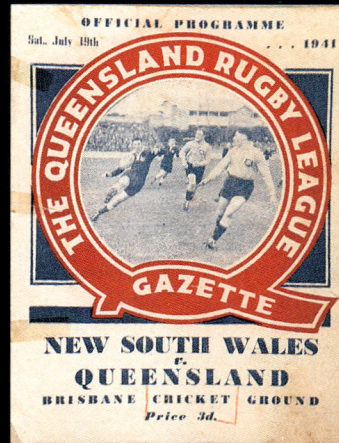

Team of the Decade...
1940-1949

MANY of Australia's leading players of the 1940s accepted lucrative offers from English clubs before the re-imposition of an international transfer ban in 1948. Stars such as Bevan, Cooper, Bath, Clues and Devery were lost to the Australian game and Churchill, too, would have followed had the ban not been imposed. Bevan and Bath win places in the team despite never representing Australia.

Fullback: Clive CHURCHILL (Central Newcastle, Souths).

Wingers: Brian BEVAN (Easts, Warrington), Lionel COOPER (Easts, Huddersfield).

Centres: Ron BAILEY (Huddersfield, Canterbury, West Maitland), Len SMITH (Newtown).

Five-eighth: Wally O'CONNELL (Easts, Christian Bros Wollongong).

Halfback: Keith FROOME (Newcastle Wests, Newtown).

Lock: Noel MULLIGAN (Port Kembla, Newtown, Captain's Flat, Bowral).

Secondrowers: Harry BATH (Brisbane Valleys, Balmain, Barrow, Warrington), Herb NARVO (North Newcastle, Newtown, St George, Cootamundra, Camden).

Frontrowers: Alf GIBBS (South Newcastle, Newtown), Frank FARRELL (Newtown).

Hooker: Kevin SCHUBERT (Wollongong, Manly).

Lionel Cooper

BALMAIN: Garry Jack, James Grant, Tim Brasher, Andy Currier, Steve O'Brien, Michael Neil, Gary Freeman, Wayne Pearce (c), Paul Sironen, Bruce McGuire, Steve Roach, Ben Elias, Steve Edmed. (Kevin Hardwick replaced Roach, Michael Pobjie replaced Sironen, Shaun Edwards replaced Pobjie). Coach: Warren Ryan.

Canberra 19 (Belcher, Ferguson, Jackson tries; Meninga 3 goals; O'Sullivan field goal).

Balmain 14 (Grant, Sironen tries; Currier 3 goals). At Sydney Football Stadium, September 24, 1989. Referee: Bill Harrigan. Crowd: 40,500.

1997 (ARL)
NEWCASTLE 22, MANLY 16

IT was the day that virtually saved rugby league. The ARL-Super League war had caused severe divisions in the game with rugby league's popularity decreasing significantly.

The game needed a lift – and Newcastle delivered.

The win has been described as one of the 'greatest fairytale victories in the long history of grand finals'.

Newcastle's winning try, quite remarkably, came with just six seconds of the match remaining.

The try to winger Darren Albert prevented the grand final going into extra time.

Halfback Andrew Johns initiated Albert's try after being hospitalised with a perforated lung earlier in the week.

Johns darted out of dummy-half down the blindside and dummied before off-loading to speedster Albert who scored.

What followed were scenes of hysteria and sheer euphoria. Manly had entered the grand final as red-hot favourites only to be beaten.

The Sea Eagles had actually led 16-8 at halftime but could not halt a rampaging finish by Newcastle.

'It was a fairytale come true. It seemed to be fate toward the end,' said Manly coach Bob Fulton.

Newcastle fullback Robbie O'Davis, who scored two decisive tries as the Knights hauled in the Sea Eagles, was voted man of the match.

Newcastle coach Mal Reilly added: 'I'm just ecstatic. I've never been involved in a game that has had such a dramatic finish.'

The Newcastle celebrations continued long into the next week.

Fairytale ... Newcastle captain Paul Harragon hoists the premiership trophy

NEWCASTLE: Robbie O'Davis, Darren Albert, Adam MacDougall, Owen Craigie, Mark Hughes, Matthew Johns, Andrew Johns, Tony Butterfield, Bill Peden, Paul Harragon (c), Wayne Richards, Adam Muir, Marc Glanville. Interchange: Troy Fletcher, Scott Conley, Lee Jackson, Stephen Crowe. Coach: Malcolm Reilly.

MANLY: Shannon Nevin, Danny Moore, Craig Innes, Terry Hill, John Hopoate, Geoff Toovey (c), Craig Field, David Gillespie, Anthony Colella, Mark Carroll, Steve Menzies, Daniel Gartner, Nik Kosef. Interchange: Neil Tierney, Cliff Lyons, Scott Fulton, Andrew Hunter. Coach: Bob Fulton.

Newcastle 22 (O'Davis 2, Albert tries; A Johns 5 goals)

Manly 16 (Hopoate, Innes, Nevin tries; Nevin 2 goals). At Sydney Football Stadium, September 28, 1997. Referee: David Manson. Crowd: 42,482.

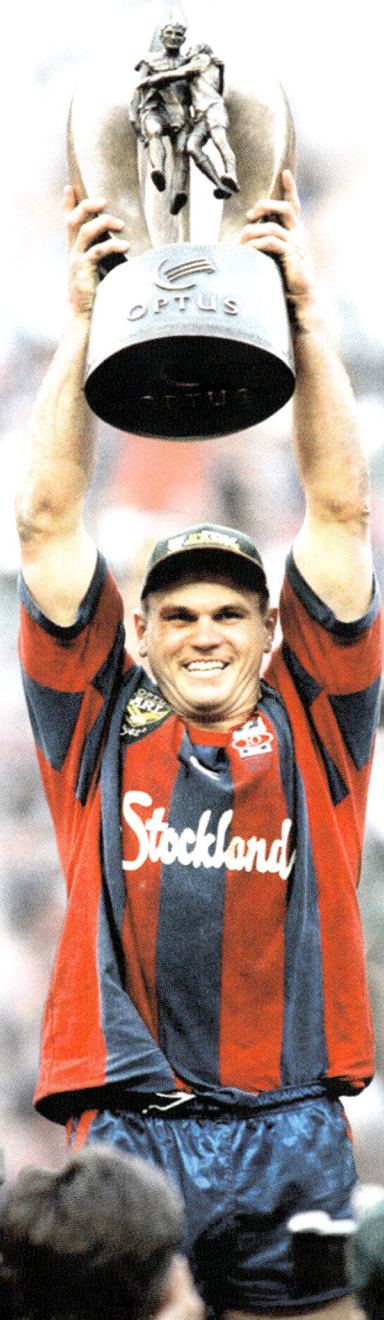

Man on Man
Harold Horder vs Wendell Sailor

Born: Feb 23, 1894. **Died:** Aug 21, 1978.
Played: 1912-26.
Clubs: Souths, Norths, Coorparoo (Brisbane).
Position: Wing.
Weight: 10st 9lb (67kg).
Height: 5ft 6ins (168cm).
Tests: 13. **Career games:** 194.
Career points: 1140 (239 tries, 203 goals).

Born: July 16, 1974.
Played: Since 1993.
Club: Brisbane Broncos.
Position: Wing.
Weight: 16st 5lb (104kg).
Height: 6ft 3ins (191cm).
Tests: 7. **Career games:** 172.
Career points: 364 (91 tries).

IT is a one-on-one duel to fire the imagination. On one hand there is the speed, deception and daring of Harold Horder and on the other the sheer size and power of Wendell Sailor.

What would be the outcome if these two grand wingers of different eras and vastly different styles were to meet on some remote plane?

Would Horder, a diminutive man with an uncanny try-scoring ability, bamboozle Sailor, or would the giant Bronco stampede his opposite?

Horder, who played from 1912-26, was described as a football wonder. 'No eel ever slipped through man's hands so exasperatingly,' wrote one observer.

In Sailor's game there are very few subtleties – it is all a matter of physics.

WHAT A GAME!
NEWTOWN v ST GEORGE
1973

JACK Gibson's Newtown Jets hold the distinction of producing the lowest scoring win in the history of Australian Rugby League.

In a dour, yet memorable clash at the SCG early in the season of 1973, the Jets downed St George by the soccer scoreline of 1-0.

For 69 of the 80 minutes, the game was deadlocked, with neither side able to score. Played in heavy conditions, the match wasn't pretty. Referee Keith Page packed down a stunning 41 scrums – more than one every two minutes – during the battle.

Coach Gibson, desperate to get his team ahead, sent replacement five-eighth **Ken Wilson** into the game after 68 minutes.

Wilson, a renowned kicker, both for goal and in general play, had earlier played in reserve grade. His arrival took the Dragons by surprise and before they knew what hit them, Wilson had calmly potted the decisive one-pointer with his first touch.

The match wasn't over, however, with veteran halfback Billy Smith immediately plotting Saints' reply.

Smith sent winger **John Chapman** charging downfield with a clever long pass that out-flanked the Jets' defence.

Chapman looked certain to score but a marvellous last-ditch tackle by Newtown fullback John Floyd brought him down agonisingly shy of the line.

Newtown held on under intense pressure in the final minutes to score an invaluable two competition points.

Under Gibson's charge, the Jets were the surprise packet of the 1973 season, reaching the finals and winning the club championship for the only time in their long history. 🏉

1940-49

FEBRUARY 10, 1948: The International Board is formed at a meeting between British, French and New Zealand delegates in Leeds. New Zealand officials represent Australia at the meeting.

JUNE 14, 1948: One of the most baffling selection decisions in the history of the game is played out when **Len Smith** is omitted from the Kangaroo team to tour England. Captain-coach of Australia in their one-all series draw with New Zealand earlier in the season, Smith is mysteriously overlooked for the Kangaroos.

OCTOBER 9, 1948: The first Test between Australia and Great Britain at Headingley is described as one of the most brilliant of all time. Twelve tries are scored in the Test, won 23-21 by the home side.

SEPTEMBER 10, 1949: St George outlast South Sydney 19-12 in one of the toughest grand finals on record. Sportswriter Jim Mather said of the match: 'Players were thrown to the ground with a venom that broke all rules of decent, hard football and almost every tackle was accompanied by a display of petty spiteful punching that would have won honours in a pub brawl.'

Michael O'CONNOR
Born: 1960

60 STYLISH centre who represented Australia in both rugby codes in the 1980s. After 13 union Tests, O'Connor signed with St George in 1983, established himself in the top grade, then moved to Manly in 1987. Earned dual international status in 1985, but forced to wait until 1986 to play first Test. Great pace, footwork and ball-handling abilities and was a goalkicker of rare talent. Scored 190 points in 17 Tests. Glut of Test-quality centres forced him to play much of international career on the wing. 17 Tests (1986-90), Kangaroo 1986.

Keith BARNES
Born: 1934

56 DID not play league until aged 15 after migrating to Australia from Wales. Quickly developed into an outstanding goalkicking fullback and was signed by Balmain from Wollongong in 1955. Although slightly built, Barnes had a great capacity to handle pressure and was a natural leader. Played 14 seasons with the Tigers, scoring a club record 1519 points. Captained the 1959-60 Kangaroos at the age of 24 and topped a century of points in Test matches – all from his 'Golden Boots'. Played in grand finals for Balmain in 1956, 1964 and 1966. 14 Tests (1959-66), Kangaroo 1959-60.

Noel KELLY
Born: 1936

54 ONE of Australia's longest serving frontrowers, Kelly played 25 Tests (1959-68) and is the only prop to tour three times with the Kangaroos. Began career in Ipswich and after a season at Ayr in North Queensland in 1960, joined Sydney's Western Suburbs. One of the roughest, toughest forwards to play the game. Statistics that summed up his career were not measured in metres gained or tackles completed. The final count for Kelly was 16 broken noses and 15 send-offs. 25 Tests (1959-68), Kangaroo 1959-60, 1963-64, 1967-68.

Cecil BLINKHORN
1892-1977

59 TRYSCORING machine of the code's first two decades, Blinkhorn was famous for his devastating fend which captivated English crowds on the Kangaroo tour of 1921-22. Scored 39 tries in 30 tour matches, a record likely to stand forever. Wing partnership with Harold Horder for Souths, Norths, NSW and Australia remains one of the most famous in game's history. Played in both of Norths' premiership sides of 1921 and 1922 and had two stints with the Rabbitohs. 4 Tests (1921-24). Kangaroo 1921-22.

THE Daily Telegraph

WE SELECT THE BEST OF THE CENTURY

Barry MUIR
Born: 1937

53 AUSTRALIA has had few more aggressive or competitive halfbacks than Barry Muir, who was unrivalled as the country's premier No 7 (1959-64). Although born in Tweed Heads, Muir was a staunch Queenslander who played most of career with Brisbane Wests. Feisty, arrogant and a persistent niggler, Muir also possessed outstanding talent and his duels with English half Alex Murphy were features of Ashes Tests of the period. Captained Australia in one Test. 22 Tests (1959-64), Kangaroo 1959-60, 1963-64.

The Great 100

Bradley CLYDE
Born: 1970

58 TALENTED, athletic back-rower, who played significant role in Canberra's rise in the late 1980s. Made top grade debut in 1988 and starred for Australia on tour of New Zealand a year later. Played in Canberra's maiden grand final win in 1989, but a knee reconstruction cost him a second premiership medal – and Kangaroo tour – in 1990. Returned to top level in 1991 and achieved career highlight of Kangaroo selection in 1994. Injury cost him a return to rep football in 1999 after transferring to Canterbury. 18 Tests (1989-94), Kangaroo 1994.

Tom RAUDONIKIS
Born: 1950

57 SON of a top Lithuanian soccer player who emerged from a migrant hostel in Bathurst to represent his parents' adopted country in 20 Tests. Raudonikis (Wests and Newtown) was no stylist, possessing none of the artistry of some of the other great halfbacks, but was resourceful, determined and never let his opposite get the better of him. Achieved career highlight in 1973 when he captained Australia in the Ashes-winning third Test against Great Britain. Played in inaugural State of Origin match in 1980. 20 Tests (1972-80), Kangaroo 1973, 1978.

Ray PRICE
Born: 1953

55 KNOWN during his playing days as 'Mr Perpetual Motion', Price set incredibly high standards for fitness and endurance following his switch from rugby union in 1976. A lock forward of all-round ability, Price adapted remarkably to the 13-a-side code. A first-grader with the emerging Parramatta club from the outset, he became a dual international after just two seasons. Played 258 first grade games for the Eels and is the only player to appear in all seven of the club's grand finals. Price had an obsessional drive that inspired teammates. 22 Tests (1978-84), Kangaroo 1978, 1982.

Billy SMITH
Born: 1942

52 SMITH was a brilliant and brave performer for St George, NSW and Australia throughout the 1960s and 1970s. Played all club football in the St George district, appearing in a record 296 grade games (1961-77). Saints coach Norm Provan encouraged him to switch from centre to half early in career, which turned out to be a masterstroke. Played in four winning grand final sides but career highlight was courageous effort in brutal 1970 World Cup final against Great Britain. 18 Tests (1964-70). Kangaroo 1967-68.

Howard HALLETT
1890-1970

51 FROM Australian Rules background, Hallett developed into a champion fullback of the game's early years. Began career as a centre but switched to fullback on the 1911-12 Kangaroo tour, where he earned rare praise from English critics. Dubbed the 'Rock of Gibraltar', Hallett was a determined defender and a mainstay of the early Souths teams in a career which spanned 16 seasons. Until the arrival of Clive Churchill, was regarded by many as the finest fullback of all-time. 6 Tests (1911-14), Kangaroo 1911-12.

CHAPTER SIX

The Back Page

BY IAN HEADS

The Back

The way we were...

1950: Actor **Chips Rafferty** announces the formation of a company to make films in Australia. Prime Minister Menzies introduces legislation to outlaw the Communist Party. Australia, with 34 medals, emerges as the top country in the Empire Games. Rising opera star Joan Sutherland, 24, wins Mobil Quest.

1951: The price of tea increased by sixpence to three shillings and ten pence a pound. CSIRO reports success with a rabbit-killing virus called myxomatosis. Frank Sedgman becomes first Australian to win US tennis singles title. **Ben Chifley** dies aged 65.

WHATEVER the reasons, rugby league has always been the most sensational of games, its rawness on and off the field leading to many extraordinary and enduring stories.

In one painful week at the start of the 1999 season, league made the major newspaper front pages five days out of seven – all of them for the 'wrong' reasons, during a disreputable period of player misbehaviour off the paddock.

None of it was good news for the game but all of it reflected accurately the intensity of media focus in 1999 on the 'old working man's game'.

The Australian media's embrace of the game happened very early – before a ball was kicked in fact, in 1907, when there was great excitement and speculation about the new movement's bold plans and the games against the All Golds.

It's fair to say that league has never been out of the media since – although there have been flat spots in the love affair, with rugby league now and then just another game on just another newspaper page.

In The Back Page we have identified 20 seminal moments (sifted from literally thousands) in the game's passing parade – big stories, great stories.

Some of them changed the game and the sporting landscape forever.

Six stand above the rest, each one imposing profound effect on the sport and its future directions:

■ The beginning in 1907 – the clandestine meeting in a Sydney pub which set rugby league on its way.

■ The spectacular coup of 1909 when a Sydney entrepreneur, James Joynton Smith, funded a raid on rugby union's finest players, luring them en masse to league and securing the game's future in a single bound.

■ The introduction of the four-tackle rule in 1967 – the most dramatic on-field innovation in the game's history – bringing perfectly-timed change and freshness.

■ The single-minded drive of 'Gentleman' Jim Comans, judiciary chairman from 1981, to crack down on foul play. Comans brilliantly read the signs – that in the television age, league could no longer tolerate the 'old ways'.

■ The resignation of Kevin Humphreys (ARL and NSWRL chairman) in 1983, ending an era – and leading directly to necessary administrative and promotional change which readied league for sport's brave new world.

■ The Super League-ARL War of 1995 and beyond – ripping the game asunder and shaping very different directions for its future after all the pain and profligacy.

These then, are the game's big stories down the years.

Stop the presses ... and hold the back page. 🏉

War torn ... ARL chief executive John Quayle in a sea of media at the height of the rugby "legal" battle

Page

THE NIGHT IT ALL BEGAN

BATEMAN'S Hotel, George Street, Sydney, which stood for many years on the block between King and Market, is no more. Its shingle carried different names over its life, spanning more than a century: Bateman's Crystal Hotel, then just Bateman's, later, The Tatler.

Early on a wintry evening on August 8, 1907, a group of men, around 50 in number, met in a downstairs room at the hotel in the most important get-together in Australian rugby league history.

Some time during the evening the group, headed by the likes of James Giltinan, Henry Hoyle, Victor Trumper and Peter Moir, voted to form a body to be known as the NSW Rugby League, with those present urged to keep secret what had taken place.

The night is a moment frozen in history for the two rugby codes. It followed weeks of turbulence and uncertainty in the football world. On a single night one game became two – and rugby league in this country was born.

Tradition ... some of the First Kangaroos relax in England

THE FIRST KANGAROOS

IT was rugby league's founding father and manager of the first Kangaroos (1908), James Joseph Giltinan, who approached Captain Bennett, skipper of the RMS *Macedonia*.

'Was there a chance that the Aussie players could stoke the boiler to help keep them fit?' he asked.

'Some of the boys stood on their dignity,' Giltinan was to recall years later.

But with tough forwards Jim Abercrombie and 'Sandy' Pearce leading the way the Roos were soon mustered into teams of six and rostered on.

So it was that the brave pioneers, 34 players and manager Giltinan, worked their way to England to begin a wonderful tradition of 'The Tours'.

Confronting the blackest northern winter in years, meagre financial returns and a cotton mill strike which crippled Yorkshire and Lancashire, the First Kangaroos somehow laid down a magnificent foundation for all the teams that followed.

GREAT COUP OF 1909

THE great entrepreneurial coup of Australian rugby league's history came when the game was in its infancy.

In the league's second year, 1909, the new code was on its knees, laid low by internal dissent, poor crowds, empty coffers and threats of withdrawal by several of the foundation clubs.

A single, brilliant stroke, bankrolled by flamboyant Sydney businessman James (later Sir James) Joynton Smith, secured the game's future virtually for the rest of the century, leaving rugby union lamenting in the new game's wake.

Offering a reported £1500 ($3544), Smith enticed across to rugby league 15 players from the outstanding Wallaby team of 1908 (*pictured above*), virtually the cream of the rugby union crop, including the 15-man game's captain and champion Chris McKivat.

Four Wallabies v Kangaroos matches were played – the last of them leading to a great sensation, when Balmain refused to play the 1909 final against Souths in protest at the match being played as a curtain-raiser to the main event.

In the long view, even that high-principled stance fades.

Via the Wallabies coup rugby league now had virtually all of football's finest men – and was on its way.

1950-59

APRIL 22, 1950: St George play first game at a new venue, Kogarah Oval. Crowd of 12,500 turn out for clash between Saints and Souths, won 17-15 by the Rabbitohs.

JUNE 3, 1950: Crowd of 70,419, at the time the biggest crowd to pack into the SCG, watch Ernest Ward's British tourists beat NSW 20-13.

JULY 22, 1950: St George winger **Ron Roberts** scores try that clinches Ashes for Australia for first time in 30 years on a SCG mudheap. Scores are locked 2-all when Roberts makes historic dash 15 minutes from time.

SEPTEMBER 6, 1950: James Joseph Giltinan, founding father of NSWRL, dies in Sydney, a week after his 84th birthday.

JULY 21, 1951: Highly entertaining French touring side, inspired by the charismatic fullback **Puig-Aubert**, wins Test series against

Australia with 35-14 third Test victory. Over 67,000 people pack the SCG for Test.

SEPTEMBER 23, 1951: Fledgling club Manly-Warringah are thrashed 42-14 by Souths in the grand final, played on a Sunday for the first time, at the Sydney Sports Ground. Souths become the first holders of the Giltinan Shield, commemorating game's founder.

The way we were...

1952: King George VI dies and **Queen Elizabeth II** ascends to the throne. Women win four of Australia's six gold medals at Helsinki Olympics. Boxing star Dave Sands dies after road accident. Former PM William Morris Hughes dies aged 90.

1953: Sydney's **Ken Rosewall**, aged 18, wins Australian tennis championship at Kooyong. The 100,000th Holden rolls off assembly line. Movie-goers in Melbourne given special glasses to view 3-D films. After three years of fighting and nearly two million casualties, the Korean War is over.

EVERYBODY OUT!

THE first and only player strike in premiership history took place in 1917.

Glebe was the club involved and the issues several – including the life suspension of Dan 'Laddo' Davies, a Newcastle player, who joined Glebe but was ruled to be not residentially qualified.

Discontent at the Davies suspension and other simmering points of conflict with the NSWRL led to the boilover, on July 21, 1917, when the Glebe first graders went on strike, refusing to play a scheduled match against Balmain.

At a subsequent inquiry, 14 Glebe players were suspended until the start of the 1919 season – among them the great lock forward Frank Burge and his brothers Albert and Laidley.

In April and May of 1918 the suspensions were lifted. But the banned Laddo Davies' return to Newcastle was to spark an even bigger split – leading to further strikes and eventually the formation of two separate competitions: the 'Lilywhites' and the 'Bolsheviks'.

UNKINDEST CUT OF ALL

IN the 1920s the NSW Rugby League dumped two clubs from the premiership – Annandale (formed 1910) and Glebe (1908, *pictured below*).

Annandale lasted only until the end of the 1920 season, axed then on the vote of the NSWRL general committee.

In the previous three seasons they had won only one of 41 matches played. Further, they were regarded as an over-rough and unattractive side which tended to field players who were not residentially qualified.

The axing of Glebe, the first club formed back in 1908, was a far more contentious issue when it came in November, 1929.

The vote couldn't have been closer, 13-12. Glebe, 'the Dirty Reds', had been without a home ground for two years, had run near the bottom the previous three years and drawn meagre crowds.

Glebe fought hard to have the decision reversed but to no avail.

THE GREAT STAMPEDE

IT was a harsh winter's day that led to one of the great crowd upheavals of the game's history.

Grand final day, 1942. As the wind whipped icy rain in beneath umbrellas, fans on the Sydney Cricket Ground hill *(above)* looked longingly across at the acres of unoccupied seats in the brand new MA Noble Stand.

Affected by the weather and the wartime conditions, the crowd was only 26,171 for the Canterbury-St George decider.

Legend has it that a diminutive soldier started the great invasion during the reserve grade grand final when he hopped the fence and, notwithstanding heavy army boots, dodged a couple of gendarmes to make it safely to the comfort of the Noble Stand. Soon it was a stampede as other soldiers and those on the hill flattened fence panels and headed across the muddy surface.

Police and league officials were powerless to stop the small army on the move, some of whom paused to chat with the reserve graders as they passed by.

In the second half thousands strayed back on to the field, and referee Jack O'Brien had to halt play at one stage.

Canterbury won the title 11-9.

THE EAR-BITE INCIDENT

TO the day he died Frank 'Bumper' Farrell *(pictured top right)* denied he had bitten the right ear of St George frontrower Bill McRitchie at Henson Park on July 28, 1945.

But Bumper, a tough cop (chief of the vice squad at Darlinghurst Station for years) and a very tough frontrower with Newtown, is linked irrevocably with what was to become known, infamously, as 'The Ear-Bite Incident'.

The story dragged on for many months in 1945, with Saints' McRitchie spending 22 weeks in hospital having his damaged ear repaired with skin grafts. After a long and sensational investigation the NSWRL cleared Farrell of the charge laid against him – by 15 votes to 12. Bumper argued that he had left his dentures in the Henson Park dressing room and therefore could not possibly have bitten McRitchie.

Fifty-four years later the mystery of McRitchie's injury remains officially unsolved – although those in the know have few doubts.

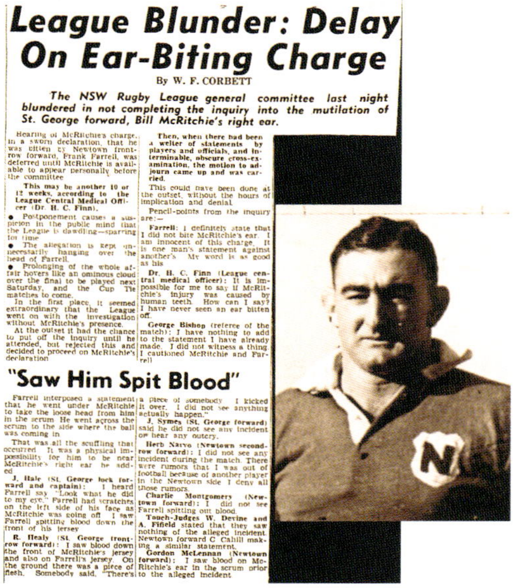

League Blunder: Delay On Ear-Biting Charge

By W. F. CORBETT

The NSW Rugby League general committee last night blundered in not completing the inquiry into the mutilation of St. George forward, Bill McRitchie's right ear.

Hearing of McRitchie's charge, in a sworn declaration, that he was bitten by Newtown front-row forward, Frank Farrell, was deferred until McRitchie is available to appear personally before the committee.

This may be another 10 or 12 weeks, according to the League Central Medical Officer (Dr. H. C. Finn).

- Postponement causes a suspicion in the public mind that the League is dawdling—sparring for time.
- The allegation is kept unnecessarily hanging over the head of Farrell.
- Prolonging of the whole affair hovers like an ominous cloud over the final to be played next Saturday, and the Cup Tie matches to come.

In the first place, it seemed extraordinary that the League went on with the investigation without McRitchie's presence.

At the outset it had the chance to put off the inquiry until he attended, but rejected this and decided to proceed on McRitchie's declaration.

Then, when there had been a welter of statements by players and officials, and interminable, obscure cross-examination, the motion to adjourn came up and was carried.

This could have been done at the outset, without the hours of implication and denial.

Pencil-points from the inquiry are:—

Farrell: I definitely state that I did not bite McRitchie's ear. I am innocent of this charge. It is one man's statement against another's. My word is as good as his.

Dr. H. C. Finn (League central medical officer): It is impossible for me to say if McRitchie's injury was caused by human teeth. How can I say? I have never seen an ear bitten off.

George Bishop (referee of the match): I have nothing to add to the statement I have already made. I did not witness a thing. I cautioned McRitchie and Farrell.

"Saw Him Spit Blood"

Farrell interposed a statement that he went under McRitchie to take the loose head from him in the scrum. He went across the scrum to the side where the ball was coming in.

That was all the scuffling that occurred. It was a physical impossibility for him to be near McRitchie's right ear, he added.

J. Hale (St. George lock forward and captain): I heard Farrell say "Look what he did to my eye." Farrell had scratches on the left side of his face as McRitchie was going off. I saw Farrell spitting blood down the front of his jersey.

R. Healy (St. George front-row forward): I saw blood down the front of McRitchie's jersey and also on Farrell's jersey. On the ground there was a piece of flesh. Somebody said, "There's a piece of somebody." I kicked it over. I did not see anything actually happen."

J. Symes (St. George forward) said he did not see any incident or hear any outcry.

Herb Narvo (Newtown second-row forward): I did not see any incident during the match. There were rumors that I was out of football because of another player in the Newtown side. I deny all those rumors.

Charlie Montgomery (Newtown forward): I did not see Farrell spitting out blood.

Touch-Judges W. Devine and A. Fifield stated that they saw nothing of the alleged incident. Newtown forward C Cahill making a similar statement.

Gordon McLennan (Newtown forward): I saw blood on McRitchie's ear in the scrum prior to the alleged incident.

THE DAY THEY SNUBBED LEN SMITH

THE omission of the then Australian captain Len Smith from the Kangaroo touring team of 1948 is perhaps the greatest of all rugby league scandals. Len, a decent and honourable man, captain of NSW in 1948 and skipper of Australia in a two-Test series against New Zealand that year, was dumped from the team in a monumental shock that has never really been explained.

His omission would be akin to Brad Fittler missing a 28-man touring party today. Smith's own view is that religion was a factor, at a time in the game's evolution when there was fierce Catholics v Masons rivalry.

'In my view, religion was one aspect of what happened,' Smith, a Catholic, has been quoted as saying several times.

There are other theories: one of them being that the hard-nosed Norman 'Latchem' Robinson had been a conspirator behind it, driven by his ambition to coach the team.

Another is that it was no more than an unbelievable mix-up, that the selectors simply got it wrong – somehow not realising they had missed Smith as they named the four centres.

Whatever the reason, it was a tragedy which scarred both Len Smith ... and the game he played.

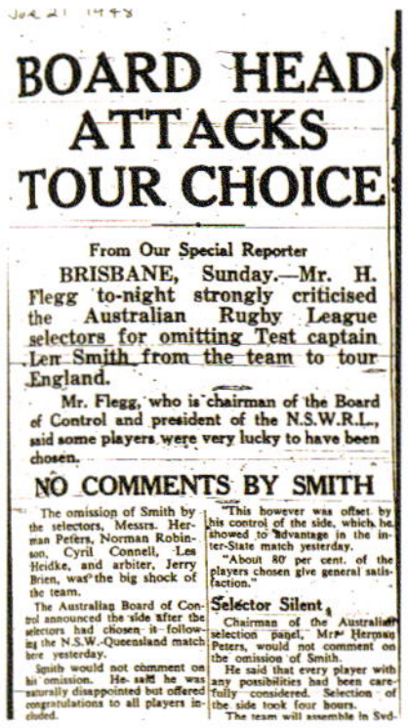

BOARD HEAD ATTACKS TOUR CHOICE

From Our Special Reporter

BRISBANE, Sunday.—Mr. H. Flegg to-night strongly criticised the Australian Rugby League selectors for omitting Test captain Len Smith from the team to tour England.

Mr. Flegg, who is chairman of the Board of Control and president of the N.S.W.R.L., said some players were very lucky to have been chosen.

NO COMMENTS BY SMITH

The omission of Smith by the selectors, Messrs. Herman Peters, Norman Robinson, Cyril Connell, Les Heidke, and arbiter, Jerry Brien, was the big shock of the team.

The Australian Board of Control announced the side after the selectors had chosen it following the N.S.W.-Queensland match here yesterday.

Smith would not comment on his omission. He said he was naturally disappointed but offered congratulations to all players included.

"This however was offset by his control of the side, which he showed to advantage in the inter-State match yesterday.

"About 80 per cent. of the players chosen give general satisfaction."

Selector Silent

Chairman of the Australian selection panel, Mr. Herman Peters, would not comment on the omission of Smith.

He said that every player with any possibilities had been carefully considered. Selection of the side took four hours.

The team will assemble in Syd-

THE DAY WE WON THE ASHES

ON the day we won the Ashes in 1950, grown men wept unashamed tears and countless thousands of hats flew high into the air over the SCG.

What an afternoon it was – on a ground churned to deep, sticky mud by a week of torrential rain.

The notable league man Harry Sunderland called the game for the BBC and recalled the spectacle when right winger Ron Roberts scored the winning try in the 65th minute: 'The confetti that was hurled in the air presented a sight like a snowstorm.'

Roberts, a big lump of a bloke from St George, rated as being an uncertain handler, sped down the western side towards the Randwick end on the end of a perfect dry-weather backline movement.

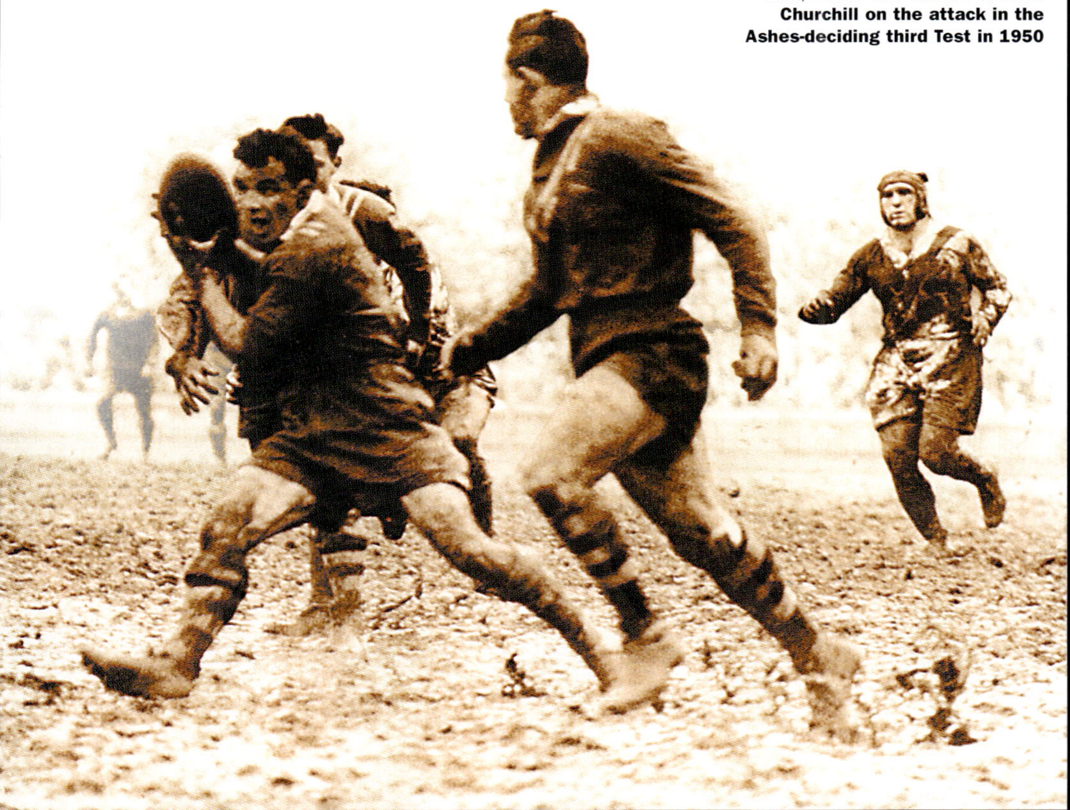

Mud, sweat and cheers ... Clive Churchill on the attack in the Ashes-deciding third Test in 1950

1950-59

NOVEMBER 17, 1951: Australian winger **Lionel Cooper** scores astonishing 10 tries in one match playing for Huddersfield against Keighley in English competition.

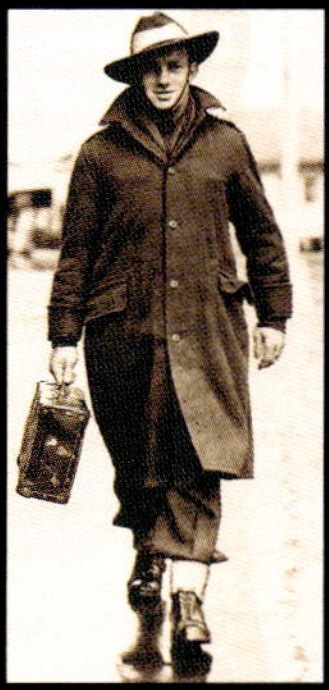

JUNE 28, 1952: Australia suffer heaviest Test match defeat when thumped 49-25 by New Zealand at the Brisbane Cricket Ground. Kiwi fullback Des White kicks a world record 11 goals.

SEPTEMBER 20, 1952: Wests beat Souths 22-12 in one of the most controversial grand finals ever played. Referee George Bishop makes two highly contentious decisions against hot favourites Souths and penalises them 15-4.

DECEMBER 13, 1952: Having lost the Ashes series 2-0, Clive Churchill's Kangaroos score their biggest win over Great Britain in 40 years, winning a violent third Test 27-7 at Odsal Stadium.

MAY 30, 1953: A curious crowd of 65,543 watch the touring **American All Stars** play their first match at the SCG. The tourists, with next to no rugby league experience, are beaten 52-25 by a 'generous' Sydney side.

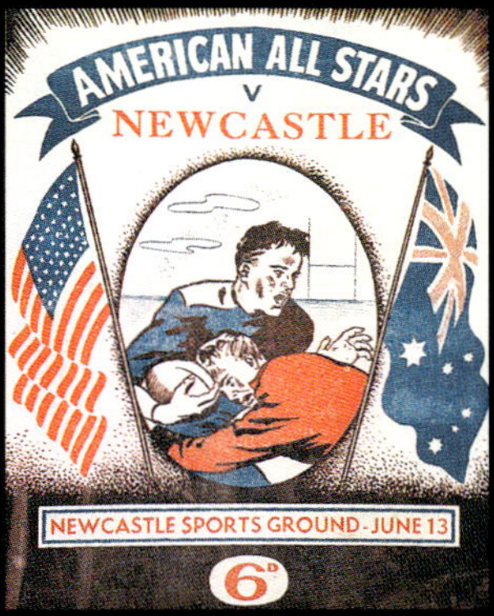

The way we were...

1954: **John Landy** runs the mile in world record time of 3min 58sec at Turku. Census reveals Australia's population is 9,025,849. Aussie golfer Peter Thomson becomes youngest British Open winner. Cyclone causes widespread flooding in NSW with 26 lives lost.

1955: Petrov Royal Commission ends (no prosecutions are considered warranted). Barry Humphries' character Edna Everage makes her stage debut. US entertainer **Frank Sinatra's** popularity soars.

Years later a magazine poll rated his try the greatest moment in Australian league history.

It was an extraordinary day for Australia's team, under the captaincy of Clive Churchill and the coaching of Vic Hey. Not since 1920 had Australia won the Ashes.

In 1950 they did it on a surface which wore a coating of 40 tonnes of river sand, the ground spiked in an attempt to drain the water.

To the 47,178 who braved the conditions only one thing mattered – Australia had regained the Ashes.

THE TRY OF THE CENTURY

THE try that has been called 'the greatest ever scored' lives only in memory and legend now.

Now and then English league journals still re-run the famous diagram which outlined the passage taken by Australia's Brian Bevan – 'The Wizard of Aus' – in his amazing try for Warrington against Wigan in the Wardonia Cup at Central Park in 1948.

Bevan's own modest recall of his amazing dodging, weaving effort which English scribes tagged 'the try of the century' is contained in a rare personal journal, made available to *The Daily Telegraph* for *100 Years of Rugby League*.

The late, great 'Bev' *(pictured below)* wrote: 'The score at the time was 5-5. A scrum had been formed five yards from the Warrington line, about a quarter of an hour into the second half ... Dave Cotton won the scrum ... the ball was passed to

Albert Pimblett, who drew the Wigan winger Hill and served me at precisely the right moment.

Instead of making for the touchline I decided to head for the centre of the field. Martin Ryan, the Wigan fullback, barred my progress on the 25, Ashcroft and Mountford ran in to support him.

Somehow I avoided all three and, in a diagonal direction, I made for the Wigan line. It seemed an eternity before I reached my goal but the next thing I knew I was placing the ball over the try line on the opposite side of the field from where I had begun my run.

I had covered, in the course of the movement, approximately 125 yards. To this day I can still remember the excitement of the crowd as I touched down.'

THE BIGGEST, BADDEST BRAWL OF ALL

EVEN 45 years on, Clive Churchill's colourful words still bring back a sense of the depth of the infamy the day referee Aub Oxford left brawling NSW and Great Britain players to it – and walked from the Sydney Cricket Ground.

Saturday, July 10, 1954. 'Well done Oxford,' called SCG m embers as Oxford headed to the referees room, shame-faced players dragging well behind, with NSW ahead 17-6 on the scoreboard.

ALL-IN BRAWL ENDS BIG GAME

REFEREE WALKS OFF THE FIELD

A brawl in which nearly every player of both teams joined stopped the Rugby League match between New South Wales and England at the Sydney Cricket Ground yesterday.

Suicide After Parking Fault

In his 1961 book, NSW captain Churchill called the match 'a filthy brawl of backlane thuggery'.

He wrote: 'The sending off of (British five-eighth) Ray Price was the spark that lit the gunpowder which went off like a hydrogen bomb. It was then that (Alf) Burnell aimed a wicked punch at me. I ducked and the blow missed – but Burnell's fist went crashing into the back of the head of an unintended victim, poor Noel Pidding.'

It was 'on' all right. Harry Wells and 'Bad Man' Douggie Greenall, who used to encase his arm with a sort of concrete plaster to make his stiff-arm tackle more effective, became locked in a terrifying punching duel like a couple of enraged beasts of the jungle.

Players of both teams sprang with bared teeth at one another ...'

At its regular meeting the next Monday night, the NSWRL passed a motion deploring what had taken place.

The comments of mild-mannered league scribe Tom Goodman capture the general disgust at league's only abandoned match. He wrote: 'The disgrace of last Saturday sickened rabid followers and the effects will linger for a long while.'

HOT OR NOT?
Grand final of 1963

THE passing years have progressively clouded the sensational St George-Western Suburbs grand final of 1963.

Fitting really, considering that the match was played on an SCG bog and produced the game's most famous image – John O'Gready's muddy, marvellous photo of Norm Provan (St George) and Arthur Summons (Wests) at game's end, a picture immortalised as 'The Gladiators'.

In a fiercely fought match laced with controversy Saints beat Wests 8-3, avenging three successive losses to the Magpies that season.

Increasingly in the passing years the focus has turned to referee Darcy Lawler, a highly contentious figure that day. In recent times respected Wests men, Jack Gibson and Noel 'Ned' Kelly, have gone public with their belief that Lawler did not give Wests a fair go – and in fact had BACKED St George.

The story has now become public knowledge of how prop Gibson had said to Kelly in the dressing room before the game: 'Mate, we can't win ... Darcy has backed them.'

Kelly told the story in full in his 1996 book 'Hard Man', concluding 'I will never forgive Darcy Lawler for what he did that day. I have no doubt we were robbed.'

Penalties in the game ran 18-7 to Saints and Ian Walsh whipped Kelly two-to-one in the scrums.

The key moment was Saints winger Johnny King's match-winning try – with Wests claiming that King had been fairly held before being allowed to get up and run.

St George to this day are just as adamant it was a fair try.

Focus on the ref ... Darcy Lawler leads out the players for the controversial 1963 grand final

1950-59

MAY 5, 1954: Australian forward **Harry Bath** captains Warrington to victory over Halifax in a replay of the Challenge Cup final, before a then world record crowd of 102,569 at Bradford's Odsal Stadium.

JULY 10, 1954: Infamous day in the game's history unfolds at the SCG when referee Aub Oxford abandons international match between Great Britain and NSW after 56 minutes of brawling and violent play (NSW led 17-6). NSW fullback Clive Churchill describes the match as a 'filthy brawl of back lane thuggery'.

SEPTEMBER 18, 1954: Souths beat Newtown 23-15 in the first 'automatic' grand final. New system determining premiership ensures a grand final is played every year.

OCTOBER 31, 1954: Clive Churchill leads Australia into first World Cup campaign, against Great Britain in Lyons, France. The Australians are beaten 28-13.

NOVEMBER 27, 1954: Australia and New Zealand play the first rugby league match on American soil. On their way home from the World Cup, Australia beat the Kiwis 30-13 before a crowd of 1000 at Long Beach Memorial Stadium, California.

AUGUST 13, 1955: Souths fullback **Clive Churchill**, playing with a broken arm, lifts his team to a crucial 9-7 win over Manly at Redfern Oval by booting a conversion from the sideline.

Churchill Kicks Goal With Wrist Broken

MOVERS & SHAKERS

RUGBY League has had eight major powerbrokers in Australia since its formation in 1908.

Entrepreneur, **James J Giltinan**, a Sydney man well known in rugby union, cricket and horseracing circles, was the driving force behind the movement which broke away from rugby union in 1908. Giltinan was manager of the First Kangaroos to England but lost the NSW secretaryship while he was away.

It has been described as one of the worst backhanders in sporting history and it took 25 years before Giltinan received due and proper recognition for his pioneer work.

In 1909, newspaper baron James Joynton Smith made a significant contribution to the code's development by arranging for the Kangaroos to play four exhibition matches against the Wallabies. Those games actually put league on the map and it has rarely looked back.

Harry 'Jersey' Flegg was a wonderful league character whose career began as a player with Easts in 1908. Flegg became a State and Australian selector in 1909 and held those posts for 19 years.

He was elected NSW president in 1929 and held the position for 31 years. Flegg also became head of the Board of Control in 1941. The junior representative competition for under-19s still carries his name.

FOUR IS THE LAW

THE greatest on-field revolution in rugby league's 92 seasons came in 1967 – with the trialling, assessment and acceptance of the four-tackle rule. The game has had no more profound change in its history, and season 1967 can be identified with clarity as the beginning of league's New Era.

Limited tackle football came from England, brainchild of the urbane ERL secretary Bill Fallowfield *(left)*. It was not, as is sometimes suggested, a device contrived to stop St George's seemingly endless run of premierships (even though the Saints' run did end in 1967).

Rather, it happened at a time that Australian league was ready for change. Fallowfield hatched his limited tackle plan 20,000km away – specifically to open up the game at a time when bash and barge football had imposed a steely grip on rugby league.

Trialled in England in the northern winter of 1966-67, the four-tackle rule was first aired in Australia on Friday, February 24, 1967 – in a pre-season match between competition new chums Penrith and Cronulla-Sutherland.

A mixed reception gradually grew into wider – although never unanimous – acceptance.

The four-tackle rule became six tackle in season 1971 – and rugby league had set its sails for the future.

A MAN OF PRINCIPLE

TOUGH, principled Dennis Tutty did every professional footballer in the years since a profound favour with the brave stand he took in seasons 1969-70.

Almost single-handedly Tutty, a blond, athletic secondrower who was a great crowd favourite at Balmain, tackled rugby league's iniquitous transfer system. His stand sent him broke, caused the break-up of his marriage and left him with an ulcer.

But Tutty stuck to what he believed – that clubs should have no rights to the services of a player once he had completed a contract, the system that had been in place since 1960.

Tutty began his fight at the end of 1968 when he sought a release from Balmain after completing a contract. In the seasons that followed, 1969-70, he gave up two full years of football and potentially tens of thousands of dollars while the battle was waged through the courts.

In 1971, his money gone, he came back to football on a match-by-match arrangement.

Not until December, 1971, was it settled – when the High Court upheld a 1970 Equity Court decision that the league's transfer system was invalid and a restraint of trade.

Dennis Tutty had won ... and lost plenty. To the players of the 30 years since he should stand tall as a heroic figure. All of them are free to ply their trade – to move on when contracts are ended.

A MAN FOR HIS TIME

LIKE Dennis Tutty, 'Gentleman' Jim Comans *(below left)* was the right man at the right time for rugby league. A former player with the old Sydney University club (104 games) and a Battle of Britain pilot, solicitor Comans was a man with a mission when he took over as chairman of the newly constituted NSWRL Judiciary in 1980.

Comans knew rugby league, and understood that television was to be a huge factor in whatever future the game was to have. He set out to eliminate thuggery from the playing field, believing a game so widely shown and publicised could no longer afford the brutality of earlier times.

To Comans, head-high tackles, use of elbows, gouging, biting and spear tackles had no place in the modern game.

Conducting his hearings with courtroom attention to fine detail, Comans displayed steely resolve in his six years at the helm.

Many players felt the sting of his tough judgments – some of them famously so (Les Boyd, 12 months suspension, then 15 months; Bob Cooper, 15 months).

By 1985 the number of players appearing before the man who some called 'The Hanging Judge' had been dramatically reduced.

Winner and loser ... Dennis Tutty and lawyer outside court during the transfer wrangle

Comans' premature resignation from the judiciary in April, 1986, on a point of principle, was the game's loss. But by then, Gentleman Jim had changed the game.

Lasting image ... Easts' captain Arthur Beetson offers an encouraging word to Graeme Langlands after the 1975 grand final

THE SADDEST FINALE OF THEM ALL

THERE are no fairytales guaranteed at the end of football careers. Just occasionally, the ending can take a player deep into nightmare territory.

So it was with the great St George warrior, Graeme 'Changa' Langlands, when the 1975 grand final – his last – turned into a horror story.

The image remains a quarter of a century on: one of the game's greatest champions stumbling and unco-ordinated in his flashy white boots as Jack Gibson's Eastern Suburbs team destroyed the Saints 38-nil.

'Langlands must play one more game of football,' wrote Frank Hyde later, appalled by the thought that such a career could end in such a way.

For 'Chang', it was the day when everything went wrong – and there is no doubt the event scarred him deeply.

It was Ken Irvine, a close pal working for the firm adidas at the time, who talked him into wearing the white boots – the enduring symbol of his bad day, although certainly in no way the reason for it.

Langlands' dilemma lay in a pain-killing injection which went wrong. Instead of dulling the ache of a groin muscle injury, the needle virtually caused Langlands to lose control of his right leg.

Over the years there have been further suggestions – that a 'go-fast' tablet taken before the game may have added to his disorientation.

At halftime there was a furious argument in the Saints dressing room – with Langlands insisting that he return to the field, against the wishes of Dragons secretary Frank 'Fearless' Facer.

The image of Arthur Beetson (Easts captain) offering his commiserations to one of the greatest of all the game's players after the decider is about as poignant as it gets.

The white boots of 1975 ended up in faraway Bradford, draped over the crossbar of the goal posts at a training ground during the World Cup late that year.

Langlands played the first four rounds of the premiership the next year (1976), contemplated his future and quietly retired.

THE RISE AND FALL OF KEVIN HUMPHREYS

KEVIN Humphreys, a strong leader with a deep passion for rugby league, dominated the game in the decade 1973-83. When he resigned in dramatic circumstances, on May 2, 1983, the reverberations reached way beyond football's world, lacerating both government and the judiciary.

Humphreys, Balmain to the bootstraps, was the seventh president of the NSWRL, elected on the death of Bill Buckley in 1973. Inspiring important change in the game as it headed towards the modern era, he fell with an almighty crash on the evening of May 2, 1983, victim of an ABC Four Corners program, 'The Big League'.

Chris Masters (brother of Roy, then coaching St George) had changed the original focus of his program to home in on the circumstances of Humphreys' acquittal in August, 1977, on charges of misappropriating $52,000 from Balmain Leagues Club.

Swept aside ... league boss Kevin Humphreys resigns
Photo: *Rugby League Week*

MOVERS & SHAKERS

Bill Buckley, a Newtown forward whose career was terminated by a broken leg in 1928, was the man who succeeded Flegg.

Buckley oversaw the development of the code (new teams and rule changes) and steered Australia to a position of dominance on the international scene.

His autocratic but authoritative period of rule took rugby league to the Kevin Humphreys era which began in 1973.

Humphreys was a prime mover in the birth of the State of Origin concept and got numerous other league projects off the drawing board and into reality.

His administrative career came crashing down in 1983 when the Four Corners TV program screened an expose into the misappropriation of money from the Balmain Leagues Club.

Manly boss Ken Arthurson then entered the scene and became one of league's finest and most powerful statesmen.

John Quayle, a former Easts lock, took league into the 1990s with his business approach and was ultimately succeeded by Neil Whittaker who had to deal with the considerable fallout from the Super League v ARL war.

The way we were...

1956: Australian television's first broadcast by Channel 9 on September 16. Sir Frank Beaurepaire dies months before Melbourne Olympics. NSW Cabinet legalises poker machines in clubs. Melbourne Olympics a huge success. Australia wins 13 gold medals, seven better than previous effort. Local stars include Betty Cuthbert, Dawn Fraser, Lorraine Crapp, Murray Rose, Jon Henricks and David Thiele.

1957: Betty Cuthbert named ABC Sportsman of the Year. Danish architect Joern Utzon wins £5000 for his design of the Sydney Opera House. Tulloch blazes to eight-length win in the Caulfield Cup. Reg Ansett buys Australian National Airways.

I was there...

'The Kevin Humphreys affair was a huge blow and came in the middle of a bad period for the code. I always felt great sympathy for Kevin. He was a bloke who did a great deal for rugby league, he was a fine administrator. After I was elected to office we held a huge public forum involving players, supporters, referees and the media. We listened to everybody and formulated deep-seated plans to lift the standards and image of the game right across the board.'

Ken Arthurson, ARL chief of the 1980s and 90s.

The program ultimately led to the setting up of a Royal Commission, to NSW Premier Neville Wran standing aside for a time and to the jailing of former NSW chief stipendiary magistrate Murray Farquhar.

Sweeping Humphreys aside in the tidal wave (the league president resigned, aware that his continued presence at the helm would inevitably damage the game) – the ABC program also triggered vast change in rugby league itself.

Building on the positive aspects of the Humphreys era, in hand with ongoing radical change, the likes of Tom Bellew, John Quayle and Ken Arthurson superintended a profound shake-up – the likes of which the game had never seen.

In hindsight, the ending of the Humphreys era on that Monday night in 1983 can be seen as a seminal moment in league's story.

BYE BYE BLACKBIRDS ... AND BLUEBAGS

THE NSWRL sacked foundation clubs Western Suburbs and Newtown on the night before John Bertrand and Australia II united the nation in joyful celebration by winning the America's Cup in September, 1983.

The Newtown Jets, $1.5 million in debt at the time, never came back to big-time football – although their enduring presence in league's Metropolitan Cup competition is testimony both to an ancient spirit and an unbreakable connection with rugby league.

On the night that the NSWRL general commitee made its agonising decision (by secret ballot, 29 votes to 12) not to invite Wests and Newtown into the 1984 premiership, Magpies president John Brooks declared: 'We're finished – the door has closed on us.'

Yet, from that point, Wests became the club that refused to die. The original plan was that Newtown would relocate to Campbelltown and be born again in 1985.

Yet in the end, after fierce scrapping in the court and the exercise of a will that simply refused to bend, it was Wests who survived to take the opportunity at Campbelltown.

Twice the NSWRL voted the Magpies out of the competition. Twice Equity Court decisions saved the Magpies' necks.

In late 1985 the High Court finally upheld the League's right to hire and fire clubs – but by then the decision had been made at Phillip Street that, with the need to get the competition set up in 1986, Wests would be in.

So, with a little bit of luck, Wests survived – managing to stay alive in all the seasons since ... although as a merged entity with Balmain (Wests Tigers) in season 2000 and beyond.

THE WAR

THE breakaway that ripped American football apart in the 1960s lasted six years. In its story are uncanny parallels with rugby league's own 'Great War' three decades later.

The Aussie version, exploding into the public consciousness on April Fool's Day, 1995, with the sensational News Limited-backed raids on established ARL clubs and players followed by the ARL's vigorous response, proved just as bitter.

Two months before (February 6, 1995), the 20 ARL clubs had rejected News Limited's proposal for a 'Super League'.

At the heart of the furious battle that ensued in the wake of the April raids was a remarkably complex mix of factors, including the big ones: an appealing, popular and marketable game at the height of its powers, seething discontent with the ARL (and NSWRL) that existed within at least one club (Brisbane Broncos) and the arrival of pay-TV as a big player on the sporting scene.

History records the gigantic split that followed, with roughly half a competition joining the breakaway born in the Broncos boardroom – and the other half sticking fast to the ARL.

In the short term, the game went mad – with vast and unrealistic sums of money thrown at players, who either jumped or stayed.

Footballers became millionaires overnight, player managers found themselves rolling in money beyond belief, friendships of long years in football were abruptly, bitterly ended, promises were made then broken, new clubs were born only later to die.

Then, it was over to the lawyers – to begin courtroom battles unprecedented in Australian sport, costing the game, its clubs and its backers,

Great crowd, great spectacle ... Stadium Australia hosts its first rugby league extravaganza to launch the 1999 season

Optus and Kerry Packer's Australian Consolidated Press on one side, News Limited on the other, countless millions of dollars.

Rugby league became rugby legal for almost two full years – the High Court having the final say in November, 1996, when its judgment opened the door for the rebel Super League competition to go ahead.

In 1997, rugby league was played for the first time in split competitions – the flak continuing to fly between opposing forces.

On December 19, 1997, a promising, if precarious, settlement rejoined the game, leading to the formation of a new body (the National Rugby League) to run the premiership.

In late 1999 the shaky peace holds, although with palpable unease as the progress to the News-determined rationalisation (to 14 teams) continues.

Many of the key players in the Super League War

Courting change ... News Limited executives Ken Cowley (left) and Lachlan Murdoch (right) with Tom Hughes QC and John Ribot

– the ARL's John Quayle and Ken Arthurson and SL's Paul 'Porky' Morgan – by then had long since departed. Clubs too – Perth, Adelaide, Hunter Mariners, Gold Coast, Crushers – all of them no more than memories.

The cost of it all was beyond measure – perhaps a ballpark figure of $400 million?

The war altered rugby league forever and only the seasons ahead will determine the success, or otherwise, of the changes wrought.

OLYMPIAN HEIGHTS

RUGBY league has placed its first footprint on many fine and famous sporting arenas in the past – Sydney Cricket Ground (1911), Sydney Sports Ground (1911), Melbourne Cricket Ground (1914), Sydney Football Stadium (1988) among them.

But never has there been an occasion to match the once-in-a-lifetime opportunity offered in March, 1999, when the old working man's game christened Sydney's spanking new Olympic stadium (Stadium Australia) and galvanised a whole city.

The night was unforgettable – a doubleheader (Newcastle v Manly, St George-Illawarra v Parramatta), the excitement in the vast crowd growing as the filling stands edged the occasion close to the world record crowd of 102,569 (Warrington v Halifax, Odsal Stadium Bradford, 1954) and then past it, to 104,583.

'Great crowd, great spectacle, great atmosphere,' said Prime Minister John Howard, one of the multitude.

The fine details of a glowing night will be soon forgotten – that Newcastle beat Manly 41-18 and Parramatta beat the Dragons 20-10 – but never the occasion itself. 🏉

The way we were...

1958: Menzies Government elected for fifth term. Eight firefighters burn to death in bushfires near Mount Gambier, SA. Champion cyclist Russell Mockridge killed when struck by bus on outskirts of Melbourne. Antarctic explorer and geologist **Sir Douglas Mawson** dies aged 76.

1959: Gregory Peck and Ava Gardner arrive in Melbourne to film *On The Beach*. Darwin wins city status. Australia's population hits 10 million. US evangelist Dr Billy Graham attracts Sydney crowd of 150,000.

WHAT A GAME!
PENRITH v ST GEORGE 1967

TO fans of the Penrith Panthers, two matches stand out in the club's history. The first, naturally enough, was the club's epic grand final win over Canberra in 1991.

The second came many years earlier – in the Panthers' debut season in the big league.

The date was Saturday, April 23, 1967 ... and it was the day the mighty St George Dragons made their first trip to the foot of the mountains.

Premiers for the past 11 seasons, the Dragons team featured a who's who of that era ... Johnny Raper, Reg Gasnier, Graeme Langlands, Brian Clay, Billy Smith, Dick Huddart and Johnny King.

The Panthers, struggling to find their feet after being controversially promoted from second division, were a team of cast-offs and youngsters ... the likes of **Laurie Fagan** (top right), Bob Landers, and Dave Applebee.

This match was the official opening of Penrith Park and over 12,000 fans turned up to mark the special event.

Two weeks earlier, on the same ground, the Panthers had won their first game 16-10 against Newtown. Despite that early success, the Panthers were expected to be cannon fodder for Saints.

But with Fagan calling the shots and the eager young Penrith forwards rising to the occasion, the Panthers produced the upset of the year ... or perhaps the decade.

Cheered on by a disbelieving crowd, the Panthers led from start to finish, thrashing the greatest team league had seen 24-12 and earning the Panthers instant respectability throughout the league world.

"It was truly one of those great matches," recalled current club boss Roger Cowan, then a young official of the club.

"That day convinced me and just about everyone at Penrith that we could be competitive."

Birth of a club...

Rugby league had been played in Penrith since 1912, but it was not until the 1960s that serious consideration was given to promoting a local team to the elite division. In 1966 Penrith were playing in the second division wearing blue and white jumpers. In the same year the NSW Rugby league voted to admit the club into the competition for the following season.

The first premiership game was against Canterbury and after leading 12-10 with 15 minutes to go, the side lost 15-12. The club's first win came when they christened their home ground, Penrith Park, with a 16-10 win over Newtown. In their first year the club finished second last, with 12 competition points.

COLOURS: Brown and white. Changed from blue and white because Canterbury and Cronulla had those colours.

NICKNAME: The Panther was chosen as the emblem in 1964 after a public competition.

Birth of a club...

IT took nine years for Manly to win a place in the competition. Attempts had been made to get a team north of the Spit Bridge from 1937, but it was not until 1947 they finally got a start. The North Sydney RLFC committee held a meeting on October 29, 1946 which generously authorised the separate establishment of Manly and in November the same year the NSWRL approved their entry into the competition. In their first game Manly were beaten 15-13 by Wests at Brookvale Oval, despite scoring three tries to one. Manly won their first game in round eight when they defeated Parramatta 15-7.

COLOURS: Maroon and white, the same as their junior representative sides had worn since the 1930s.

NICKNAME: There was some anecdotal evidence the club was first known as the Seagulls. Officially they have always been the Sea Eagles.

I was there...

'Sadly, it was a very emotional period but I believed at the time what we were doing was right and I have not changed my mind. League in this country needed to streamline its organisation ... to make many tough decisions in order to prosper. I was often portrayed as the bad guy and there were plenty of people who tried to make life tough for me ... but I survived. The game is now in a very exciting phase and the next few years will see further change, but they'll be for the better.'

John Ribot, front man for Super League during the battle with the ARL.

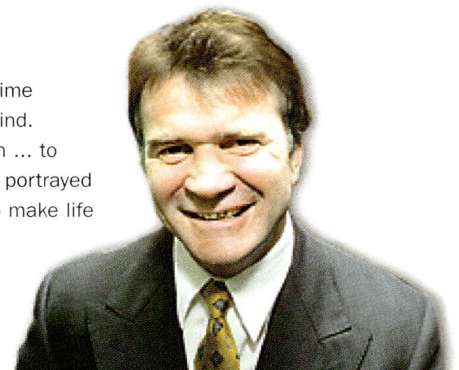

Man on Man
Vic Hey vs Brad Fittler

Born: November 18, 1912.
Died: April 11, 1995.
Played: 1933-49. **Clubs:**
Wests, Toowoomba, Leeds,
Dewsbury, Hunslet,
Parramatta.
Position: Five-eighth.
Weight: 11st 11lbs (75kg).
Height: 5ft 8ins (173cm).
Tests: 6. **Career games:** 307.
Career points: 427.

Born: February 5, 1972.
Played: Since 1989.
Clubs: Penrith, Sydney City.
Position: Five-eighth or lock.
Weight: 15st 1lb (96kg).
Height: 6ft (184cm).
Tests: 26.
Career games: 286.
Career points: 407.

THEY may have emerged from different generations, but as footballers Vic Hey and Brad Fittler have much in common. One writer said of Hey: "He possessed speed, weight, strength, a dazzling sidestep and a pair of wonderfully safe hands". It is a description that could have been written for the prodigiously talented Fittler. Both were outstanding schoolboy footballers – and both rose to Test level early. Hey played just six Tests before spending some of his most fruitful years in England. By the time his career wound up in 1949 he was acclaimed as one of the very best this country has produced. Fittler, who has captained NSW and Australia and is still just 27, is well on the way to the same acclamation.

Team of the Decade...
1950-1959

THE 1950s were one of the golden eras of the famous South Sydney club. The Rabbitohs won five out of six premierships between 1950-55 - the sixth they lost in controversial circumstances. With a resolute pack of forwards, Souths were blessed with the incomparable Clive Churchill at fullback and prolific tryscoring wingers in Ian Moir and Johnny Graves. The South Sydney era ended in 1955, giving way to an emerging St George juggernaut.
Fullback: Clive CHURCHILL (Souths, Brisbane Norths).
Wingers: John GRAVES (Souths, Charleville, Cootamundra, Camden Haven), Ian MOIR

Harry Wells

(Wollongong, Souths, Wests). **Centres:** Harry WELLS (Souths, Wollongong, Wests), Brian CARLSON (North Newcastle, Wollongong, Norths, Blackall). **Five-eighth:** Frank STANMORE (Wests, Maitland, Smithtown). **Halfback:** Keith HOLMAN (Wests). **Lock:** Les COWIE (Souths).
Secondrowers: Brian DAVIES (Brisbane Brothers, Canterbury), Kel O'SHEA (Ayr, Wests).
Frontrowers: Duncan HALL (Home Hill, Toowoomba, Brisbane Wests), Roy BULL (Manly).
Hooker: Ken KEARNEY (Leeds, St George).

I was there...

"I really felt sorry for Changa. He had such a wonderful career and even though I was on the other side, it was terribly sad to see such a champion play that way in a grand final. We all knew that something was amiss but didn't know what. I just went over to him at fulltime and gave him a handshake and a pat on the back. It's a shame that Graeme Langlands, one of the best players we've ever had, is often remembered as 'the guy who wore the white boots.' He deserves a lot better than that."
Arthur Beetson, Easts' 1975 grand final skipper.

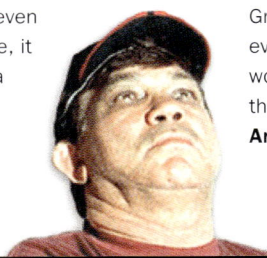

1950-59

SPORTS NOVELS 2/- For AUGUST

Is Tulloch greater than Phar Lap?

INSIDE: JIM BROUGH tells his own story

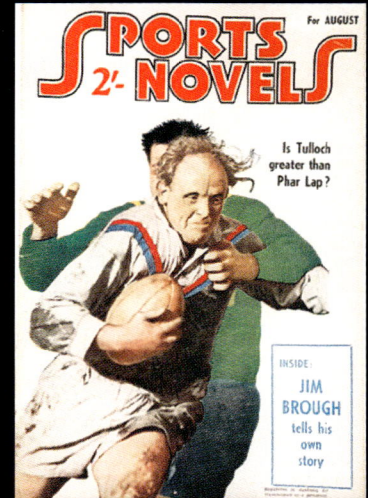

JULY 5, 1958: Great Britain captain **Alan Prescott** earns a place in league folklore with his heroic effort to play nearly the entire second Test of the Ashes series with a broken arm. In one of the epic Test matches, Prescott leads Britain to a 25-18 victory at Brisbane Exhibition Ground.

AUGUST 16, 1958: Clive Churchill plays his final match for South Sydney. A dispute over money forces his departure from the club after 12 seasons and 157 games.

AUGUST 15, 1959: St George complete an undefeated season with a 20-0 grand final victory over Manly, their fourth consecutive premiership.

OCTOBER 17, 1959: Emerging St George centre Reg Gasnier scores three tries in his debut against Great Britain at Swinton's Station Road ground.

NOVEMBER 24, 1959: Rugby league's first true superstar, **Herbert Henry 'Dally' Messenger**, dies in the north-western NSW town of Gunnedah, aged 76.

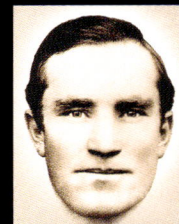

Andrew ETTINGSHAUSEN
Born: 1965

50 CLASSIC centre with superb speed and balance, will be remembered as one of the true champions of modern era. Debut for Cronulla at 17 and celebrated 300th first grade game in 1999. Prolific tryscorer, notched over 150 tries in club football and many more at State of Origin and international level. Surplus of top class centres forced him to play much of Test career on wing. Star of Australia's Ashes triumph in 1990. Played a record 27 Origin matches for NSW 1987-98, figuring at fullback, centre and wing. 25 Tests (1988-94), Kangaroo 1990, 1994.

Harry BATH
Born: 1924

46 BATH'S name figures high on the list of greatest players never to represent Australia, but national selection would have been a formality if not for a decade in English football. Injury cost him Test berth in 1946 and later that year he accepted lucrative English offer. Achieved career highlight when he led Warrington to victory before crowd of 102,569 in 1954 Challenge Cup final replay. Had a perfect record in Sydney football – five premierships in five seasons (with Balmain and St George). Outstanding ball player and prolific goalkicker. 12 matches for Other Nationalities (1949-55).

Ian Moir
1932-1990

44 GENUINE speedster, who had pace and finishing ability to capitalise on creative work of champion fullback Clive Churchill. Scored 105 tries from 110 games for Souths, before playing out career with Wests. Combination with Churchill produced large proportion of his tries, but teamwork was no fluke. Pair spent hours together to perfect timing. Clocked at 10.4 secs for 100 yards, putting him in the same category as Irvine and Cleary, athletic wingers who followed Moir into Australian teams in the 1960s. 8 Tests (1956-59), Kangaroo 1956-57.

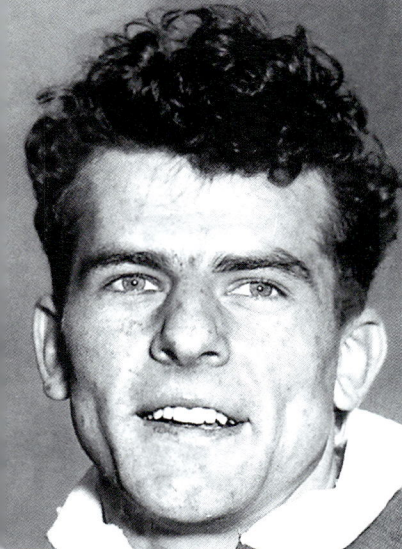

Les COWIE
1925-1995

49 BORN in Rockhampton, but favourite son of South Sydney, where he played entire senior career (1947-1957). Lock forward of all-round ability, scored 66 tries for Souths, including four in beaten side in 1956 final. Classic cover-defender who was once reputed to have scuttled entire Newtown three-quarter line in one sweeping move at the SCG. Played leading hand in Australia's Ashes win in 1950, but surprisingly overlooked for second Kangaroo tour in 1952-53. Member of five premiership-winning Souths sides. 6 Tests (1949-53), Kangaroo 1948-49.

THE Daily Telegraph

WE SELECT THE BEST OF THE CENTURY

Ken THORNETT
Born: 1937

43 LACKED kicking game of many of his predecessors, but was a peerless attacking fullback with dependable defence and safe hands. Emerged from ranks of Randwick rugby union in late 1950s, representing NSW, before accepting offer from Leeds rugby league in 1960. Signed with Parramatta in 1962 and quickly established himself in the top bracket. Played first of 12 Tests against South Africa in 1963 and member of first all-Australian side to win Ashes in England the same year. 12 Tests (1963-64), Kangaroo 1963-64.

The Great 100

Charles 'Chook' FRASER
1893-1981

48 PLAYED fullback, centre and five-eighth for Australia in Test career that covered the years immediately before and after World War I. Quick-thinking and innovative player, Fraser was one of Balmain's all-time greats, figuring in their first six premiership wins. Early experience in Australian Rules, where he learned to leap for the ball and kick effectively. Toured with 1911-12 Kangaroos at 18 and made second tour in 1921-22, captaining Australia in all three Tests. Central figure in Ashes victory against touring English side of 1920. 11 Tests (1911-22), Kangaroo 1911-12, 1921-22.

Harry WELLS
Born: 1932

47 TOUGH-TACKLING centre who reserved best football at international level for the 'old enemy', Great Britain. Made debut for Australia on 1952-53 Kangaroo tour and made second trip seven years later, where he formed one of the country's great centre partnerships with rising star, Reg Gasnier. Pair played 11 Tests together, with Wells' strength providing the ideal foil for gazelle-like Gasnier. Wells played senior football with Souths, Wollongong and Wests and continued in country football until he was 40. 21 Tests (1952-60), Kangaroo tourist 1952-53, 1959-60.

Herb NARVO
1912-1958

45 ONE of Australia's greatest secondrowers, Narvo may never have played for his country had it not been for an injury to Joe Pearce. Narvo was called into the 1937-38 Kangaroo side when Pearce broke his leg in New Zealand. Played four of the five Tests on tour, but outbreak of World War II ended international career. Came to notice as a constructive attacking forward with North Newcastle in 1930s, also had stints with Newtown and St George. Australian heavyweight boxing champion, but scrupulously fair on the football field. 4 Tests (1937-38), Kangaroo 1937-38.

Sid 'Joe' PEARCE
1910-1995

42 BELONGED to one of Sydney's most famous sporting families. Son of first Kangaroo Sandy Pearce and cousin of Olympic sculling champion Bobby Pearce. Played first grade Aussie Rules before switching to league with Easts in 1929. A big man, Pearce could hold the opposition off with one palm, enabling him to offload. Star of infamous Battle of Brisbane Test in 1932 and automatic selection in Test sides until 1937. Played in Easts' title treble 1935-37. 13 Tests (1932-37), Kangaroo 1933-34, 1937-38.

George TREWEEK
1905-1991

41 TREWEEK started out as a fullback with Adelong in NSW, but when he moved to Souths in the mid-1920s, he developed into a secondrower of world class. Broke into Souths first grade in 1926 and became an integral member of one of the great club teams of all time. Relatively short career for Australia and missed 1933-34 Kangaroo tour for business reasons. Had speed to run with three-quarters and toughness to match it in tight. Tall and long-striding, Treweek regularly left defenders in wake. 7 Tests (1928-30), Kangaroo 1929-30.

CHAPTER SEVEN

Masters of the Art

BY RAY KERSHLER

Masters of

New breed ... Brisbane coach Wayne Bennett

COACH? What coach? Modern rugby league fans will be amazed to know that in the 'good old days' there sometimes was no coach.

None of the scientific, tactical brains. None of the $10,000 fines for ranting and raving about the referees. None of the bonding sessions. None of the six-figure annual salaries.

No, in the olden days when rugby league split from rugby union, some of the teams did not even have a coach.

The transformation of the coach from a nonentity to one of the most powerful men in any modern rugby league club is more remarkable than any story of the transformation of the modern player.

No role in rugby league history has changed more than that of the coach. Initially, once all teams decided one was necessary, he was a senior player and generally, but not always, the captain.

His position of authority was based almost totally on his playing ability or his club loyalty.

The captain-coach was for decades the appointment around which the basic team was chosen.

Only later when it came to representative fixtures was the coach divorced from the captaincy.

And only in the late 1960s and early 1970s did the coach universally emerge from the playing field to sit and critically analyse his players from the sidelines.

So, for nearly 70 years the coach's influence on rugby league games could be said to have been, with a few exceptions, minimal.

Even in the era of the great St George teams which won 11 consecutive grand finals, the coach's role was underplayed because he was also the captain.

His off-field role at times looked simply to be that of the chap who made sure the balls turned up at training, ordered the lap running and, generally speaking, led the lads to the pub for a few beers.

That is not to say he had no influence on the field when the game was being played; only that his role as captain and coach blurred the definition of his authority.

For instance, when the St George captain-coach Ken Kearney was ordered from the field for any number of infringements he would give departing instructions to his players on how the game should continue. But was he giving them as coach or captain?

The need for a coach was questioned right at the start of St George's golden run. Kearney had been captain-coach for two years when, in 1956, Norm Tipping was appointed as coach. Although St George won the first of 11 straight premierships that year under Tipping's guidance, he was sacked and Kearney reinstated as captain-coach.

Kearney – and Norm Provan who would follow – were shrewd, insightful leaders who, as captains, almost made coaches redundant.

After the revolution of the role of coach (which is widely considered to have started with two visionaries, Terry Fearnley and Jack Gibson) there evolved a different type of man.

No coach in the early days of rugby league could have succeeded without the respect of his players because, almost certainly, it was from their ranks that he had sprung.

But the modern-day coach in more ways than one seeks to divest himself from the emotions and even the actions of his players. Modern-day coaches no longer feel the need to be liked by their players. Indeed, it is usually considered requisite for a coach to spend a few years in the wilderness between the end of his playing days and the start of his coaching career just to break the bond.

In creating the divide between the two groups, modern-day coaches sometimes feel no compulsion to explain their decisions to their players.

One of the few men who changed the game in its infancy was Arthur Hennessy, said to be the father of coaching. A rugby union convert, he was influential at the South Sydney club from its inception. Even in the early days of the revolution Hennessy was a radical.

the Art

He had Souths playing with a strict 'no kick' policy and played one of his forwards in the backline, believing that any five South Sydney forwards were worth six of the opposition.

Another was Pony Halloway (*left*), a Kangaroo tourist in 1908 and 1911 whose coaching career spanned 19 seasons and eight premierships.

Halloway first coached Balmain as captain in 1916 and closed his career as coach of Canterbury in 1948.

In between he coached Easts, Norths, Newtown and Ipswich and, in one glorious period between 1935-37 when coaching Easts, lost only one match.

Duncan Thompson, a top player of the 20s, was recalled to coach in the 50s and amazingly instigated many theories on coaching which later, trendy coaches claimed as their own.

But Thompson, Hennessy and Halloway could be considered the exceptions rather than the rule.

Many captain-coaches were to make a name for themselves in the years which followed, notably Jack Rayner, Kearney and Provan, whose runs of success elevated them above others.

Statistically Provan, who guided St George, Parramatta and Cronulla in the 60s and 70s, is the most successful coach ever with a winning record of 68.5 per cent.

But a time was around the corner when men like Rayner, Kearney and Provan would be considered dinosaurs in coaching terminology.

The catalyst for change was American football in general and one man, Vince Lombardi, in particular.

Lombardi's well-worn philosophy – 'Winning isn't everything, it's the only thing' – became the catchcry not only for rugby league but all professional sport in Australia.

Parramatta coach Fearnley is credited as the first to click with the motivational style of coaching which was to swamp rugby league for the next 30 years.

Fearnley saw Lombardi's film Second Effort which lauded attributes such as discipline, pride and 'mental toughness'. He showed it to Jack Gibson, then the St George coach, who was instantly hooked.

Gibson showed it to the three grades at St George who were in a slump and none of them lost a game for seven weeks.

The rugby league coaching revolution had begun. It included sprint trainers, skills coaches, nutritionists, sports psychologists and conditioners.

With them came a new breed of coaches. The coaches who would take rugby league to the end of the century were expected to move with the trends. Those who did not perished in the interim.

The new breed of successful men like Warren Ryan, Bob Fulton, Tim Sheens and Wayne Bennett were highly individual and highly paid – but they had one thing in common.

The coach was now the supreme commander of the club's football team. He lived and died by his results.

Shrewd leader ...
Ken Kearney lays down the law as guest St George forward coach in 1973. Halfback Billy Smith looks on

1960-69

MAY 29, 1960: Balmain fullback **Keith 'Golden Boots' Barnes** kicks one of the game's greatest goals (six metres inside his own half and out wide) in a 19-15 win against St George at Leichhardt.

JULY 16, 1960: After suffering the biggest defeat in Test match history (56-6), France perform an astonishing turnaround to upset Australia 7-5 in the third Test at the SCG.

AUGUST, 1960: Harry 'Jersey' **Flegg**, president of the NSWRL since 1929, dies in office aged 82. He is replaced by former Newtown forward Bill Buckley.

APRIL 15, 1961: Balmain and Norths play in rugby league's first televised game on Channel Nine. The NSWRL allow half a match to be televised each weekend as a trial.

JULY 1, 1961: Wests fullback **Don Parish** becomes the first fullback to score a try in a Test when he crosses in Australia's 12-10 loss to NZ at Carlaw Park.

SEPTEMBER 16, 1961: St George create history by becoming the first side to win six consecutive premierships when they defeat Wests 22-0.

APRIL 1, 1962: Canterbury defeat Wests 14-10 in the inaugural pre-season final at Sydney Sports Ground.

JUNE 2, 1962: Referee **Cliff Brown** sends off six players in a sensational NSW v Great Britain match at the SCG.

JUNE 9, 1962: Centre Reg Gasnier becomes Australia's youngest captain (23 years and 28 days) against Great Britain in the first Test at the SCG.

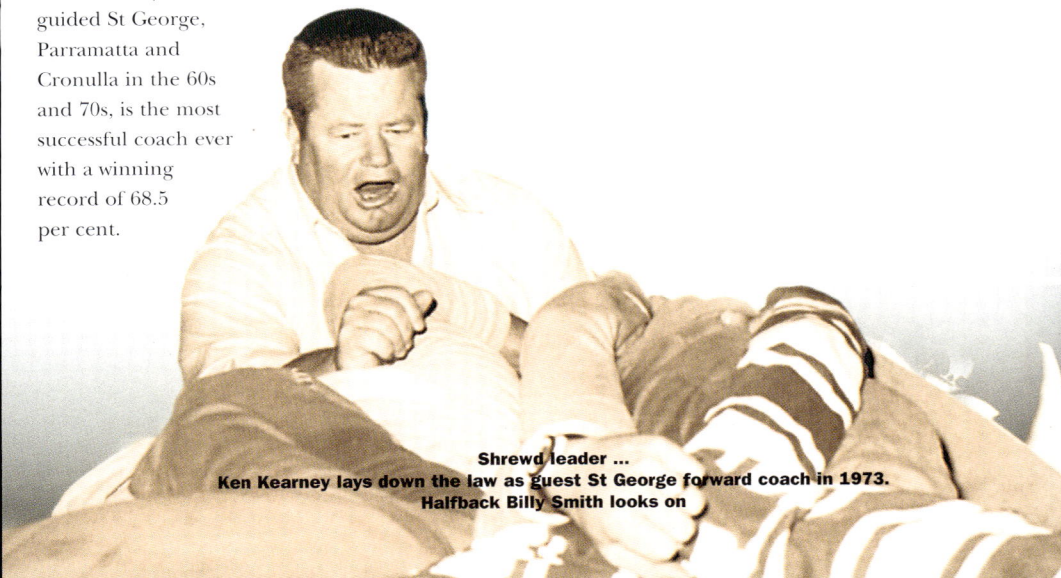

The way we were...

1960: Victorian Government passes bill to establish the TAB. Neale Fraser wins men's singles at Wimbledon. Bill Roycroft, **Dawn Fraser** and Herb Elliott star at

Rome Olympics. Police in Ceylon arrest Stephen Bradley for kidnap and murder of eight-year-old Sydney schoolboy Graeme Thorne. West Indies and Australia tie cricket Test in Brisbane.

1961: Last Sydney tram runs from La Perouse to Randwick workshop. *Four Corners* first screened on ABC-TV.

I was there...

'Wayne Bennett is the best coach I ever had. He was a father figure off the field and a brilliant schemer and motivator when it came to matters on it. 'Benny' has the knack of getting the very best out of players, be it with a kick in the bum or a quiet, calming word moments before you run out to battle. He's a brilliant reader of the game, a man who does plenty of homework to counter the opposition. He has never been a rant-rave style of coach but when he talks, players listen.'

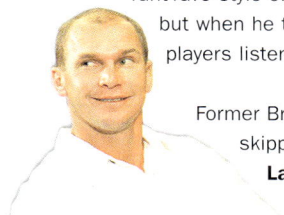

Former Brisbane skipper **Allan Langer**

Arthur HENNESSY

BOTH rugby league and rugby union owe a great debt to Arthur Hennessy, a rugby union prop who converted to hooker in league.

Hennessy is credited with formulating the famous South Sydney style of running football – which in turn is said to have influenced Randwick rugby union team's running rugby.

Arthur 'Ash' Hennessy was a foundation member of the breakaway rugby league and upon reading the rules of the game in 1907 declared: 'This is a game for racehorses.'

Hennessy decided from that day that while soccer and Australian rules were kicking games, rugby league should be a running game.

The South Sydney style which saw them become 'The Pride of the League' was based on a no kicking policy. Indeed Hennessy was known to drop players who disregarded his instructions.

In the 1920s Hennessy successfully introduced the five-man pack and emphasised attack. 'Keep it moving, run from your own goal line if you can and back up, back up, back up.'

Hennessy was the first of the specific national coaches when he took the 1929-30 Kangaroos to England. The team lost the fourth and deciding Test for the Ashes 3-0 in a game made necessary by the famous Chimpy Bush 'no try' ruling in the third Test.

Not until 30 years later, when Clive Churchill was made coach of the 1959-60 Kangaroos, was another coach deemed good enough to be appointed specifically for the task.

Frank BURGE

NOT every great coach can win premierships. Frank Burge was such a man.

Still Australia's greatest try-scoring forward, Burge can be said to be the man who instilled pride into the St George club.

Known as a dapper dresser, Burge was also a very tough man who first coached St George as captain in 1927.

He took a listless, losing club to the final that year, semi-finals in 1928-29 and the final again in 1930. But the premiership eluded him.

Frank 'Chunky' Burge came back to coach the club again in 1937, lifting a team which had finished second last the year before to equal second.

He was much sought-after as a coach and also teamed up with Newtown, Canterbury, Western Suburbs and North Sydney.

In 1937 Burge was lionised in a sporting newspaper as a 'super coach' 40 years before the term became commonplace.

Burge's coaching style was based on discipline and pride.

He told his players he wanted them to *look* like rugby league players – meaning they should be immaculately presented.

'Pride in yourself and your club' became his catchcry and he is largely credited with imbuing these characteristics in the St George teams he coached.

Others in the club continued the practice until by the 1950s and 60s pride was the club's trademark.

Duncan THOMPSON

DUNCAN Thompson never coached Australia yet even today his influence on the game is omnipresent. If there was ever a coach before his time it was Duncan Thompson.

As a player Thompson was a dazzling halfback nicknamed 'The Fox' who played nine Tests for Australia.

He was a member of the 1921 and 1922 North Sydney teams which won the Sydney premiership and captain of the 1922 team.

Born in Queensland, he returned to Toowoomba after being, in his eyes, unjustly suspended from the Sydney competition on a charge of kicking.

He played and coached the Galloping Clydesdales, Toowoomba's famous team, and guided Queensland

Ahead of their times ... (from above left) Arthur Hennessy, Frank Burge and Duncan Thompson, with Ken McCaffery

1960-69

JULY 14, 1962: After losing the Ashes with consecutive defeats, Australia salvage pride in the third Test, winning 18-17 after a last-minute try and conversion to **Ken Irvine**.

JULY 18, 1962: St George suffer rare humiliation when beaten 33-5 by the touring British side at the SCG, watched by a midweek crowd of 57,895.

JULY 1, 1963: St George Leagues Club (the 'Taj Mahal') opens for business on the Princes Highway, near Kogarah Oval.

JULY 27, 1963: Ken and **Dick Thornett** become first brothers to play in a Test for Australia since 1912 – against South Africa in the second Test in Sydney.

AUGUST 24, 1963: St George march on to their eighth consecutive premiership. On SCG mudheap, Saints beat Wests for third successive year, winning controversially 8-3.

NOVEMBER 9, 1963: The Kangaroos waltz away with the Ashes after thumping 50-12 (12 tries) victory over Gt Britain in second Test at Swinton. Australia become first all-Australian team to win the Ashes on British soil.

AUGUST 29, 1964: Newcastle score one of the city's most famous victories when they defeat Parramatta 14-7 in State Cup final. Earlier, they account for St George 5-3 in a semi-final.

SEPTEMBER 18, 1965: The SCG stretched to breaking point when a record crowd of 78,056 cram in for grand final between St George and Souths. Thousands climb on to roofs of grandstands for glimpse of the action. After leading Saints to their 10th successive grand final win, captain-coach Norm Provan retires.

‹ **115** ›

The way we were...

1962: Cahill Expressway opens. NSW wins Sheffield Shield for ninth season in a row. Rod Laver wins tennis grand slam. Southern Aurora links Sydney and Melbourne on uniform gauge line.

1963: Coroner returns open finding after investigating Sydney's mysterious **Bogle-Chandler** case.

Aussie Rules hero Roy Cazaly dies aged 70. Humorist Barry Humphries creates the character of uncouth ocker **Bazza McKenzie**.

Birth of a club...

The Sharks were coached by Ken Kearney in their debut season and captained by Monty Porter, both stalwarts of 'big brother' club St George.

Cronulla won their first competition game – an 11-5 victory over 1966 wooden spooners Eastern Suburbs.

The club's first home ground was Sutherland Oval and they later moved to Endeavour Field (Shark Park) adjacent to the current leagues club. In their first year the team finished as wooden spooners, with seven points.

COLOURS: Blue, white and black are the same as the South Cronulla Surf Lifesaving Club.

NICKNAME: The side originally had the Endeavour ship as their logo because they wanted to be associated with the sea. They became the Sharks shortly after.

in a golden era when the Maroons won nine of 11 games against NSW between 1922 and 1925.

Thompson was recalled to coach Toowoomba from 1951 to 1956 where he nurtured the talents of stars such as Des McGovern, Ripper Doyle, Duncan Hall, Ken McCaffery, Bobby Banks and Don Furner. He moulded their careers.

This was the period in which the term 'contract football' was introduced. Thompson explained the theory as being a contract between two players – the man with the ball and the man in support.

Future generations of football coaches were to reintroduce this theory, telling their players to 'keep the ball alive'.

Many of the tactics modern coaches claim to have introduced, Thompson had already pioneered. The Brisbane coach Wayne Bennett, a student of Thompson's game, concedes: 'He was talking about quick play-the-balls in the 50s'.

Thompson's strategies on diet, training times, gang tackling and motivation were all advanced thinking and through people like Don Furner, were translated to modern teams.

Ken KEARNEY

KEN Kearney brought a lot of things back from his career in England. Baggy shorts, a crewcut – and attitude.

'Compared to English league, I couldn't believe how rudimentary Australian football was in those days: no tactics, no finesse, no defensive or attacking strategy,' he would later recall.

A rugby union convert, Kearney was the brains behind the early days of the great St George run from 1956 to 1966, a man of such stature as captain-coach that even stars like John Raper and Reg Gasnier pale to insignificance.

Ken 'Killer' Kearney switched to rugby league after the 1948 Wallaby tour of the British Isles and played for Leeds where, because he could not find a decent barber, he wore his hair in crewcut style.

Kearney learned his trade as a hooker in Leeds and became a master craftsman when he returned to sign with St George in 1952.

His catchcry, learned from painful experience with Leeds, was: 'Retaliate first. Thump them before they thump you.'

He elaborated: 'Back then, British league ruled the world and there was no better place to learn scrummaging, defence, ball skills, tactics, conditioning – and not turning the other cheek. I learned well.'

A roly-poly figure, the hard-working Kearney could have been the inspiration for the Peanuts comic character Pigpen such was his dishevelled appearance after a game.

Kearney was appointed captain-coach of St George in 1954 and 1955 and was captain (under Norm Tipping's coaching) in 1956 before resuming the reigns as captain-coach from 1957-1961.

Kearney *(above)* led from the front and inspired fierce loyalty in his players.

In the days of unlimited tackle football, Kearney's philosophy was simple enough: keep the ball in the forwards until the opposition tires and then let the backs have a run.

He instituted the straight-line defence and St George mastered the art of sending an attacking player through a gap.

Kearney went on to coach Parramatta to their first semi-finals from 1962-64 and then Wests and Cronulla, retiring after the 1969 season.

Frank STANTON

FRANK Stanton was the first coach to take a Kangaroo tour undefeated through England and France.

This feat in 1982 led to his team being labelled 'The Invincibles'.

Canny guidance ... Frank Stanton gesticulates from the sideline in his time with Norths

On that score alone, Stanton earned a reputation as a superb coach.

But 'Biscuits' created the foundations with two Sydney premierships as a coach, guiding Manly to success in 1976 and 1978.

Stanton retired from playing in 1970 and the next season was coaching the Manly reserve grade side.

He was first grade coach from 1975 to 1979 when the club was one of the leading lights in the Sydney competition.

Although a loyal clubman at Manly, he later also coached Balmain, Norths and Redcliffe in Brisbane.

Considered at times to be an irascible character, he hid a wry humour behind a policy of discipline for his teams, on and off the field.

Stanton, like Bob Fulton, was guided in all stages of his career by the top-flight league executive Ken Arthurson but was also influenced as a coach by Wally O'Connell.

His greatest achievement in Australia came in 1978 when Manly came through six finals matches in 24 days, five of them sudden-death, including two replays.

The season climaxed when Manly and Cronulla drew 11-all in the grand final and, after the replay on the following Tuesday, Manly triumphed 16-0.

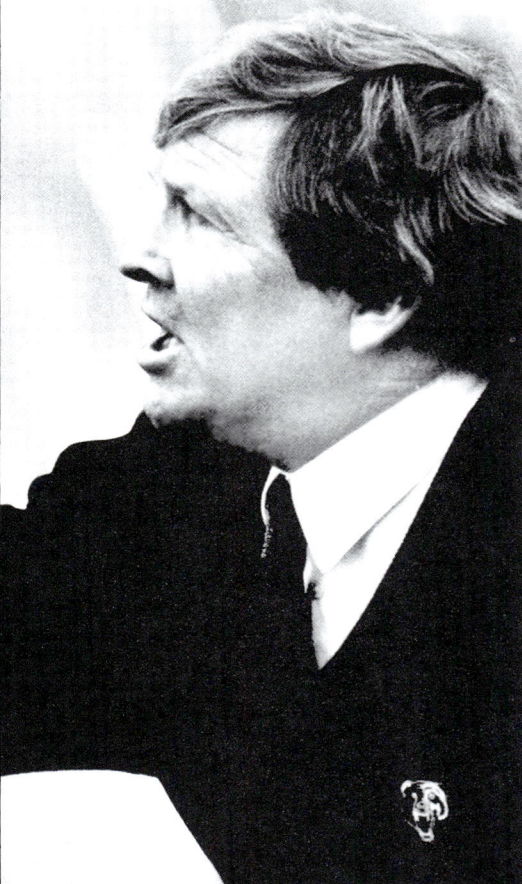

Stanton's effort in getting his 'crippled' team to back up and win ranks as one of club football's greater coaching feats.

Stanton's Invincibles set the bar for performance as high as it ever could be when they won all 22 games on their 1982 tour.

Stanton described the players as 'a beautiful football team' but it was his canny guidance through the pitfalls that only an overseas tour can provide which smoothed the path for one of rugby league's dream teams.

Smell of success ... Harry Bath anxious on the St George bench

Harry BATH

HARRY Bath was known as a great coach of forwards and, while he doesn't entirely agree with that analysis, his success does suggest that was his strength. As do the cauliflower ears, which made him a caricaturist's delight.

For a start, Bath confessed that in his early days he 'loved every bump and bruise' of the game. Only a forward would say that.

Bath spent most of his playing career in England for the Warrington club where he established himself as a ball-playing forward.

He used those skills to great effect when he returned to play with St George near the beginning of their historic 11-year premiership run.

Bath coached three clubs: Balmain, Newtown and St George and, if he brought with him one trait, it was the smell of success.

The Balmain winger Paul Cross said of him: 'He thought like a winner, he walked like a winner and he talked like a winner. And it rubbed off.'

Bath coached two St George teams to grand final success including the team known as 'Bath's Babes' in 1977. But he also coached Australia in 1962 and won the World Cup with Australia in 1968 and 1970.

He was hired as coach of the Australian World Cup team for 1968 after the then chairman of the Australian Rugby League, Bill Buckley, found him driving a cab.

But in his later years he did not relish the emerging independence and larrikinism of some players.

Bath maintains most of the teams he coached were 'babes' in that he never had an experienced team with which to work.

He also reckoned he could coach backs as well as forwards and perhaps he was right because he was, with all his experience, inspirational before big games.

Probably his finest hour was the 1977 grand final success when, after a historic 9-all draw with Parramatta, he coached a young St George side to a comprehensive 22-0 win in the replay.

Bath quit coaching after a losing season in 1981. He is a harsh critic of the modern game, declaring it owes too much to the influence of American football and is played by 'robots'.

Jack GIBSON

JACK Gibson is known as the master coach. It is not a term with which he is ever comfortable.

For Gibson, arguably the most influential man in rugby league over the past 30 years, is a man of simple words, almost to the point of being blunt.

Gibson rang the bell of change from the moment he took an Eastern Suburbs team, which had not won a game the previous season, to the semi-finals of 1967 on the back of improved defence.

Much has been made of Gibson's American odysseys which resulted in radical changes to rugby league coaching theory from the 1970s but, in truth, Gibson's philosophy for his players could be summed up in two words – pride and discipline. Everything else was peripheral.

Gibson coached five premiership-winning teams and was primarily responsible for the use of video equipment, motivational speeches and computers in rugby league training.

But it was his straight-forward manner which endeared him to his players and later his one-liners for TV commentaries, when he was known as Cardigan Jack, which broadened his public appeal.

As much as he is lauded as a trendsetting revolutionary, the colourful Gibson was a straight shooter who, among many other initiatives, insisted the coach should have the final say on team selections.

On that score alone, modern coaches have him on a pedestal.

Gibson's motivational methods were not as complicated as sometimes suggested, being based more on a theme of commonsense.

His philosophy of professionalism at all times was encompassed by his theory 'winning starts on Monday' and in the quote: 'People can't get motivated by a five-minute speech.'

Gibson won premierships with Easts and Parramatta. Parramatta's success was the club's first and his pronouncement 'ding, dong, the witch is dead' at the victory party in 1981 is still celebrated.

Gibson never claimed that he didn't make mistakes. But he did learn from them.

At first he eschewed professional fitness instructors for his teams. When he realised the need he got the best, starting with the famed George Daldry.

The long-time Australian coach Bob Fulton best summed up Gibson's contribution to the game: 'Any coach who says he hasn't been influenced by Jack Gibson is kidding.'

Bob FULTON

NO coach has had his results analysed more than Bob 'Bozo' Fulton. A fiery character as a player, Fulton retained the emotion when he took up coaching.

Fulton (right) coached Easts and Manly, two of the code's least-popular clubs in the eyes of the wider rugby league public, and he believes critics of his career load their guns with ammunition from that antagonism.

Born in Lancashire, Fulton would grow to torment his native land. As a young player he was brought to Manly from Wollongong by top administrator Ken Arthurson and matured into one of the game's great players.

Ironically, Fulton's career as a coach began when he was lured away from Manly to the powerful Eastern Suburbs club.

His first year as captain-coach was, in his own view, ordinary. Then, over a total of 16 years, only once did he fail to get his team to a finals series.

What his critics overlook is that Fulton was the 'winningest coach' in the 1980s – an era when his opposition included Jack Gibson, Warren Ryan and Tim Sheens.

Fulton guided teams to four grand finals, winning two premierships – with Manly in 1987 and 1996.

His international record is hard to question. He coached Australia from 1989 to 1998 and never lost a Test series.

Almost as if they were raising the bar higher, Fulton's Australian teams did lose the first Test on two tours of Britain but fought back to win both series 2-1.

By his own admission Fulton did have the players. So the proudest moment in his international career came in 1995 when Australia, split by the Super League war, sent an inexperienced team to the World Cup.

After losing their first match to England the young Australians rallied to win the Cup.

'What we did over there against supreme adversity was just magic,' Fulton said later.

He gave his critics as good as he got but one simple off-the-cuff remark will go down in league folklore.

In 1987 he was fined for a caustic comment about referee Bill Harrigan, saying: 'I hope he gets hit by a cement truck.'

Straight shooter ... then Cronulla coach Jack Gibson

1960-69

JUNE 24, 1967: Queensland end run of 18 losing matches against NSW with 13-11 victory in fourth match of interstate series at Lang Park.

SEPTEMBER 9, 1967: After 11 glorious seasons, **St George** era finally ends when Saints are beaten 12-11 by Canterbury in preliminary final.

GREAT SAINTS LEAGUE ERA CLOSES

SEPTEMBER 16, 1967: The grand final, won 12-10 by Souths over Canterbury, is televised 'live' (on all channels) for first time.

DECEMBER 21, 1967: Crowd of just over 1000 in Avignon watch incomparable Reg Gasnier in action for last time. Gasnier, captain of the 1967-68 Kangaroos, limps from field nine minutes from the end of a tour match.

MARCH 16, 1968: Referee **Laurie Bruyeres** sends off seven players in an ill-tempered pre-season clash between Balmain and Manly at Brookvale.

JUNE 10, 1968: Johnny Raper leads Australia to a 20-2 win over France in World Cup final at SCG.

AUGUST 27, 1968: Cronulla halfback Terry Hughes wins inaugural Rothmans Medal, a best and fairest award voted by referees and touch judges.

JULY 27, 1969: Calls for the devaluation of the field goal strengthen when Eric Simms kicks five in Souths' 40-18 defeat of Penrith.

AUGUST 30, 1969: St George legend Johnny Raper plays last match for the club in a 19-10 semi-final loss to Manly.

SEPTEMBER 20, 1969: Balmain score what is regarded as greatest upset in grand final history when they down 1/3 favourites Souths 11-2.

The way we were...

1964: Aircraft carrier **HMAS** Melbourne collides with destroyer HMAS *Voyager* in Jervis Bay, killing 82. Midget Farrelly wins world surfboard championship at Manly Beach.

The Beatles leave Australia in June after hectic concert tour. Rupert Murdoch publishes national newspaper *The Australian* for first time.

1965: First hydrofoil service on Sydney Harbour. Margaret Smith wins Australian tennis singles for sixth successive year. PM Menzies declares Australia is in a state of war with Vietnam. Jean Shrimpton's fashion sense wows crowd at Melbourne Cup. Peter Thomson wins fifth British Open golf title.

1966: After 16 years in office, Robert Menzies retires as PM and is succeeded by **Harold Holt**. Australia changes to decimal currency. The Beaumont children – Jane, Arnna and Grant – go missing in Adelaide. Jack Brabham takes world drivers' title in Italy.

1967: The Seekers attract crowd of 200,000 to concert at Myer Music Bowl, Melbourne. Galilee becomes first horse to win Caulfield, Melbourne and Sydney Cups in one season. Prime Minister Holt drowns in surf at Portsea and despite extensive search his body is never found.

Australian coach Bob Fulton with Laurie Daley

That was a vintage year for Fulton because it was also the year he won the premiership.

Warren RYAN

NO rugby league official or journalist will ever die wondering what Warren Ryan thinks of them.

Ryan has coached five teams in the Sydney competition, making six grand finals and winning two.

But his feuds with the press and the acrimony with club officials tend to overshadow the career of a man who took the ideas of Jack Gibson a few steps further along the path to success.

While the tag 'genius', attributed to him by one of his proteges, might be stretching things a bit,

there is no doubt Ryan is one of the game's more astute thinkers.

Not many coaches can say the rules of the game were changed because of their tactics. But Ryan can.

After his Canterbury team constantly bombed St George in the 1985 grand final, league officials changed the rule so the defending team retained possession if the defender caught the ball on the full behind the goal line.

Similarly, the 5m gaps between attacking and defending teams was increased to 10m, largely after the 1986 grand final resulted in a tryless 4-2 loss to Ryan's Canterbury, which had officials questioning the entertainment factor of the game.

Criticised for being too defensive, Ryan once said: 'You work to the nth degree within the fairness of the rules.'

Ryan was a journeyman first grade player who made a name for himself coaching the Wests under-23 squad in 1978. From there he went on to successful first grade stints with Newtown, Canterbury, Balmain, Wests and currently Newcastle, achieving his two grand final successes with Canterbury in 1984 and 1985.

Ryan is never far from controversy. At times scathing in his criticism of others he can be, nevertheless, thin-skinned when under the blowtorch himself.

Whenever he and a rugby league club were divorced it was, in Ryan's eyes, rarely his fault.

A few quotes give some indication as to the reasons why Ryan is deemed so controversial.

Of Wests: 'There wasn't a person there with the faintest idea how to mount a premiership challenge.'

Of Balmain: 'Keith (Barnes), your forwards will retire before you get a decent backline.'

Of Canterbury: 'The *family* was more important than the club.'

Play it again ... Warren Ryan explains a strategy to Balmain skipper Wayne Pearce

Penny for your thoughts ... Brisbane coach Wayne Bennett with then captain Allan Langer

Wayne BENNETT

H E has an expression which could have been carved out of Easter Island rock. But it is a public face.

Wayne Bennett, fans are assured by those who know him, smiles regularly and does have a sense of humour.

No coach in Australian rugby league has been in charge of a single first grade NRL or ARL rugby league team longer than Bennett (over 300 games since 1988), nor can any of his contemporaries match his 68 per cent win ratio, which is just below the great Norm Provan's record.

With four premierships (including the 1997 Super League title) in that period it seems harsh crticism indeed from those who believe Bennett should have done better with 'the cattle'.

Bennett played one Test match for Australia and first made a name for himself when he coached Brisbane Souths to a grand final victory over then glamour club Wynnum-Manly, just a year after having been thrashed 42-8 by the same club.

After one year as joint coach of Canberra with Don Furner in 1987, Bennett took over new ARL club Brisbane.

Initial suggestions the club would carry all before them fell flat as the team failed to adapt their undoubted talent to the high pressure of weekly competition.

He knew he had a hell of a football team but he also had problems.

In 1989, he sacked Brisbane captain Wally Lewis in one of the greatest shocks of modern rugby league. In doing so he proved who was boss in Queensland football.

Bennett is described as a man of routine and in those years his dour demeanour gave rise to fascinating analyses. Was he brooding or just thinking deeply?

Bennett and Furner went close with a youthful Canberra in 1987 but it was not until 1992 that Bennett won his first ARL premiership. He parlayed that success into back-to-back titles a year later, both against St George.

Bennett coached the Queensland State of Origin side for three years, winning back-to-back series in 1987 and 1988.

In 1998, as if to reinforce his stature in the game, Bennett coached Brisbane, Queensland and Australia to victory.

Bennett may well be the greatest of all footballing generals in that he allows players, within the framework of a rigid game plan, to make the most of their individual talents.

Yet he remains an enigma.

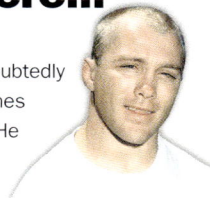

Birth of a club...

ILLAWARRA STEELERS

The Illawarra region unsuccessfully applied for entry into the Sydney premiership in 1954 and 1966.

On December 13, 1980, a meeting of the NSWRL general committee admitted Illawarra as the 13th team in the premiership.

They made their debut in the 1982 competition.

The side lost their first game against Penrith at Wollongong Showground, but recorded their first win two weeks later against Souths at Wollongong.

COLOURS: Scarlet and white, depicting the Illawarra flame tree which blossoms on the escarpment overlooking Wollongong each year.
NICKNAME: The Steelers, because the BHP steel plant is the most dominant industry in the region.

I was there...

'Jack Gibson's strength was the aura of fear he put into people. We had a couple of near misses in grand finals and Jack, with his right hand man Ron Massey, put certain structures in place that helped us take the next step to the premiership. He had plenty of talented players at his disposal but almost invariably picked the right combination and the titles came in a rush. He was a truly great coach and it was a pleasure to be associated with him.'

Ray Price, the Eels' Trojan lock from 1976 to 1986.

Man on Man
Ray Stehr v Mark Carroll

	Ray Stehr	Mark Carroll
Born:	January 24, 1913.	February 26, 1967.
Died:	June 2, 1983.	
Played:	1929-46.	Since 1987.
Clubs:	Easts, Mudgee.	Penrith, Souths, Manly, London Broncos.
Position:	Front row.	Front row.
Weight:	13st 2lb (84kg).	17st 13lb (114kg).
Height:	5ft 11ins (181cm).	6ft 4ins (193cm).
Tests:	11.	12.
Career games:	271.	217.
Career points:	107.	57.

RAY Stehr was one of the toughest men ever to lace on a football boot. Confrontations with his English counterparts during the 1930s have been written into league folklore. But if Stehr were to stand alongside the prototype frontrower of the 1990s, he would be dwarfed. Modern day frontrower, Souths' Mark Carroll, has built both his attack and defence on size, strength and power.

More often than not, he takes a personal battering. Modern weight training techniques were unheard of in Stehr's day – natural strength, an uncompromising nature and "street cunning" were the chief attributes of successful props of the 1930s. Match wits with your opposite and the battle was half won. Black eyes and broken noses, though, are occupational hazards in any era.

WHAT A GAME!
SOUTHS v MANLY 1984

Sudden-death football invariably produces memorable matches – and that can certainly be said about the semi-final between Souths and Manly in 1984.

Down 14-0 in even time, the Rabbitohs looked set to cop the mother of all hidings.

But calling on their renowned spirit and courage, the Rabbitohs turned it all around to score a memorable 22-18 win over one of their most loathed rivals.

Grand finalists the two previous years, Manly were expected to make short work of Souths, a team lacking big names, but not grit and determination.

When internationals **Chris Close** (above right) and Kerry Boustead crossed for tries, Souths' early exit from the finals seemed assured.

But the tide turned after a scrum flare-up in which Souths clearly had the upper hand.

Big Bill Hardy put Souths in the picture when he scored from a Neil Baker bomb, then Craig Coleman put up another high kick for captain **Ziggy Niszczot** (left) to cross.

With two Baker conversions and a penalty goal, it was suddenly 14-all at halftime, with Manly on the backfoot.

The dreaded bomb produced the try that broke Manly's spirit just four minutes after the break, with Hardy again crossing.

Souths' discipline and defence did the rest. Manly crossed for another try through replacement Steve Hegarty late, but after that Souths repelled everything Manly could throw at them.

Fans danced on the famous SCG Hill, while in the dressing rooms, big men shed tears as they contemplated one of league's bravest fightbacks.

The Whistle Blowers

Refereeing has had many changes down the years but there has always been one constant – the man in charge has never been far from controversy.

Whistle-blowers rarely please everyone. Where there are winners and losers there are grins and grimaces. Rugby league chronicles since 1908 have often portrayed referees as controversial figures and it is doubtful that will ever change.

League fans love to paint them as villains but in the majority of cases, the man with the whistle has always tried his best to present a good, hard and fair contest.

In the earliest years, refs went about their business in white jerseys with high, starched collars. They often wore caps and their white shorts were contrasted by navy and sky blue socks.

The most prominent referees in the pioneer years included William Beattie, Jack Fihelly, **Tom McMahon Sr** *(left)*, Charles Hutchison and Tom Costello, while in the 1920s it was Laurie Kearney, Lal Deane and Webby Neill. In the 1940s and 50s, the main men were Tom McMahon Jr, Darcy Lawler, Aub Oxford, George Bishop, Jack Casey and Eric Cox.

In the 1960s, Lawler, Jack Bradley and Col Pearce ruled supreme while Don Lancashire, Keith Page, Laurie Bruyeres, Keith Holman, Jack Danzey and Gary Cook became big names in the decade that followed.

In the mid-70s, it was Cliff Brown who greatly helped refs along the road to professionalism by introducing compulsory weekly training sessions.

As the game got faster, the need arose for greater fitness and stamina levels from the men in the middle.

Saturation print, TV and radio coverage in the 1980s and onwards placed referees in the spotlight like never before.

Like them or loathe them, Greg 'Hollywood' Hartley, Kevin Roberts, Michael Stone, John Gocher, Greg McCallum and **Barry 'The Grasshopper' Gomersall** *(left centre)* became talked about almost as much as the games themselves.

In the 90s, the super fit Bill Harrigan has reigned supreme but men such as Graham Annesley, David Manson, Eddie Ward and **Steve Clark** *(left centre)* have also made their mark.

Sweeping on-field changes were made in the late-1980s and early-1990s as league continued its boom.

In-goal touch judges were introduced to relieve the burden on the centre men.

Then followed radio communication between referees and touch judges and finally, perhaps the most valuable of all aids, the video referee.

Pay scales have escalated enormously as referees now move towards full-time professionalism. 🏉

Team of the Decade...
1960-1969

Johnny Raper

THE team of the 1960s is dominated by St George selections, and why wouldn't it be? Saints were at the height of their powers, winning the first seven premierships of the decade. Nine of the all-star 13 were involved in the red and whites' premiership dynasty, with Les Johns, Ken Irvine, Brian Hambly and Noel Kelly the only 'outsiders'. The decade showcased some of the truly great players of the game. Gasnier, Raper and Langlands will remain household names while ever league is played. The team also includes nine 1963-64 Kangaroos, one of the finest outfits to leave our shores.

Fullback: Les JOHNS (South Newcastle, Canterbury).
Wingers: Ken IRVINE (Norths), Eddie LUMSDEN (St George).
Centres: Reg GASNIER (St George), Graeme LANGLANDS (Wollongong, St George).
Five-eighth: Brian CLAY (St George).
Halfback: Billy SMITH (St George).
Lock: Johnny RAPER (St George).
Secondrowers: Norm PROVAN (St George), Brian HAMBLY (Wagga Magpies, Parramatta).
Frontrowers: Kevin RYAN (St George, Canterbury), Noel KELLY (Ayr, Wests).
Hooker: Ian WALSH (Eugowra, St George).

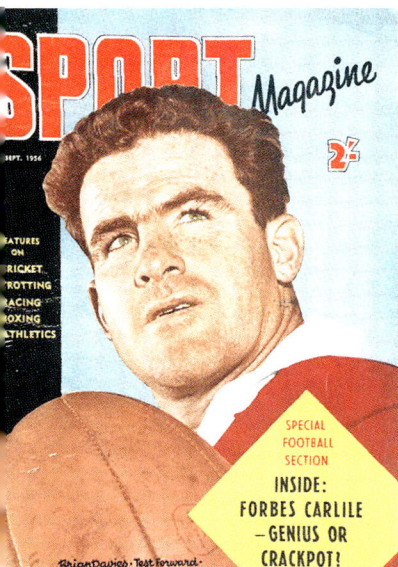

Brian DAVIES
Born: 1930

40 TOUGH and uncompromising secondrower or prop, Davies was one of few Queensland-based players to break into Australian Test sides of the 1950s. From time of Australian debut in 1951, was a regular in green and gold for next eight years. Crowning moment came in 1958 when he captained Australia in Ashes series against Gt Britain. Strong-running forward and clever distributor, rated one of the world's best secondrowers of era. Four overseas tours and played in World Cup in 1954 and 1957. 27 Tests (1951-58), Kangaroo 1952-53, 1956-57.

Laurie DALEY
Born: 1969

36 IDENTIFIED as teenager of exceptional talent playing at Junee. Joined Canberra 1987 and quickly established first grade position. Five-eighth with speed and power, added class to Canberra side that broke through for first premiership in 1989. Made State of Origin debut in 1989 and played first Test for Australia, 1990. By early 1990s was automatic selection in rep sides and captained NSW to series wins 1992-94. Captained Australia twice. Lived up to expectation he was the man to succeed Wally Lewis as game's premier five-eighth. 20 Tests (1990-99), Kangaroo 1990, 1994.

Jimmy CRAIG
1895-1960

39 RATED the most versatile of all players, Craig could fill almost any position. During 16-year career (1915-30), played fullback, wing, centre, five-eighth, halfback, lock and hooker. In one match for Wests in 1930, Craig played in four different positions. Won five premierships with Balmain in first six seasons, before playing significant role in Queensland's rise to prominence in the 1920s. Teammates on 1921-22 Kangaroo tour attested to his amazing adaptability and legendary Dally Messenger believed he was the greatest player he ever saw. 7 Tests (1921-28), Kangaroo 1921-22.

The Daily Telegraph

WE SELECT THE BEST OF THE CENTURY

Sid 'Sandy' PEARCE
1883-1930

34 FAMOUS teammate Frank Burge said of 'Sandy' Pearce: 'Football never had a gamer, rougher, nor more loyal team player.' Pearce was league's first great hooker, playing in first matches in 1907 and touring with Kangaroos of 1908-09. Made second tour at age 38 in 1921-22, after declining 1911-12 tour for business reasons. Used immense strength to dominate scrums and create havoc in open. Versatile sportsman, Pearce often acted as sparring partner for Les Darcy when legendary boxer trained in Sydney. 14 Tests (1908-21), Kangaroo 1908-09, 1921-22.

Chris McKIVAT
1879-1941

33 CHAMPION union halfback, made switch to league in great Wallaby raids of 1909. Toured England with 1908-09 Wallabies and won Olympic Gold medal at 1908 Games in London. Returned as Kangaroo captain in 1911-12, becoming first Australian skipper to win Ashes. One correspondent on that tour wrote: 'At halfback he stands alone in the whole world of Northern Union football. Without McKivat the Australasian team would never have been so successful'. Excellent tactician, robust, durable and inspiring leader. Played for Glebe 1910-14. 5 Tests (1910-12), Kangaroo 1911-12.

The Great 100

Les JOHNS
Born: 1942

38 SPECTACULAR attacking fullback, whose impact on game would undoubtedly have been greater had he not arrived at same time as Graeme Langlands. Emerged from Newcastle to join Canterbury, under coaching of fullback great Clive Churchill, in 1963. Toured with Kangaroos after one season in Sydney and made second trip four years later. Noted for his counter-attack, Johns excelled under the high ball and had uncanny ability to find the line with stabbing kicks. Injuries restricted career and forced an early retirement in 1971. 14 Tests (1963-69), Kangaroo 1963-64, 1967-68.

Bob McCARTHY
Born: 1946

37 FIRST of the wide-running secondrowers. Broke into first grade in 1963, but wasn't until introduction of limited tackle rule in 1967, that he was seen at his best. Under coaching of Clive Churchill, McCarthy was allowed to run among the three-quarters, where he wreaked havoc with pace and power. Scored over 100 tries for Souths and Canterbury. Played just 10 Tests for Australia, but regarded as one of this country's greatest secondrowers. Appeared in five grand finals for Rabbitohs, including three winning sides (1967, 1970 and 1971). 10 Tests (1969-74), Kangaroo 1973.

Joe 'Chimpy' BUSCH
1907-1999

35 FEW players experienced such a meteoric rise as Joe 'Chimpy' Busch, who went from barefoot country centre to Test halfback in four months in 1928. Made Test debut against England in 1928 and toured with Kangaroos the next year. His 'no-try' in the third Test at Swinton, 1930, ranks as most controversial incident in history of Tests. Played four seasons at Leeds before playing out career with Balmain. Tall halfback, exceptionally fast, he possessed bullet-like pass and was master of blindside play. 6 Tests (1928-30), Kangaroo 1929-30.

Norm PROVAN
Born: 1932

32 GIANT secondrower of 50s and 60s, Provan enjoyed great success in international arena, playing 14 Tests and four World Cups. Best remembered, though, for epic deeds with St George, where he played in 10 consecutive grand final-winning sides (1956-65). Captain-coach for last four. Pinnacle was finale before then record grand final crowd of 78,056 in 1965. Image immortalised in Gladiators photograph (with Arthur Summons) following 1963 grand final. Tall, strong and intelligent, Provan played record 256 first grade games for Dragons. 14 Tests (1954-60), Kangaroo 1956-57.

Brett KENNY
Born: 1961

31 LAIDBACK Brett Kenny's off-field demeanour belied his class and natural ability. First grader at 19 and, in second season, starred in Parramatta's maiden premiership. While Eels achieved rare premiership treble, Kenny wrote history of his own, scoring two tries in three successive grand finals. Played mostly five-eighth for club, but versatility allowed a shift to centre for much of Test career. Confrontations with Wally Lewis were highlight of Origin contests between 1982 and 1987. 17 Tests (1982-87), Kangaroo 1982, 1986.

CHAPTER EIGHT

The Tough Guys

BY IAN HEADS

The Tough

ARTHUR Hennessy in the early days called it 'a game for race horses' but rugby league, with its furious 80 minutes of action, has always been just as much a game for hard cases and brave hearts.

Hennessy, league's foundation coach, saw the potential for speed and movement of the ball when he first glimpsed the new 'Northern Union' game in the early 1900s.

But league has always mixed the physical with the athleticism that first caught Hennessy's eye: on its toughest days down the years it has asked profound questions of the men who chose to play it. Tales of breathtaking skulduggery and immense bravery litter its history, balanced one against the other.

Who could forget Geoff Toovey taking a smashed cheekbone into a grand final? Garry Hughes (Canterbury) doing the same? Andrew Johns, nursing a punctured lung, somehow making magic in

Newcastle's fairytale grand final win of 1997?

Or the fearless Ron 'Hit Man' Hilditch at the apex of a flying wedge of 100 stone or more in one of the boldest ploys of grand final history (Parramatta v Manly, 1976)? Or Earl Park, Arncliffe, on a Saturday afternoon in the mid-20s?

A St George player can be seen acting strangely, bumping a shoulder against one of the wooden goal posts.

He is Aubrey 'Jockey' Kelly, a lock forward also known as 'The Terror' because of his demon tackling and all-round toughness.

Moments before Kelly had dislocated a shoulder in a tackle.

Against the post, he knocks it back into place ... and rejoins the play.

There is no question that the toughness of league offers some of Australian sport's most captivating stories.

Our focus in the pages that follow, on 10 of the game's hardest men – tough guys who carved their paths in the most direct manner imaginable – is no more than a splinter off a very large and rough-hewn block. The 10 chosen to represent the genre were wielders of the broadsword rather than the rapier on football's fields; men of direct action.

So were the next 10 who stand alongside them ... and the next.

Stories of brawn and bravery positively leap from league's pages down the decades:

■ Dan Dempsey's immortal (apocryphal?) plea as ambulancemen worked to stem the blood flow from a wicked eye cut during a vicious match against St Helens in 1933: 'Stick a safety pin in it and let me get back into the game!'

■ Eric Weissel's long and famous run on a ruined ankle to win the Battle of Brisbane Test of 1932.

■ Clive Churchill kicking a famous, winning goal for Souths in 1955 – a broken arm hanging limply by his side.

■ Balmain's Arthur Patton playing more than half a game on a broken leg so that his team wouldn't be left short-handed in the 1948 final against St George.

■ Souths' Greg Hawick playing 70 minutes with a broken jaw against St George in 1951 – refusing point blank to leave the field.

■ Manly skipper Fred Jones, losing a handful of teeth one day, courtesy of an opposing elbow. Back at the club Freddo couldn't get a glass to his lips. He chose instead to drink his beer through a straw.

■ Matches of R-rated brutality: The Battle of Bradford in 1952; the Battle of Leeds, World Cup final of 1970; the Battle of Brisbane II, 1970, when Britain's Cliff Watson introduced Australia – and Jim Morgan – to the 'Liverpool Kiss'; the ferocious Cronulla-Manly grand final of 1973.

And so it goes ... the Rorke's Drift Test (1914) and its postscript when Australian and English players fought furiously in Melbourne; the Earl Park riot (1928); the infamous Malcolm Reilly-George Piggins feud that shook the SCG to its rafters in 1973; the Manly-Wests 'wars' of the 1970s; the Newtown-Norths Amco Cup melee of 1976 (Bears president Harry McKinnon wryly blamed it on the full moon); the violent SCG explosion of 1981 when Newtown played Manly in a semi-final; Kevin Tamati and Greg Dowling brawling on the sidelines at Lang Park while a Test match continued nearby ...

Raging bulls ... Brisbane's ferocious backrower Gorden Tallis and (opposite) Manly's Malcolm Reilly and Souths' George Piggins exchange pleasantries at the SCG in 1973

Guys

Let us now praise tough men and many hard days of skirmish and stoush.

Our chosen 10 in no way stand above the others – the likes of Billy 'Captain Blood' Wilson, Piggins and Reilly, Brian Hambly, Herb Steinohrt, Dan Dempsey, Peter Dimond, Herb Narvo, Duncan Hall, Arthur Beetson, John Elford, Gary Stevens, Trevor Gillmeister, Steve 'Blocker' Roach, Les Davidson and so many more.

Or today's heroes: Mark Carroll with his kamikaze charges, Martin Lang – ditto; hard-as-nails Dean Pay; the Broncos' raging bull Gorden Tallis; and a quieter achiever, Balmain's Mark Stimson, on feet unsuited to anything vaguely athletic ... but ploughing on all the same.

Sometimes, as with Stimson, the bravery has been of a more complex mix.

Ian Roberts (194 first grade matches, 13 Tests) stands tall among the hard men of the modern game.

But there are many who believe his greatest show of courage came when, while still a first grade frontrower, he wrote bravely and honestly of his homosexuality in the book *Finding Out.*

That, in its different way, was true grit.

1970-79

MARCH 29, 1970: Norths captain Ken Irvine attempts to lead team from the field in protest at control of referee Keith Page in sensational match against Canterbury at North Sydney Oval. Norths players claim Page 'treated them like adolescents'.

MAY 2, 1970: Balmain and Souths play in first league match in Australia to be attended by

royalty. **Queen Elizabeth**, Prince Philip and Princess Anne watch an entertaining game at the SCG, won 14-5 by the Rabbitohs. Almost 38,000 fans turn out.

JUNE 6, 1970: The **first Test** between Australia and Great

Britain at Brisbane's Lang Park turns into bloody war, and although copping a belting, Australia take first honours in Ashes series with 37-15 win.

SEPTEMBER 19, 1970: Souths captain John Sattler shows remarkable courage by playing majority of grand final against Manly with badly broken jaw.

The way we were...

1970: Poseidon nickel shares reach $280 in February but are $145 towards the end of March. Bob Hawke takes over as ACTU president. Tullamarine Airport opened. Australians in huge

street protests against Vietnam war. **Westgate Bridge** collapses, killing 35 workers.

1971: John Gorton votes himself out of office, **William McMahon**

elected PM. Evonne Goolagong, 19, wins Wimbledon. Actor Chips Rafferty dies aged 62.

Strength of 10 men ... Easts and Australian forward legends Sandy Pearce (right) and (top) Ray Stehr

Sid 'Sandy' PEARCE

THE great lock forward Frank Burge once wrote of Sandy Pearce: 'Football never has had a gamer, tougher, rougher or more loyal player.'

Burge, Pearce's roommate on the 1921-22 Kangaroo tour of England, gave a captivating insight into old Sandy, a 1908 Kangaroo 'original' who, remarkably, was 38 when he toured for the second time in 1921.

'Pearce had the strength of 10 men, if ever a man did,' wrote Burge.

'He neither drank nor smoked to any extent and seldom swore.

'As part of his training he would spar two or three rounds with six or seven of us in succession, finishing each spar by allowing us to whale into his body with punches that he made no attempt to block.'

Pearce, who boxed with the legendary Les Darcy, was Australia's first great hooker.

A quiet man, much admired for his personal qualities, he acquired his prodigious natural strength from his life as a fisherman and boat-rower at Double Bay.

On the football field he would play it hard but fair – until stirred.

Easts teammate Larry O'Malley recalls an opposing forward belting Pearce on the nose – twice – in a club game on the 1908 Kangaroo tour.

'Sandy bellowed and tore right through that and subsequent packs like an enraged bear,' said O'Malley.

Burge remembered Pearce, with his immense strength, terrorising the English forwards in 1921.

'He would have those English hookers eating out of his hand after half an hour.

'He would pack in with one arm loose and as the ball came in would whack the opposing hooker on the ear.'

Born in 1883, Sandy Pearce died early, of 'heart strain', in 1930 – and so never got to see his son Sid 'Joe' Pearce, another tough customer, play for Australia.

Ray STEHR

PROBABLY only the wild and colourful Ray Stehr himself knew the answer to the appealing mystery which highlighted a monumental career.

Was Stehr knocked cold by the raw-boned Englishman John Arkwright in the Third Test of 1936 ... or was he foxing? Stehr himself gave varying versions over the years, claiming that he 'took a dive', 'tried my Barrymore act', 'was spreadeagled with the most perfect right hand', 'was knocked unconscious on the ground'.

It is a famous moment in league – referee Lal Deane waiting until Stehr 'comes around' – and then sending him off in the wake of Arkwright.

The grainy film of the incident that still exists adds weight to the theory that Stehr was truly in Disneyland, as two 'zambuks' escort him from the arena.

The story is somehow typical of Stehr: larger than life.

Cured by a Chinese herbalist of a mystery back ailment which threatened to cripple him permanently, he played first grade for Eastern Suburbs at 15 – and went on to become one of the roughest, toughest front row forwards of them all, sent off in successive Tests against the 1936 Englishmen.

Stehr always reckoned he developed his 'retaliate first'

style after tasting the scientific foul play tactics of the English forwards on the Kangaroo tour of 1933.

Just 15 minutes into his first tour match – against St Helens – he was knocked cold by a stiff-arm tackle.

Stehr played in the historic match which kicked off rugby league in France and was a pillar in the unbeatable Easts sides of the 1930s (he played 184 games for the Tricolours).

Footballer, boxer, commentator, coach, club president and trenchant critic of league administrators, Ray Stehr, with his ever-present cry 'Easts to win', lives on in memory and legend as one of the giant figures of the game.

Frank 'Bumper' FARRELL

A prominent Sydney sporting identity has known for half a century the answer to one of league's great secrets – did Frank 'Bumper' Farrell bite the ear of St George's Bill McRitchie in a match in 1945? The sporting man was an 11-year-old boy when he accompanied his father to Lewisham Hospital to visit McRitchie.

There, the stricken forward told the story: that Bumper had just been in to see him, had apologised profusely for what had happened and had appealed for the truth of it to be kept quiet.

Otherwise, said Bumper, he would lose his job (in the police force).

The story accompanied tough, genial Bumper Farrell down the years.

An acutely awkward matter at the time (Farrell was cleared of the charge) it became eventually no more than a part of colourful rugby league folklore, adding to the legend of 'Bumper' (a nickname from schooldays when he was sneaking smokes).

After the incident, Bumper had to live with taunts of 'cannibal' from the crowd.

Frank Farrell, for Newtown and Australia, was one of the toughest of them all – a barrel-chested, cauliflower-eared frontrower of the old school in which the motto was: take no prisoners.

A late 1940s magazine article wrote of his approach to football as: 'a sort of good-humoured, bare-gummed ferocity ... an amiable grin upon his battered Irish countenance'.

Clive Churchill called him: 'The forward most feared – either in club or international football'.

Churchill would recall his first on-field meeting with Bumper.

Take no prisoners ... 'old school' frontrower, Newtown's Frank 'Bumper' Farrell

1970-79

NOVEMBER 7, 1970: World Cup final between Australia and Gt Britain deteriorates into wild

brawl after Australian halfback **Billy Smith** and Great Britain's Syd Hynes are sent off for fighting. Australia win 12-7.

MARCH 26, 1971: After trials at end of 1970 and through pre-season of 1971, a six-tackle rule is introduced for start of premiership. Field goal is reduced from two points to one.

DECEMBER 13, 1971: In historic decision, full High Court of Australia rules the NSWRL's transfer system invalid. System had been challenged by Balmain forward Dennis Tutty, costing him two years of his career and possibly a premiership with Balmain in 1969.

SEPTEMBER 16, 1972: Captained by international hooker Fred Jones, Manly break through for their first premiership title after 25 seasons in the competition, accounting for Eastern Suburbs 19-14 at the SCG.

APRIL 30, 1973: Receivers take over **South Sydney** Leagues Club after serious financial problems beset club. Two months later, club closes doors, only to reopen on September 30 after enthusiastic 'Save Souths' campaign.

The way we were...

1972: Snowy River Scheme completed. Shane Gould wins five gold medals at Munich Olympics. Rock opera Jesus Christ Superstar opens in Sydney. **Edward Gough Whitlam** and his Labor party sweep to power on the back of inventive 'It's time' advertising campaign. Risque TV show *Number 96* shown five nights a week on Channel 10.

1973: Fire bomb kills 15 at Brisbane's Whisky Au Go Go nightclub. Queen opens **Sydney Opera House**. Australia's first legal casino opens at Wrest Point.

1974: January floods cause havoc in eastern states. Saturday mail deliveries cease. **Cyclone Tracy** flattens Darwin: 66 die, 25,000 left homeless in one of Australia's worst natural disasters. **Sir Frank Packer** dies. Visiting Frank Sinatra insults Australian journalists.

1975: Family Law Court established. Medibank starts. Kings Cross publisher Juanita Nielson vanishes. Papua New Guinea proclaimed an independent nation. Governor general Sir John Kerr sacks Gough Whitlam and appoints Malcolm Fraser PM.

A Souths player finds himself on the end of a Brian 'Poppa' Clay blockbuster

'I was rising to play the ball,' wrote Churchill, 'I heard a deep voice over me exclaim: "Hello son".

'Almost at the same time I felt Bumper Farrell's big powerful hands around my head, screwing it off.'

Bumper, almost as famous as a hard-nosed police officer on the tough Darlinghurst beat, eschewed all ambulance treatment on the field.

The story is told of him lashing out with his feet at a zambuk who had dared to approach him with the smelling salts after he had been felled.

An iconic figure with the Newtown Bluebags, Farrell played 250 games with the club, his last in 1951.

Brian 'Poppa' CLAY

AS has sometimes been the way over the seasons it was Jack Gibson who summed up Brian Clay more succinctly than anyone.

Talking about the genuinely tough players of his experience, Gibson made the observation: 'If Clay was on the left, the natural inclination was to veer right'.

The words left unsaid are the key: the nod in the direction of Clay's ability as one of the fiercest tacklers in the game's history *(see picture above)*.

Short, stocky, tremendously powerful, 'Pop' Clay was the rock in the St George backline in seasons 1957-67.

He played 200 games with the Saints, mainly at five-eighth, and was in eight of the 11 straight grand final victories.

Queensland halfback Barry Muir, sometime (Australian) teammate of Pop's, commented that taking a Clay tackle was like being 'knocked over by a tank'.

Any opposition player giving St George trouble would generally find himself on the end of a Clay blockbuster.

'One of Poppa's specials would generally bring them back to the field,' said his former captain Ian Walsh.

The bald-headed Clay was the perfect team man, the faultless link in a virtuoso Saints backline.

'If there was the chance of a teammate being dumped Poppa would take the tackle himself,' said Reg Gasnier.

Clay has been called 'the fulcrum around which the Saints wove their magic'.

His courage was never in question. In the Second Test of the bruising 1959 Ashes series a pair of English knees smashed two of his ribs.

Pop just got on with the job.

When he died prematurely in 1987 of heart problems the men of St George mourned one of the Special Ones.

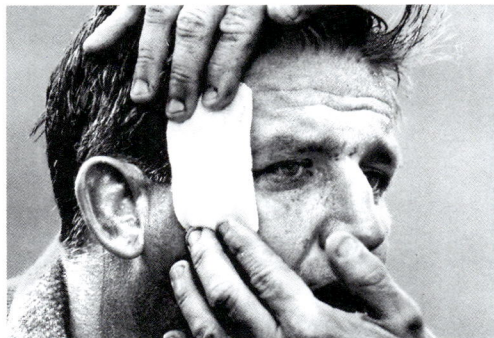

Wests' hard man Noel Kelly

Noel 'Ned' KELLY

NOEL Kelly was sent from the field 17 times in his career.

But who's counting?

Arriving in Sydney from Queensland in 1961 when the game was at its hardest, Kelly – already an established Australian player – quickly worked out he would have to adopt a personal survival code if he was to last in Sydney.

'I realised I was going to be a target every time I walked out there,' said Kelly.

That code, which was to underpin an enormously colourful (and successful) career, could be roughly translated as "do unto others before they do unto you'.

His meaty fists flailing at the times that it had to

be that way, Kelly – with Wests and Australia – built a reputation as one of the toughest and most ruthless forwards to ever play the game.

In the midst of all the hard stuff was a hooker-prop of considerable ball-handling skill, a key figure in great Australian sides of the time.

But it was more often the 'hard man' side of Kelly's game that captured the headlines.

When Ned flattened British secondrower Bill Robinson with a whistling right hand in the Third Test of 1966, Tommy Bishop suggested that Kelly had a better knockout record than (boxing champion) Rocky Gattellari.

Kelly explained how he had copped four stiff-arm tackles in the first 10 minutes before eventually 'popping one' on Robinson.

'I did what I had to do,' he said.

'I played the game hard and I played for keeps,' Kelly reflected in later years.

'If an opponent was worrying me with illegal tactics I would set out to stop him in the most direct way possible.

'Over the seasons I copped it and I dished it out ... and I didn't whinge.'

With 25 Tests, three Kangaroo tours and the 1960 World Cup, Kelly carved out a particularly fruitful career amidst the mayhem.

St George enforcer Kevin Ryan

Kevin 'Kandos' RYAN

FRAGMENTS of stories help shape the legend of single-minded Kevin Ryan – perhaps the most feared frontrower of them all:

■ In an Eastern Suburbs dressing-room after a match in the mid-1960s a distressed forward is telling officials 'I will never play front row again'. The forward has just played 80 minutes against the might and power of Ryan, contesting fierce scrums in which Ryan, boring relentlessly in, has worn him down to a numbing state of pain and exhaustion.

1970-79

MAY 9, 1973: Former Balmain frontrower and club secretary Kevin Humphreys unanimously elected seventh president of the NSWRL, following death of Bill Buckley, who had been at helm since 1960.

MAY 12, 1973: Newtown replacement halfback **Ken Wilson** etches name in history books when he lands a 68th minute field goal to secure an historic 1-0 victory over St George in club match at SCG.

SEPTEMBER 15, 1973: Manly and Cronulla battle out one of most savage grand finals of all time. Ironically, it is the football genius of Manly centre Bob Fulton that decides issue. Fulton's two tries give the Sea Eagles a 10-7 victory.

DECEMBER 1, 1973: Tommy **Raudonikis** captains Australia and secondrower Ken Maddison enjoys greatest day of football career when he scores twice in Australia's 15-5 Ashes-deciding win on an ice-covered Wilderspool Stadium.

AUGUST 21, 1974: Coached by former Test star Johnny King, Western Division complete fairytale run when they defeat Penrith 6-2 in final of inaugural Amco Cup midweek knockout competition.

JULY 20, 1974: Graeme Langlands becomes first player to score 100 points in Anglo-Australian Tests when he leads Australia to famous 22-18 third Test victory at the SCG. British hooker John Gray sparks revolution with successful 'around the corner' goalkicking style.

Birth of a club...

IN 1981 the Queanbeyan Blues made a formal application to have a Canberra club admitted to the competition the following year. Canberra joined the competition along with Illawarra. But they were a Queanbeyan-based club, with their home ground at Seiffert Oval and their administration operating from Queanbeyan Leagues Club. The side was coached by Don Furner and captained by former Balmain forward David Grant. In their first season the team won four matches and finished 14th.

COLOUR: Lime green. In the early years they were known as the 'Lime Splices' because they melted under pressure.

NICKNAME: The Raiders, with a Viking as the jumper logo.

I was there...

'Noel Kelly was among the toughest I've seen ... a hard man who never contemplated taking a backward step. I once got knocked out by this big Kiwi prop. Ned turned to him and said: "You can't do that to my mate" and dropped him on the spot with a single punch. He was greatly protective of the younger players and fiercely proud to wear the Australian jumper. Ned gave his all every time he laced on the boots. A great player in his day, he remains one of my closest friends.'

League Immortal **Johnny Raper**

■ A journalist visits Ryan at the time he is both footballer and law student.

Recuperating from a knee problem Ryan nurses a heavy law tome while relentlessly "working" the bad leg, a brick strapped to his foot.

Recommended to St George by journalist Alan Clarkson in 1960, Ryan was still raw for league's demands – immensely powerful but with suspect hands – even though already a rugby union international (1957 Wallabies).

With Saints it could never be said that Ryan evolved into a 'sophisticated' front-rower but his power and strength, in scrums and open play, added up to the stuff of nightmares for Dragons' rivals.

His speciality was full-frontal 'body' tackling – a jarring confrontation which dazed countless rivals.

Ryan went on to play 106 first grade games with Saints and helped the Dragons win seven grand finals.

He was the cornerstone of the pack – raw-boned, strong, fearless.

His front row peers of the time almost unanimously nominate him as 'the man' when it came to toughness.

In his story there lies a final irony – of Ryan leaving Saints (1967) to captain-coach Canterbury.

And of Canterbury beating St George 12-11 in the final of 1967, to bring to an end the greatest winning run in history.

John SATTLER

JOHN Sattler lived by the sword in the way he played his football; in the grand final of 1970 against Manly he simply refused to die by it.

The effort of the South Sydney captain in playing on for 70 minutes with a badly shattered jaw lives on in the annals of rugby league – and Australian sport – as one of THE great feats of courage.

'Satts', a punishing player who dealt out pre-emptive strikes on many opponents during those tough days, found himself on the receiving end in the 1970 grand final.

Manly secondrower John 'Sleepy' Bucknall caught him with a wicked right hand 10 minutes into the match, breaking his jaw ... but not his spirit.

The minutes that followed onfield were amazingly dramatic as the realisation sunk in with Souths players.

Winger Mike Cleary remembered: 'He kept saying to me, "hold me up, hold me up ... I'm feeling crook, I'm going to faint". He looked at me, and I said, "what's wrong?" He said "I've broken my jaw".

'When he said that, the jaw dropped about half an inch.

'I said ... "you'd better hold me up".'

When Bucknall hit Sattler, he struck virtually the entire Souths team in a single blow – and the rallying call amongst troops of the likes of O'Neill, McCarthy and Stevens resounded through the match that afternoon.

In the end it was Bucknall who had to go off – smashed in a tackle by McCarthy and Stevens.

Sattler was there to the end as the Rabbitohs triumphed 23-12.

To those at the SCG, the polished, precise words of his victory speech – in the light of the later revelation of his shocking injury – rank among the true wonders of rugby league.

Living by the sword ... Souths strong-arm leader John Sattler (left) never said die and (below) teammate of the late 60s and early 70s John 'Lurch' O'Neill forced to leave the field with a fractured arm

1970-79

SEPTEMBER 20, 1975: Easts thrash St George 38-0 in the greatest whitewash in grand final history. Wearing a pair of new white boots, St George fullback

Graeme Langlands cuts despairing figure after painkilling needle for groin injury goes 'wrong'.

APRIL 26, 1976: All-time great Langlands announces retirement following club match between St George and Wests.

MAY 12, 1976: 'Wild and disgraceful brawl' erupts in Amco Cup clash between Newtown and Norths at Leichhardt. Three players are sent off by referee Col Turnell and a further three cited by NSWRL judiciary. First time video is used to highlight foul play.

JUNE 26, 1976: Wests halfback Tommy Raudonikis admits in a newspaper article biting nose of Manly opponent John Gibbs in club match at Lidcombe. He is fined $200 by the NSWRL.

JUNE 29, 1976: Sydney premiers Easts beat English champions St Helens 26-2 in one-sided match billed as the 'World Club Championship' at SCG.

SEPTEMBER 20, 1976: Coached by Terry Fearnley, Parramatta make first grand final appearance. Despite scoring two tries to one, the Eels are beaten 13-10 by a more experienced Manly.

The way we were...

1976: Blue Hills, Australia's longest running radio serial, ends after 27 years on the ABC. Mudrunner Van Der Hum wins Melbourne Cup. Aussie pop group **Skyhooks** leave for tour of US.

1977: **Granville train disaster** claims 83 lives when Blue Mountains express is buried under a collapsed overpass. 'Advance Australia Fair' wins poll to become national anthem. Centenary Cricket Test won by Australia at MCG. World Series Cricket begins.

1978: Hilton Hotel bombed during Commonwealth Heads of Government Meeting (CHOGM). Sir Robert Menzies dies aged 83. Rocker **Johnny O'Keefe** dies at 43 of heart attack. Sydney rugby league player Paul Hayward and two accomplices arrested for heroin smuggling in Bangkok.

1979: Sydney's Eastern Suburbs railway is opened. Man, six children die in Luna Park fire. Mel Gibson stars in box office smash, **Mad Max**. Computerised ticket selling network Computicket goes into receivership.

John 'Lurch' O'NEILL

JOHN O'Neill was from the old frontrowers' school – travelling the well-worn route from country town (Gunnedah) to city club, to build a reputation and a life in football.

There is not a lot of coincidence about O'Neill's brilliant grand final record (six wins in eight deciders).

Great teams are built around great frontrowers and, with Souths (1967-68-70-71) and Manly (1972-73), O'Neill was akin to the pillar of Hercules.

Absolutely uncompromising in approach, O'Neill worked on a philosophy that front row play was almost totally about gaining the physical ascendancy over your rival.

'The hard stuff is part of the game – you've got to accept it,' he would say.

The frontrowers then adhered to a code of silence; whatever happened on the football field, stayed there.

If 'Lurch' lacked the ball skills of an Arthur Beetson, he made up for it with the absolute fearlessness and robustness of his approach.

Through the later 1960s and into the 1970s one of the great sights of football was the big bloke charging furiously into the ruck.

The young carpenter who came from Gunnedah to try his luck in the Big Smoke ended up playing in two of the toughest games in the history of the code – the 1970 World Cup final and the 1973 grand final (Manly v Cronulla).

Australian team manager at the Leeds final in 1970, Ken Arthurson, called it: 'Desperate, dangerous, dastardly football'.

O'Neill's incredibly brave performance as the Englishmen turned him into a punching and kicking bag was the stuff of sporting legends.

Afterwards, his eye split, his ankle gashed to the bone, filling his boot with blood, O'Neill was a mess. But triumphant. O'Neill's legendary bravery faced a different test in recent times as he fought the ravages of cancer, losing a long battle in, August, 1999

Terry 'Igor' RANDALL

IN 50-plus years of playing, coaching, managing, administering and watching football, ex-ARL boss Ken Arthurson says the two hardest tackles he ever saw were made by the one man.
Terry Randall.

Wrote Arthurson in his book, *Arko*: 'One was in a World Cup match in Wales in the 1970s when Randall almost snapped Jim Mills in two.'

Mills played his football around 17-18 stone.

The other was on Bob 'The Bear' O'Reilly at Sydney Sports Ground.

'Randall hit O'Reilly just beneath the short ribs, driving in with his shoulder.

'The ball flew out as if it had been fired from a gun.'

Then there was the tackle on big John 'Dallas' Donnelly as Manly headed through a minefield of sudden-death matches in 1978 towards the premiership.

Randall's murderous hit drove Donnelly back metres, freeing the ball for a Manly possession in a tight game.

Randall, starting his life in the backline, was a genuine demon tackler, a bone-and-muscle athlete who loved nothing better than wiping out an opponent.

Demon tackler ... Terry 'Igor' Randall who had opponents looking over their shoulders for most of his career

Randall played his football in the fast lane – never sparing himself and inevitably taking a toll on his own body (as well as those of his opponents) with the way he played.

He was a 1973 Kangaroo but never played a Test – successive injuries wrecking his tour.

But with Manly he was a devastating cog in the machine – linking with Allan Thomson and Mal Reilly to make up a particularly punishing back row.

In Manly's remarkable run in 1978 he showed courage way beyond the call; carrying injuries, he was needled match after match – and somehow drove himself through.

Said coach Frank Stanton: 'I'll take to my grave the vision of Terry Randall getting up for the last game, needing not one but several pain-killing injections.

'It was sheer mind over matter.'

Paul 'Chief' HARRAGON

THE collisions between Paul Harragon (111kg) and Mark Carroll (110kg) are among the most discussed and famous events of modern rugby league. In them is a sense of nostalgia – that today's 17-a-side version of the game is still very occasionally a man-on-man game.

Crash or crash through ... Newcastle tough guy Paul Harragon in a face-to-face altercation with Manly's John Hopoate in the 1995 finals series

Photo: Grant TURNER

Harragon v Carroll was about just that – about big men stepping fearlessly forward to duel in the sun.

Headline writers colourfully likened the impact generated by the pair to a 'human train smash'.

Dr Merv Cross, who spends his working days repairing damaged footballers, gets more technical.

'Momentum equals mass times velocity,' he observed a couple of years ago, making the point that a couple of 'ordinary' big blokes colliding in such a way in the street would very likely end with one of them on a slab in the morgue.

The Paul Harragon approach to football was always crash or crash through.

A powerful athlete, passionate about his district, his team and his game, Harragon was a formidable figure from the time he burst into Knights first grade in 1989.

His unsparing defensive style was often under the microscope – and sometimes in the headlines, as when he flattened Gary Larson (Queensland) in an Origin match or Britain's Ian Lucas in a Test.

Harragon's style, sometimes taking its toll on the hitter as much as those he hit, was backed by an admirable growth in the skills side of his game.

From a forward of limited ability with the ball, he grew to one adept at hitting the line fiercely then rebounding to get his pass away.

Forced out in 1999 by an unforgiving knee, 'The Chief' will be remembered as a dominant front row forward of the modern era, a considerable 'personality' in the game and an outstanding captain.

Mal Reilly, who coached Newcastle, under Harragon's leadership, to miraculously win the 1997 (ARL) premiership has said of him: 'The Chief is very special, a man of pride and emotion, a player who puts his body on the line week in and week out.

'The tougher it is, the more he wants to put his hand up.

'The way he has played his football has guaranteed a shorter career than some ... but what a career it has been.'

1970-79

SEPTEMBER 17, 1977: Parramatta and St George fight out first drawn grand final. Parramatta hit back from 9-0 down to draw level 9-all. Twenty minutes extra-time cannot separate sides and they are forced to replay a week later. St George score a crushing 22-0 victory in the replay.

MARCH 18, 1978: Exhibition match between Manly and Wests at Junction Oval in Melbourne sparks bitter feud between clubs. For the next four years, clashes between the Manly 'Silvertails' and the Wests 'Fibros' are fierce in the extreme.

MAY 28, 1978: Scrum collapses on Penrith prop **John Farragher** in a first grade match against Newtown at Henson Park. Farragher's spine is broken and he is rendered a quadriplegic.

SEPTEMBER 16, 1978: In one of sport's great coincidences, 1978 grand final ends with same result as previous season – a draw. Manly and Cronulla are deadlocked 11-all. With no extra-time and the Kangaroos due to depart for England, a midweek replay is hastily organised and Manly prevail 16-0.

MAY 29, 1979: NSW beat Queensland 31-7 to complete two-game romp in an increasingly one-sided interstate series. 'A major suggestion now is a State of Origin series,' writes Lawrie Kavanagh in *The Courier Mail.*

JUNE 16, 1979: Australia and Gt Britain meet at Lang Park in first international match in Australia played under lights. Home side crush an inept touring outfit 35-0. **Mick Cronin** lands 10 goals from 11 attempts.

137

I was there...

'Terry Randall built his reputation on toughness, durability, the ability to withstand pain and maintain an extraordinary level of fitness throughout his career. He could be the classical defender or the damaging defender, depending on the need. He had the knack of coming up with the right tackle for the right scenario and there's no doubt he was one of the finest and hardest players of his era. And he did his tackling legally. 'Igor' was rarely in trouble with the judiciary.'

Former Sea Eagles coach
Frank Stanton

I was there...

'The Chief was a very tough, hard man who would have created respect in any era. His greatest strength was the passion he had for the game. He loved playing and was always prepared to do anything to get his team home. The Chief had the ability to play with injury. I remember one time he was instructed to miss a City-Country game but went out and won the man of the match award. It was an honour and an experience to play alongside him.'

Knights warhorse **Tony Butterfield** on Paul Harragon

Football Femmes

TWO women – one a Sydney mother, the other a grandmother – made indelible impressions on rugby league eight decades apart. Annie Messenger, the mother of the code's first superstar **'Dally'**, features prominently in the code's history for making one of the most crucial decisions of all.

It was Mrs Messenger who gave her blessing for 'Dally' to make the switch from rugby union to the fledgling, professional rugby league.

The breakaway code had lured the player they called 'The Master' to its ranks and his wonderful on-field deeds guaranteed huge support from fans.

American rock star **Tina Turner** had reached grandmotherly status by the time she was approached by the NSWRL in the late 1980s to help market the game.

Using her smash hit 'Simply The Best', Turner headed an advertising campaign featuring star players and supporters and it turned out to be a fabulous marketing tool that appealed to all ages and, most importantly, both sexes on a national scale.

There have been many other women, down through the ages, who have made vital contributions to the game.

Famous Australian swimmer Annette Kellerman was the 'celebrity' chosen to kick off a series of major Sydney matches in the 1920s.

The St George Dragons broke new ground by apppointing Jeni Saunders as club doctor in 1980.

And in 1997, the Adelaide Rams Super League club placed Liz Dawson in the powerful position of chief executive.

Since the 1970s a number of women have made their mark as league writers/columnists. Dorothy Goodwin, Debbie Spillane, Julia Sheppard, Jenny Cooke, Jacqueline Magnay and Sharon Mathieson – all broke new ground in a once male-dominated profession.

Clubs around the nation have employed female marketing/promotions and media officers including Trish Sinclair (Parramatta) and Alison Gibson (St George-Illawarra).

New ground was broken by 22-year-old **Jenny Robinson**, a highly promising referee from the Penrith district, who officiated at four Flegg Cup matches. Respected judges say she has the potential to handle a first grade NRL match one day.

Special mention must be made of the players' and coaches' wives who have had an undeniable influence on their men.

Not forgetting the countless thousands of league mums who produced their sons and allowed them to prepare for, and participate in, the 'Greatest Game of All'.

Team of the Decade...
1970-1979

ONLY four clubs won premierships in the 1970s – Souths, Manly, Easts and St George – and this team reflects the dominance of these four Sydney clubs. Six played for Easts, four for Souths, four for Manly and one for St George. Three of the 13 would have undeniable claims for selection in the greatest team of any era. Five-eighth Fulton, secondrower McCarthy and frontrower Beetson rank among the all-time greats. The champion Kangaroos of 1973 are also heavily represented. Eadie, Branighan, Cronin, Rogers, Fulton, Raudonikis, McCarthy, O'Reilly, Beetson and Walters were all members of the squad.

Ron Coote

Fullback: Graham EADIE (Woy Woy, Manly).
Wingers: Ray BRANIGHAN (Souths, Manly, Ayr), Kerry BOUSTEAD (Innisfail, Easts).
Centres: Mick CRONIN (Gerringong, Parramatta), Steve ROGERS (Gold Coast Tigers, Cronulla). **Five-eighth:** Bob FULTON (Warrington, Manly, Easts). **Halfback:** Tommy RAUDONIKIS (Wests). **Lock:** Ron COOTE (Souths, Easts). **Secondrowers:** Bob McCARTHY (Souths, Canterbury), Rod REDDY (St George). **Frontrowers:** Bob O'REILLY (Parramatta, Penrith, Easts), Arthur BEETSON (Balmain, Easts, Parramatta).
Hooker: Elwyn WALTERS (Souths, Easts, Manly).

WHAT A GAME!
NEWTOWN v CANTERBURY 1982

NEWTOWN and Canterbury earned themselves a curious piece of league history by playing out the code's only scoreless draw back in 1982.

Newtown 0, Canterbury 0.

It was a soccer score. But the name of the game was very much rugby league as the Bulldogs and the Jets fought out an amazing match before just over 6000 fans at Henson Park in late March.

With both sides renowned for their tough, defensive packs, this was always going to be a low-scoring affair.

As the match progressed, the two teams battered themselves to a standstill, with barely a tryscoring opportunity between them.

Newtown had the better of play and looked more creative than their opponents over the 80 minutes. But the tie was a credit to the Bulldogs' tenacity and ability to hang in there in tough matches.

The key moment in the game came when a scrum flared up in front of the Newtown posts.

Players traded blows for the best part of a minute, with Newtown's ironman **Steve Bowden** ending up flat on his back.

When order was restored, referee Barry Goldsworthy received reports from his two touch judges.

The man with the red flag said Newtown started the fight, while the one with the blue was adamant it was Canterbury.

In the middle of a dilemma, Goldsworthy opted against a penalty and put down another scrum, ensuring his place in history along with the 26 players.

Birth of a club...

IN early February, 1908, a move was made to entice Newcastle into the new Sydney competition. Despite some misgivings and the failure to pass a recommendation at a large gathering at Pike's Rooms in Bolton Street on February 8, it was announced on April 11 the eighth team would be Newcastle. The side lost their first game against Glebe 8-5. Newcastle withdrew in 1909 to form their own local competition. In March, 1987, after years of lobbying, the NSWRL announced Newcastle would re-enter the competition the next year. The club lost their first competition game to Parramatta 28-4 and finished 14th.

COLOURS: The team originally played in red and white bars but changed to red and blue when they re-entered in 1988.

NICKNAME: The Knights.

Man on Man
Duncan Thompson v Andrew Johns

Born: February 19, 1895.
Died: May 18, 1980.
Played: 1911-25.
Clubs: Ipswich, Norths, Toowoomba Valleys.
Position: Halfback.
Weight: 11st 3lb (72kg).
Height: 5ft 7in (171cm).
Tests: 9.
Career games: 96*.
Career points: 290*.

(*not Ipswich, Toowoomba).

Born: May 19, 1974.
Played: Since 1994.
Club: Newcastle Knights.
Position: Halfback.
Weight: 14st (89kg).
Height: 5ft 10in (179cm).
Tests: 11.
Career games: 150.
Career points: 1122.

WORDS like wizardry and genius were often used to describe Duncan Thompson. One of the game's most creative halfbacks, Thompson played at the top level before and after World War I. Respected writer Tom Goodman described him as 'an innovator ...

a quick-thinker ... who planned movements beyond the mental reach of his teammates'. If anyone in today's game possesses such qualities, it is Newcastle's Andrew Johns. Johns grew up with a football in his hands, providing him with unsurpassed handling and passing skills. Johns is considerably taller and heavier than Thompson, who believed it was improper for a halfback to expend unnecessary energy in defence. That philosophy has them poles apart, because Johns tackles as effectively as any forward. Just as Thompson was, Johns is a capable goalkicker and a champion of his time.

Eric WEISSEL
1903-1972

30 COUNTRY football has produced no more loyal or talented player than Eric Weissel. Born in Cootamundra, Weissel rejected countless offers to play in Sydney and England, preferring to stay in the bush. Said to have had technically flawless five-eighth's game. Devastating attacker with cast-iron defence. Had ability to kick with either foot and was accomplished goalkicker. Career highlight came in Battle of Brisbane Test in 1932 when he hobbled 70 metres on injured ankle to set up winning try for Australia. 8 Tests (1928-32), Kangaroo 1929-30.

Duncan HALL
Born: 1925

26 REGARDED as finest forward Queensland has produced in last 50 years. Emerged from Rockhampton, before linking with Valleys in Brisbane, where he won Test spurs in 1948. A player with superb all-round abilities, could produce toughness or finesse depending on circumstances. Played 22 Tests at a time when international football was at most competitive. Highlight was Ashes victory in third Test against Great Britain in 1950. After stints with Toowoomba and Home Hill, wound up career with Brisbane Wests in 1956. 22 Tests (1948-55), Kangaroo 1948-49, 1952-53.

Brad FITTLER
Born: 1972

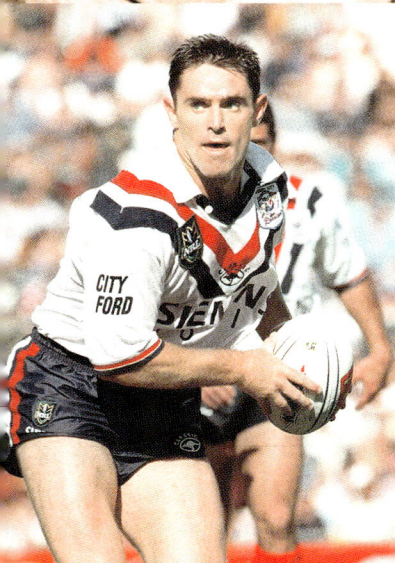

24 FITTLER has already achieved almost every honour the game has to offer. Played first grade at 17, NSW and Australia at 18 and captained his country to against-the-odds victory at 23 in 1995 World Cup. Prodigious talent as youngster, Fittler represented Australia as schoolboy then as senior international in successive years. Created and scored many tries with giant sidestep. Has strength and power to play in forwards and creativity and pace to match it with backs. Won premiership with Penrith in 1991 and joined present club, Sydney City, in 1996. 26 Tests (1991-99), Kangaroo 1990, 1994.

Tom GORMAN
1901-1978

29 HOLDS revered place in Queensland as first Maroon player to captain Kangaroos. Centre with exceptional personal qualities, Gorman led Kangaroos of 1929-30 following decade of interstate dominance by Queensland. Gorman was more than just a leader. After he retired in 1930, one reviewer rated him 'the outstanding Rugby footballer of the past decade'. Another said: 'The complete footballer in every sense ... the cunning of a fox and the driving force of a tank'. Learned football at Toowoomba before joining Brisbane Brothers in 1926. 10 Tests (1924-30), Kangaroo 1929-30.

THE Daily Telegraph

WE SELECT
THE BEST
OF THE CENTURY

Mick CRONIN
Born: 1951

23 POWERFUL ball-player, Cronin ranks high among Australia's finest centres. As a record-breaker, he has had few peers. Justified controversial selection with 1973 Kangaroos by finishing leading scorer and making Test debut against France. Lured to Parramatta in 1977. Played in six grand finals for Eels, including winning sides 1981-83 and 1986. Highest scorer in premiership football (1971 points), only player to win successive Rothmans Medals and holds world record for most points in a season (547, all matches, 1978). 22 Tests (1973-82), Kangaroo 1973, 1978.

Steve ROGERS
Born: 1954

28 OUTSTANDING centre of the 1970s and early 1980s, whose contemporaries rated him as good in defence as he was in attack. Made meteoric rise in first season of first grade, playing in Cronulla's first grand final team and touring with Kangaroos later the same year. Quick-thinking player, formed dynamic centre partnership with Mick Cronin at State and international level. Quality goalkicker, who scored over 1000 points for Cronulla. Made three Kangaroo tours and captained Australia in two Tests, 1981. 21 Tests (1978-83), Kangaroo 1973, 1978, 1982.

Graham EADIE
Born: 1953

27 GIANT, rampaging attacking player, who added new dimension to fullback play in 12 seasons with Manly. Eadie had forward's build and used it with telling effect, powering through tackles or dropping opponents. Toured with 1973 Kangaroos as understudy to Graeme Langlands, but thrown into second Test when Langlands broke his hand. Faultless debut and kicked five goals in difficult conditions. Retired in 1983, but made comeback in England with Halifax, collecting winners' medal at Wembley, 1987. 12 Tests (1973-79), Kangaroo 1973, 1978.

The Great 100

Ian WALSH
Born: 1933

25 KANGAROO selection (1959-60 tour) from the western NSW town of Eugowra. Continued to live in the country until enticed to St George in 1962, where he replaced veteran hooker Ken Kearney. Quickly warmed to dominating St George style and provided glut of possession with scrummaging skills. Took over from Norm Provan as captain-coach of Saints and led the club to 11th premiership win in 1966. Captained Australia in 10 Tests, including record-breaking 50-12 second Test win against Great Britain in 1963. 25 Tests (1959-66), Kangaroo 1959-60, 1963-64.

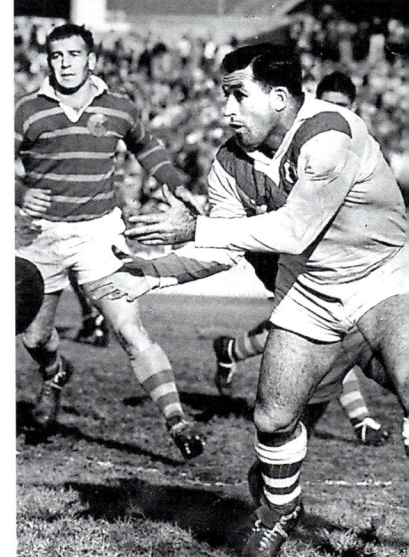

Allan LANGER
Born: 1966

22 CAME to notice when selected for Queensland in 1987. Warmed quickly to Origin football, providing brilliant foil for Wally Lewis. Test debut at 21 and made first of two Kangaroo tours in 1990. Neck-and-neck battle with Ricky Stuart for Test honours in early 1990s, but unlike Stuart, Langer prevailed at Test level until retirement in 1999. Inspiring captain, master tactician, who guided Brisbane to four premierships. Achieved rare treble in 1998, leading Brisbane, Queensland and Australia to victory. 22 Tests (1988-99), Kangaroo 1990, 1994.

Keith HOLMAN
Born: 1927

21 A SOUTHS junior, Holman was refused grading by Rabbitohs because of size. Spent season at Dubbo before joining Wests in 1948. Small stature defied heart and courage and as career progressed became renowned as best halfback in world. Forerunner of succession of tough, cheeky halfbacks which included Muir, Smith and Raudonikis. Long list of outstanding achievements with 1950 Ashes win the highlight. Toured twice with Kangaroos, played in 1954 World Cup and in 32 Tests, a record for an Australian halfback. 32 Tests (1950-58), Kangaroo 1952-53, 1956-57.

Long Enough, High Enough

BY DAVID MIDDLETON

The way we were...

Long Enough,

1980: Ten-week-old Azaria Chamberlain disappears from campsite at Ayers Rock. Australian Olympic team, weakened by some boycotts of the Moscow Games, returns with two gold medals. Merchant banker Frank Nugan found dead in his car.

1981: Australia's Trevor Chappell bowls last ball underarm against NZ at MCG, enraging fans and cricket officials. South Melbourne AFL club ordered to play 11 matches in Sydney. Cricketers

Dennis Lillee and **Javed Miandad** involved in ugly pitch clash.

1982: Lindy Chamberlain

sentenced to life imprisonment for murder of baby Azaria. *Women's Weekly* goes monthly.

Prince Philip opens Commonwealth Games in Brisbane; Australia tops gold medal tally with 39.

1983: First Australian death from

AIDS virus recorded on July 14. Australia II wins **America's Cup** in Newport. Pat Cash-led Australia defeats Sweden to lift Davis Cup. Cliff Young, a 61-year-old potato farmer, wins Sydney-Melbourne marathon.

EVERY generation of sport has produced champions who run faster, leap higher and kick further than those who went before. Cricket had W G Grace, Victor Trumper and then the incomparable Don Bradman.

Distance swimming has had Boy Charlton, Murray Rose, Kieren Perkins and now Grant Hackett.

They are sport's record-breakers, athletes at the height of their powers who rewrote the history books, etching their names into sport's pantheon until their deeds are surpassed in the years to come ... if ever.

Rugby league has had a procession of such champions, beginning with Dally Messenger in the game's infancy through tryscoring marvels Harold Horder and Frank Burge in the late 1910s and early 20s, pointscoring machine Dave Brown of the 1930s and on to such stars of the 50s and 60s as 'Golden Boots' Keith Barnes, Graeme Langlands and Eric Simms.

More recently, it has been Mick Cronin, Graham Eadie and Mal Meninga and today's stars such as Matthew Ridge, Jason Taylor and Canterbury's superboot Daryl Halligan.

Over the past century, league has also had its record-breaking teams.

The mighty St George side that won 11 straight premierships (1956-66) established a world record for the football codes that has stood for more than 30 years.

The Kangaroos of 1982, coached by Frank Stanton and ably led by hooker Max Krilich, rewrote the history books when they advanced through Great Britain and France undefeated – the first touring side to do so.

St George created a record for premiership football in 1935 that has remained unchallenged for more than 60 years.

Their 91-6 demolition of a fledgling Canterbury is the biggest win in premiership football.

In the Test arena, the Australian World Cup side of 1995 broke a world record when they despatched league novices South Africa 86-6 at Gateshead.

The great pointscoring clubs were Eastern Suburbs – 633 points in 18 games in 1935 – and the Brisbane Broncos of 1998 – 812 points in 28 games.

High Enough

In Long Enough, High Enough we have identified the 10 individuals whose ability to rewrite history has been unsurpassed.

■ Brian Bevan – the game's most extraordinary tryscorer. In 688 senior games in British football the freakish winger from Randwick notched a tally of 796 tries.

■ Mal Meninga – the only player to tour four times with the Kangaroos. Meninga played more Tests and scored more points for Australia than any other player. He holds a swag of records at club, State of Origin and international level.

■ Frank Burge – the greatest tryscoring forward the Australian game has known. He scored 146 tries in 154 games at club level and holds the premiership record of eight tries in a single game.

■ Mick Cronin – the record pointscorer in premiership football. Cronin did not begin his premiership career until he was almost 26 but in the next 10 seasons he registered 1971 points, all for the Parramatta club.

■ Dave Brown – scored more points in a match and more tries in a season than any player in premiership football. Such was his ability to accumulate points Brown was known as the 'Bradman of League' in the 1930s.

■ Terry Lamb – the most durable player in the world's most demanding rugby league competition. For 17 seasons Lamb backed up week after week to record a tally of 349 first grade games.

■ Ken Irvine – record tryscorer at club, interstate and Test level and one of the fastest men to play the game.

■ Dally Messenger – he WROTE the record books in the first place. Many of the records he established in the game's infancy took decades to surpass. He still holds the mark for most points in an interstate game and most points for NSW.

■ Daryl Halligan – kicked more successive goals than any player in top-level football. By the late 1990s he developed into possibly the most accurate goalkicker of all time.

■ Clive Churchill – captained Australia more times than any other player. An appropriate record for a man regarded by many as the greatest player in Australia's rugby league history.

These are the players that have set a standard so high it will take a player with the mark of greatness to match and perhaps surpass their feats.

They are the benchmark for all who follow.

Golden boots ... Balmain icon Keith Barnes attempts a long-range goal at the SCG (left) and (above) 'The Master' Dally Messenger who 'wrote' the record books

1980-89

JULY 8, 1980: Queensland triumph 20-10 in inaugural State of Origin match at Lang Park. Mal Meninga kicks seven from seven on his 20th birthday and Chris Close claims man of match award. Arthur Beetson cheered from the ground in his first game for home State.

SEPTEMBER 27, 1980: Canterbury winger **Steve Gearin** scores one of the most spectacular tries in grand final history in team's 18-4 defeat of Easts. Dr George Peponis leads the Bulldogs to first premiership win since 1942.

DECEMBER 13, 1980: Illawarra become 13th team included in 1982 NSWRL premiership. Team representing Canberra named 14th team early in 1981.

MARCH 29, 1981: Newtown hooker Barry Jensen the first player sent to sin bin. Sin bin rule, along with differential scrum penalty, are the significant rule changes of 1981.

JULY 4, 1981: Wally Lewis makes Test debut in Australia's 43-3 defeat of France at SCG.

⟨ 145 ⟩

The way we were...

1984: Robert de Castella named Australian of the Year. Lindy Chamberlain loses High Court appeal against life sentence. Seven people shot dead in battle between motorcycle gangs at Milperra. Batsman **Greg Chappell** becomes first Australian to score 7000 Test runs.

1985: Former chief stipendiary magistrate Murray Farquhar gets four years jail for attempting to pervert the course of justice. Finland's **Keke Rosberg** wins Australia's first Formula One Grand Prix.

1986: Lindy Chamberlain released from jail after three years and three months following discovery of new evidence at alleged murder scene of baby daughter Azaria. Car bomb explodes, injuring 22 people outside Russell St police HQ in Melbourne. **Crocodile Dundee** a box office hit around the world.

1987: Australia's population passes 16 million. Five men found guilty of murdering Sydney nurse Anita Cobby. Kensei wins Melbourne Cup. Pat Cash wins Wimbledon. Former Liberal party leader Billy Snedden found dead in Sydney hotel. Rupert Murdoch buys *Herald* and *Weekly Times* in Melbourne.

Brian BEVAN

BRIAN Bevan looked nothing like a footballer.

Slightly built, hair thinning, elbows and knees swathed in bandages and reputedly a heavy smoker – he was not, at first glance, the type of winger to inspire confidence.

But once he had the ball in his hands, Bevan was capable of freakish deeds.

Although raised in Sydney, just a stone's throw from Bondi Beach, Bevan made his indelible mark on rugby league in the northern hemisphere.

He played a handful of games with Easts before signing with Warrington late in 1945.

He retired 19 seasons later, with the phenomenal tally of 796 tries to his credit.

'Bev' had astonishing acceleration and evasive abilities that baffled his opponents.

He accumulated tries at an incredible rate.

By 1952-53 he became the highest tryscorer in the game's history when he passed the existing mark of 446.

In 1955 he scored try number 500.

By the time his career ended in 1964, Bevan had scored 796 tries in 688 first class matches.

The single try that was rated the best of his career, was once labelled the 'try of the century'.

He scored the length-of-the-field effort playing for Warrington against Wigan in the Wardonia Cup final of 1948 (see story on Page 100).

Played: Eastern Suburbs 1942-45, Warrington 1945-62, Blackpool Borough 1962-64, represented Other Nationalities 1949-55.

Played 688 career games in English football.

The Extraordinary Brian Bevan
TRYSCORING RECORDS

1945-46	0	1955-56	57
1946-47	48	1956-57	17
1947-48	57	1957-58	46
1948-49	56	1958-59	54
1949-50	33	1959-60	40
1950-51	68	1960-61	35
1951-52	51	1961-62	15
1952-53	72	1962-63	10
1953-54	67	1963-64	7
1954-55	63	Total	796

Frank BURGE

FOR sheer tryscoring volume, Frank Burge commands a place among any selection of Australian league's greatest record-breakers.

Burge was a marvel of the game's early years.

He began with the old Glebe club as a teenager in 1911 and played the final season of his career with St George 16 years later.

Between times he established tryscoring records that may never be broken.

Australia has had other great tryscorers – men such as Bevan, Irvine and Horder – but they were all wingers whose primary responsibility was scoring tries.

Burge was different; he played in the forwards.

He was predominantly a lock forward who would invariably break quickly from the base of the scrum to join attacking movements among his three-quarters. But he was also equally at home as a secondrower or prop.

None of that curtailed his prolific scoring.

In 138 first-grade games for Glebe, Burge scored 137 tries.

In one match against the University club in 1920, he ran in eight tries. It is a tally no player has bettered before or since in premiership football.

When he toured with the Kangaroos of 1921-22, Burge scored 33 tries in 23 games.

His efforts in England were of such a high standard that officials from Everton soccer club made him an offer of 3000 pounds to join the club. They figured he would make an outstanding goalkeeper!

Burge stayed in front of his contemporaries with a fitness regimen that was years ahead of its time.

He undertook regular training runs through inner-Sydney on a Sunday morning and was one of the first players to embrace pre-season training.

Only two other forwards have topped 100 tries in premiership football, but none have approached Burge's record-breaking tallies.

MOST PREMIERSHIP TRIES BY FORWARDS

Tries	Player	Years
146	**Frank Burge**	1911-27
119	Bob McCarthy	1963-78
104	Steve Menzies	1993-99
88	Ron Coote	1964-78
78	Ray Price	1976-86
60	Eddie Burns	1935-50
66	Les Cowie	1947-57
66	Rod Reddy	1972-85
63	Norm Provan	1951-65
61	Reg Latta	1916-30

Mick CRONIN

HOW wrong the critics were about Mick Cronin, the highest pointscorer in premiership football. When he was named in Australia's squad to tour with the 1973 Kangaroos his selection was ridiculed.

But just as he would do for the next 13 years, Cronin made his critics eat their words.

He returned from his first tour as the leading pointscorer, along the way winning his first Test jersey in France.

Cronin – born in Kiama and playing mostly in Gerringong – frustrated Sydney's football club secretaries for the next three years by resisting their attempts to sign him to a leading premiership club.

It wasn't until 1977, when Cronin was almost 26, that he decided to make the jump.

He joined Parramatta, whose coach Terry Fearnley had been his most persistent suitor. 'The Crow' set about his revision of the game's record books in clinical style.

His traditional 'toe-poking' style of goalkicking was unerringly accurate and in a short period with the Eels the records began to fall.

He scored most points in a season for Parramatta in his first year. Within two seasons he had scored more points for the club than any other player.

In 1978 he smashed the premiership pointscoring record of Eric Simms, set in 1969, and broke the all-games record of 572 points in the calendar year.

The same year he landed 26 successive attempts at goal, beating the previous mark set by Arthur Oxford in the 1920s.

As Parramatta soared to the top of the charts in the early 1980s, Cronin kept on piling on the points.

He passed 1000 premiership points in 1981, 1500 in 1983 and in 1985 he overtook former Manly fullback Graham Eadie as the highest scorer in premiership history.

When Cronin hung up his boots after the 1986 grand final, his final tally stood at 1971 points.

I was there...

'In my opinion, Michael Cronin's best attribute was that anyone who played around him ALWAYS played well. He might have been off-colour in a particular game but his supports were still catered for. Michael scored plenty of points, but he always considered that to be part of his job, albeit an important part. There were never any pretentions with 'The Crow', he was modest from top to toe. He also had a lot of talent in between games – the boys liked having him around. The only time I ever sent a harsh word in his direction was the day he tipped me his horse. I think it ran dead.'

Master coach **Jack Gibson**

Tryscoring freaks ... the amazing 'Wizard of Aus' Brian Bevan (opposite page top left), the equally prolific Frank Burge (opposite page), and Parramatta's record goalkicker Mick Cronin on the burst (left)

Photo: *Rugby League Week*

MOST POINTS IN FIRST GRADE CAREER

Points	Player	Years	Trs	Gls	FG
1971	**Mick Cronin**	1977-86	74	865	2
1917	Graham Eadie	1971-83	71	847	3
1841	Eric Simms	1965-75	23	803	86
1830	Daryl Halligan	1991-99	73	767	4
1760	Jason Taylor	1990-99	38	788	32
1554	Graeme Langlands	1963-76	86	648	-
1519	Keith Barnes	1955-68	11	742	1
1442	Terry Lamb	1980-96	164	386	44
1388	Steve Gearin	1976-86	78	566	-
1374	Steve Rogers	1973-85	90	543	10

1980-89

SEPTEMBER 13, 1981: Newtown and Manly fight out brutal semi-final at SCG. Steve Bowden (Newtown) and Mark Broadhurst (Manly) stand toe-to-toe in ugly and violent all-in brawl.

SEPTEMBER 25, 1981: Parramatta break through for first premiership with a 20-11 grand final win over gallant Newtown. Fans celebrate by torching old Cumberland Oval grandstand.

FEBRUARY, 1982: Rothmans announce major sponsorship for game worth $850,000 over three years. Teams now vie for the Winfield Cup, as well as Giltinan Shield.

JUNE 29, 1982: Wests second-rower Bob Cooper handed record 15-month suspension by judiciary boss Jim Comans after violent brawl in match against Illawarra in Wollongong.

MARCH 28, 1982: Newtown and Canterbury play only 0-all draw in first grade premiership history.

JUNE 8, 1982: Controversial North Qld referee Barry Gomersall makes first appearance at State of Origin level.

DECEMBER 18, 1982: Captained by Max Krilich and coached by Frank Stanton, 15th Kangaroos become first team to complete tour of Great Britain and France undefeated.

FEBRUARY 26, 1983: Value of try rises to four points for season start. FootyTAB begins.

APRIL 30, 1983: ABC screens Four Corners program which leads to resignation of NSWRL president Kevin Humphreys.

MAY 9, 1983: Tom Bellew, 60, elected eighth president of NSWRL.

JUNE 7, 1983: Queensland prop Darryl Brohman has jaw broken by elbow of NSW forward Les Boyd. Boyd later suspended for 12 months.

Prolific ... one of rugby league's leading pointscorers, Dave Brown

Dave BROWN

DURING his heyday in the 1930s, Dave Brown was variously known as 'the Bradman of rugby league' and 'the wonder man'.

He emerged from the junior ranks at Eastern Suburbs to become one of the legendary figures of the game, as much for his remarkable ability in general play as for his freakish pointscoring efforts.

As a youngster, Brown overcame a series of physical setbacks that would have thwarted lesser men.

A succession of childhood accidents and then the loss of all his hair through illness at the tender age of 18 failed to dampen his ambitions.

He made his debut for Easts when he was 17 and quickly stamped himself a player of class.

On tour with the Kangaroos of 1933-34, Brown amassed 285 points from 32 games. a Kangaroo record which remains to this day.

But it is three records which Brown set in Eastern Suburbs' extraordinary team of 1935 that set him apart.

As the Tricolours stormed to premiership honours, Brown scored 38 tries in only 15 games.

Twice he scored six times in a match, he crossed for five tries once and he scored four tries in a game on three separate occasions.

In one match in 1935, Brown scored 45 points, another premiership record that has never been approached.

As Easts put competition newcomers Canterbury to the sword with an 87-7 trouncing, Brown scored five tries and kicked 15 goals.

The 15 goals equalled the premiership record of St George winger Les Griffen, set, ironically, one week earlier.

Brown also wrote his name into the game's history books as Australia's youngest Test captain, leading the tour of New Zealand in 1935.

He was just 22 years and 177 days old.

MOST TRIES BY INDIVIDUAL IN ONE SEASON

Tries	Player	Club	Year
38	**Dave Brown**	Easts	1935
34	Ray Preston	Newtown	1954
29	Les Brennan	Souths	1954
28	Bob Lulham	Balmain	1947
28	Johnny Graves	Souths	1951
27	Rod O'Loan	Easts	1935
27	Norm Jacobson	Newtown	1948
27	Phil Blake	Manly	1983
26	Tommy Ryan	St George	1957
25	Fred Tottey	Easts	1936
25	Ron Roberts	St George	1949
25	Reg Gasnier	St George	1960

Terry LAMB

TERRY Lamb built his reputation as a relentless support player through dogged determination and boundless energy.

They were attributes that bought him a swag of tries throughout his career and ultimately led to him being recognised as the most resilient player in the history of premiership football.

Lamb was a committed first-grader for 17 seasons – from the time he broke into first grade with Western Suburbs in 1980, to the end of the 1996 season with Canterbury.

By the time he hung up his boots for good – he originally announced his retirement after leading the Bulldogs to the 1995 premiership – Lamb had played 349 first-grade games, 46 more than anyone else had played to that time.

Lamb's record pales in comparison with that set by Wigan's legendary fullback of the inter-war years, Jim Sullivan (928), but on hard Australian grounds in the most physically demanding rugby league competition in the world, Lamb's effort is worthy of undying respect.

With a powerful, nuggety build, Lamb was able to withstand the ravages of injury and time that caught

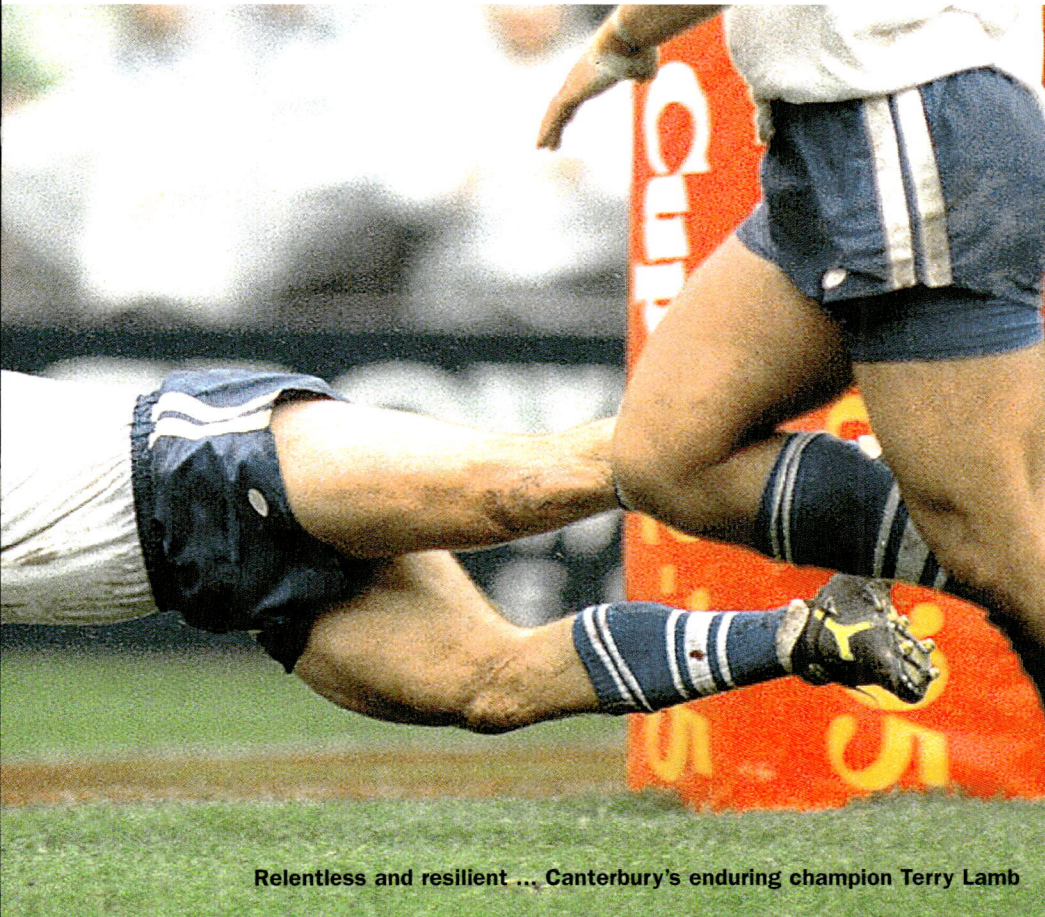

Relentless and resilient ... Canterbury's enduring champion Terry Lamb

1980-89

JULY 9, 1983: Australia's run of 16 straight Test victories ends when New Zealand upset home side 19-12 at Lang Park.

AUGUST 22, 1983: Former international lock John Quayle becomes NSWRL general manager.

AUGUST 27, 1983: Newtown play last match, beating Canberra 9-6 at Orana Park, Campbelltown.

SEPTEMBER 4, 1983: Parramatta winger Eric Grothe beats five defenders to score spectacular semi-final try against Canterbury.

SEPTEMBER 26, 1983: Wests and **Newtown** eliminated from 1984 premiership. NSWRL's general committee announce Newtown will return as Newtown-Campbelltown in 1985. It never happens.

DECEMBER 5, 1983: NSWRL reinstate Wests after Equity Court ruling.

JANUARY 23, 1984: First meeting of newly incorporated NSWRL nine-man board of directors.

JULY 2, 1984: Three matches after returning from 12-month suspension, Manly's Les Boyd charged with gouging Canterbury hooker Billy Johnstone. Subsequent 15-month ban ends his Australian career.

MARCH 16, 1985: Cronulla's **Steve Rogers** has jaw smashed in a tackle by Canterbury's Mark Bugden. Rogers later instigates civil action against Bugden.

MAY 4, 1985: Australian players Peter Sterling (Hull), Brett Kenny (Wigan) and John Ferguson (Wigan) among stars at Wembley Stadium for Challenge Cup rated greatest of all time. Wigan beat Hull 28-24.

1980-89

JUNE 11, 1985: Steve Mortimer leads NSW to their first State of Origin series victory.

JULY 2, 1985: Bitter rift splits Australian side in NZ when coach Terry Fearnley drops four players, all Queenslanders, for final Test of series.

AUGUST 9, 1985: Champion Australian and Souths fullback **Clive Churchill** dies. A huge crowd turns out for his funeral at Sydney's St Mary's Cathedral.

MARCH 16, 1986: Parramatta christen new home ground, Parramatta Stadium, with stunning 36-6 defeat of St George.

APRIL 21, 1986: Jim Comans resigns after six years as judiciary chairman.

JUNE 29, 1986: Easts defeat Norths 21-14 in final match at old Sydney Sports Ground.

JULY 1, 1986: NSW, coached by Ron Willey, complete first clean sweep of Origin series. Winning 22-16, 24-20, and 18-16 in the final match.

JULY 29, 1986: Eccentric doctor Geoffrey Edelsten makes a bizarre $2.5 million attempt to 'buy' Cronulla for his wife Leanne. Not surprisingly, deal soon collapses.

SEPTEMBER 28, 1986: Parramatta stalwarts Mick Cronin and Ray Price complete fairytale farewell when they play in Eels' 4-2 grand final win over Canterbury.

DECEMBER 13, 1986: Don Furner-coached and **Wally Lewis**-led Kangaroos complete second successive undefeated tour of Gt Britain and France with 52-0 romp in second Test against France at Carcassonne.

up to many of his contemporaries, and although he was cosseted through the final years of his career on the training paddock, he never gave anything less than 100 per cent on the field.

Lamb's resilience was evident early in his career when he played in some part of every match on the Kangaroo tour of 1986. He appeared in all 20 matches on tour, including the five Tests.

No player, before or since, has achieved such a feat.

Lamb holds second place on the list of premiership tryscorers (164), and he is Canterbury's highest pointscorer (1276) and their leading tryscorer (123).

MOST GAMES IN FIRST GRADE

Games	Player	Years
349	**Terry Lamb**	1980-96
332	Cliff Lyons	1985-99
315	Paul Langmack	1983-99
311	Andrew Ettingshausen	1983-99
303	Geoff Gerard	1974-89
287	Des Hasler	1982-97
285	Greg Florimo	1986-98
284	Bob O'Reilly	1967-82
274	Mario Fenech	1981-95
272	Steve Mortimer	1977-88
272	Ian Schubert	1975-89
272	Steve Walters	1986-99
272	Kevin Walters	1987-99

Mal MENINGA

MAL Meninga may never have scaled the heights he reached in the game had it not been for a series of broken arms in 1987 and 1988.

By that time, the big Queenslander's career had reached something of a plateau. He had toured twice with the Kangaroos, racked up a large number of Test and State of Origin appearances, achieved success in Brisbane club football and was adored in the English town of St Helens, where he spent an off-season in 1984-85.

But Meninga was only a fringe Test selection on the 1986 tour and many believed his best days were behind him.

A sickening collision with a goalpost at Queanbeyan in 1987 proved to be a defining moment in his career.

A long and frustrating convalescence refuelled his hunger for the game, and when the arm had fully recovered, Meninga was a different player.

He won back his Test jersey in 1989 and the next year succeeded Wally Lewis as Australia's Test captain.

Indeed, the years that followed the arm injury were the most fruitful of Meninga's career.

He captained Canberra to their first premiership win, became the first player to lead Australia on successive Kangaroo tours and made an unprecedented four tours of Great Britain and France.

His final Test match against France on the 1994 tour was his 45th for Australia.

Two years earlier he had surpassed Reg Gasnier's record of 36 Tests.

Big Mal's tally of 272 Test-match points is another record and so is his total of 551 points in all matches for Australia.

He scored most points in State of Origin football, played most Origin games and played in most representative matches for Queensland.

The following list outlines just some of the records Meninga continues to hold.

■ Most Tests for Australia (45).
■ Most points for Australia (272 in Tests and 551 in all matches).
■ Most Kangaroo tours of Great Britain and France (four, 1982, 1986, 1990, 1994).
■ Most Kangaroo tours as captain (two, 1990, 1994).
■ Most goals in Tests for Australia (96).

Canberra's man mountain Mal Meninga

■ Most Ashes Tests (17).
■ Most points in Ashes Tests (108).
■ Most State of Origin matches (32).

- Most representative matches for Queensland (42).
- Most points in State of Origin football (161).
- Most points in a match for Canberra (38 v Easts, 1990).
- Most tries in a premiership match for Canberra (five v Easts, 1990).

Ken IRVINE

THOSE who watched Ken Irvine at his peak swear he was the fastest man ever to play rugby league.

In the 1960s he was Australian professional sprint champion, clocking 9.3 seconds for the 100 yards.

Complementing his blinding pace was his innate footballing ability, honed by the dedicated coaching of the Marist Brothers at Mosman.

He was able to combine speed with a safe pair of hands, a strong sense of anticipation and an effective body swerve. Irvine graduated to first grade with North Sydney at the end of 1958, and after just one full season in the top grade he was selected to make the first of his three Kangaroo tours.

The rise to international class was no hurdle and he carried his exceptional tryscoring ability at club level into the international arena.

By the time his Test career wound up in 1968, Irvine had scored 33 tries in 31 Tests.

His tally is seven tries more than his nearest rival, Reg Gasnier.

In club football, Irvine scored 212 tries from a mere 236 first grade games.

Only Terry Lamb has come within 50 tries of Irvine's benchmark.

Remarkably, Irvine scored 171 of his premiership tries with North Sydney, a team which qualified for the finals only twice in the 13 seasons he played with the club.

Irvine wound up his career at Manly, adding a further 41 tries in 60 first grade outings.

More importantly, Irvine achieved one of his career highlights with the Sea Eagles – two premiership victories – something that eluded him at North Sydney.

Irvine also holds a place in the game's record books for scoring most tries in interstate matches (30) and most tries in all matches for Australia (90).

Rugby league's fastest man Ken Irvine

MOST TRIES IN PREMIERSHIP CAREER

Tries	Player	Years
212	**Ken Irvine**	1958-73
164	Terry Lamb	1980-96
158	Andrew Ettingshausen	1983-99
152	Harold Horder	1912-24
147	Bob Fulton	1966-79
146	Frank Burge	1911-27
144	Benny Wearing	1921-33
143	Johnny King	1960-71
142	Steve Renouf	1989-99
138	Phil Blake	1982-97

Dally MESSENGER

LIKE many of the game's great record-breakers, there was more to Dally Messenger's game than mere numbers.

His sobriquet, 'The Master', says it all about a player who stood head and shoulders above his contemporaries.

His freakish deeds with the football – his ability to beat an opposition fullback by diving over the top of him, his skill in kicking a field goal while one leg was pinned down by a defender – have assured Dally M a place among the game's legends.

But it is impossible to discuss Messenger without paying some attention to the records he set.

Technically, Messenger was not a record-breaker, because he was the first league player to accumulate points in great numbers.

He set the standard for ALL who followed.

1980-89

APRIL 5, 1987: Newcastle accept invitation to join 16-team NSWRL competition in 1988. Later joined by Brisbane and Gold Coast.

AUGUST 6, 1987: After highly successful State of Origin series, fourth match played at Veterans' Stadium, Long Beach, California, and won 30-18 by NSW.

SEPTEMBER 27, 1987: Last grand final is played at SCG. Manly beat Canberra 18-8.

MARCH 4, 1988: First rugby league match at $62 million **Sydney**

Football Stadium between St George and Easts. Saints win 24-14.

MARCH 6, 1988: Brisbane crush defending premiers Manly 44-10 in debut at Lang Park.

JUNE 11, 1988: Australia beat Great Britain 17-6 in 100th Test between traditional rivals.

OCTOBER 9, 1988: Australia defeat New Zealand 25-12 in World Cup final in front of 47,000 at Eden Park, Auckland.

MARCH 13, 1989: NSWRL unveil glamorous advertising campaign featuring American rock superstar Tina Turner.

JUNE 14, 1989: Queensland State of Origin captain Wally Lewis turns in one of his best performances to inspire 16-12 win for his injury-hit team.

AUGUST 11, 1989: Canterbury and Canberra meet at Perth's WACA Ground in first premiership match staged outside eastern states.

SEPTEMBER 24, 1989: Canberra upset Balmain 19-14 in extra-time to win one of the most dramatic and exciting grand finals ever.

The way we were...

Birth of a club...

IT was announced in March, 1987, that Brisbane would join the competition the following year. In his book *True Blue, The Story of the NSWRL*, Ian Heads wrote 'serious attacks of cold feet and an astonishing amount of dithering almost undermined Brisbane's acceptance of the NSWRL's invitation to "come and play".' Commonsense prevailed and an impressive consortium headed by businessman Barry Maranta won the licence. Brisbane made a spectacular debut in their first premiership game, thrashing Manly 44-10 at Lang Park. The Broncos were the top-drawing team in 1988, pulling 331,533 fans. They missed the semi-finals in their debut year, finishing just outside the five on 28 points.

COLOURS: Maroon, white, yellow. The maroon was to represent Queensland.

NICKNAME: The Broncos – chosen after a public survey.

The finest year of his relatively short rugby league career (1907-13), was undoubtedly 1911.

That year, as Eastern Suburbs won their first premiership, Messenger kicked 108 goals in 21 matches (at all levels).

He scored 270 points, including 148 for Easts.

Such figures were unique in the rugby codes to that time.

In fact, Messenger's all-games record of 1911 stood until 1935 when it was overtaken by another Easts player, Dave Brown.

Although nearly all of Messenger's pointscoring records have fallen by the wayside over time, two records in interstate football remain.

In a crushing NSW defeat of Queensland in 1911, Messenger scored 32 points from four tries and 10 goals.

And his tally of 278 points in all matches for NSW has never been beaten. The accompanying list details some of Messenger's outstanding feats and records:

- Most points for NSW (278).
- Most points in a match for NSW against Queensland (32 in 1911).
- The first player to score 100 points in a premiership season (1911).
- The only player to represent New Zealand, Australia, NSW and Queensland.
- Captained Eastern Suburbs to their first three premiership wins.
- Captained Australia in the first two Ashes Tests.

Daryl HALLIGAN

BECAUSE of the absence of a complete set of records on the subject, the question of who has been the game's greatest goalkicker remains largely a matter of opinion.

Until relatively recent times, statistics on goals kicked from goals attempted were never recorded.

But it is safe to say that improvements in ground drainage, high-tech, all-weather footballs and even tailor-made kicking boots have contributed to a generation of the finest goalkickers the game has ever seen.

Keith Barnes, Graeme Langlands, Mick Cronin and Eric Simms were all outstanding goalkickers in their day, but they would be the first to admit they could not kick the ball between the uprights as regularly as some of the modern-day masters.

Canterbury's Kiwi sharpshooter Daryl Halligan can lay claim to being the most accurate of all the kickers.

In one golden period in 1998, Halligan landed 30 successive goals for Canterbury, surpassing the record for senior football of 26 set by Mick Cronin in 1978.

The great Dally Messenger kicks downfield

Throughout his career in Australian football, Halligan has maintained remarkable standards.

In nine seasons, Halligan has kicked over 700 goals with a success rate of 78 per cent.

That's almost eight goals from every 10 attempts – from all angles, and in all conditions.

The finest goal of Halligan's career stands out like a beacon.

In the preliminary final against Parramatta in 1998, Halligan was confronted with a conversion from the sideline to put the match into extra-time.

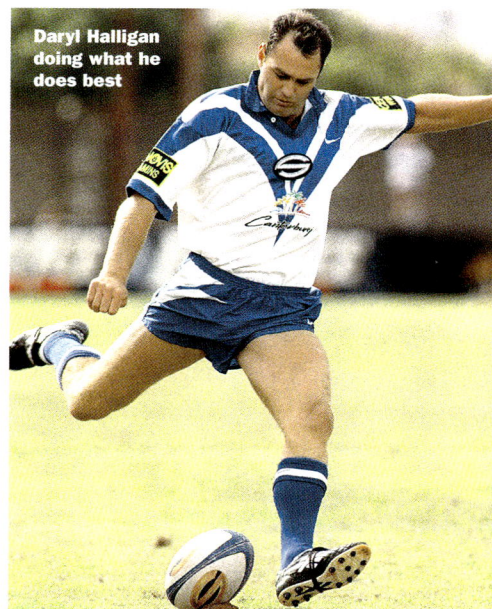

Daryl Halligan doing what he does best

Miss and the Bulldogs were eliminated from the competition.

With 37,000 people watching on, Halligan coolly potted the goal and Canterbury went on to win the match and fight their way into the grand final.

After nine seasons of premiership football, Halligan has assembled an impressive list of records and milestones:

- Most consecutive goals in first-class football (30 for Canterbury in 1998).
- Fourth on the list of premiership pointscorers (behind Mick Cronin, Graham Eadie and Eric Simms).
- Most points in a season by a winger (270 in 1994).
- Most points in a season for Canterbury (270 in 1994).
- Highest pointscorer for Canterbury.

Clive CHURCHILL

WHEN Wally Lewis was added to the list of rugby league Immortals in 1999, he humbly conceded it "wouldn't have been right" had he overtaken Clive Churchill as the most capped Australian captain.

It is a measure of the respect in which Churchill continues to be held, 14 years after his premature death.

There is a wide body of opinion that places Clive Bernard Churchill at the top of the pile among all of Australia's great rugby league players.

An attacking fullback of unequalled courage and talent, Churchill ascended to the Australian captaincy after only two seasons in the Green and Gold.

In his first series as Test captain (1950), Churchill inspired Australia to their first Ashes victory over Great Britain since 1920.

The 23-year-old was raised to the shoulders of his teammates as a wave of euphoria swept the Sydney Cricket Ground.

'That turned out to be my crowning glory,' Churchill wrote years later.

Top of the pile ... Australia's Clive Churchill makes a despairing dive for the ball in a 1952 Test in England

After captaining the Kangaroos in 1952-53, he led Australia to their second Ashes victory in four years, when Great Britain returned in 1954.

Churchill's 24 Tests as captain came in six successive seasons (1950-55).

It was a challenging period for Australia internationally, and although they won two Ashes series, they were beaten in three series against France and two against New Zealand.

Churchill's 24 Tests as captain was 17 more than the previous mark held by earlier Kangaroo captains Tom Gorman (1929-30) and Wally Prigg (1937-38).

Before Churchill came along, no Australian captain had led his country in more than three Test series.

Churchill led Australia in eight.

Just when Lewis and then Mal Meninga had Churchill's record in their sights in the 1990s, fate intervened.

Lewis failed a medical before the Kangaroo tour of 1990, while a suspension cost Meninga a Test appearance in 1993 that would have seen him equal Churchill's mark.

AUSTRALIA'S LEADING TEST CAPTAINS

Player	Tests
Clive Churchill	24
Wally Lewis	23
Mal Meninga	23
Keith Barnes	12
Brad Fittler	12
Max Krilich	10
Ian Walsh	10
Ken Kearney	9
Reg Gasnier	8
Bob Fulton	7
Tom Gorman	7
Graeme Langlands	7
Wally Prigg	7

I was there...

'Terry (a Canterbury junior) began his grade career with Wests and it was always a priority to get him back. It took three years and the $50,000 we paid was the best money Canterbury ever spent. Terry was a fantastic player, who could do anything on the football field ... a tremendous leader, the scorer of tries, the kicker of goals, an excellent defender. And there has never been a more durable customer. He played the game for 17 years and when you take all of his qualities into account, he is just about the best all-round player we've ever seen.'

Peter 'Bullfrog' Moore, Canterbury's then chief executive

I was there...

'Kenny Irvine was like a bullet, a very dangerous man to have on your team. He had tremendous acceleration, good hands, a great swerve and wonderful anticipation. If you made a break you just knew he'd be there in support. If you gave Irvine a yard, he'd take 100. He was the youngest Kangaroo tourist in 1959 and made a wonderful impression with 17 tries. 'Mongo', as we called him, was an asset to any team. He was a top fellow on and off the field. He died too young.'

League Immortal **Reg Gasnier**

Team of the Decade...
1980-1989

THIS was a period of almost total Australian dominance on the international stage. The Green and Golds won every Test series they contested, triumphed in the only World Cup of the decade and were undefeated in successive Kangaroo tours. It comes as no surprise that members of the 1982 and 1986 Kangaroos dominate the side. All 13 members toured with one or both of the champion outfits. Five players – Kenny, Meninga, Lewis, Sterling and Miles – toured with both The Invincibles (1982) and The Unconquerables (1986), making them automatic selections in an all-star team.

Wally Lewis

Fullback: Garry JACK (Wests Wollongong, Wests, Balmain, Salford).
Wingers: Michael O'CONNOR (St George, Manly, St Helens), Eric GROTHE (Parramatta, Leeds).
Centres: Brett KENNY (Parramatta, Wigan), Mal MENINGA (Souths Brisbane, St Helens, Canberra).
Five-eighth: Wally LEWIS (Valleys, Wakefield, Wynnum, Brisbane Broncos).
Halfback: Peter STERLING (Parramatta, Hull).
Lock: Ray PRICE (Parramatta, Wakefield).
Secondrowers: Wayne PEARCE (Balmain), Gene MILES (Wynnum, Brisbane Broncos).
Frontrowers: Steve ROACH (Balmain, Warrington), Greg DOWLING (Innisfail, Wynnum, Brisbane Broncos).
Hooker: Ben ELIAS (Balmain).

‹ 154 ›

WHAT A GAME!
PARRAMATTA v MANLY 1981

AN era came to an end in magical style when Parramatta and Manly lined up for the last game ever at Cumberland Oval in 1981.

With the ground set to be bulldozed and replaced by a more modern ground known as Parramatta Stadium, the game was a nostalgic occasion for Eels fans.

And the Parramatta team, cheered on by former greats Ken Thornett, Ron Lynch and Barry Rushworth, produced a memorable finale against their long-time foes.

The match – in the final round of the minor premiership – had no bearing on positions in the top five, with both Parra and Manly assured of their places regardless of the result.

So the players took the opportunity to let down their hair, with the result a modern-day classic.

In the end, it finished 20-all – a just scoreline with honours shared evenly after a superb seven-try extravaganza.

The Sea Eagles dominated the early exchanges, with tries to **Les Boyd** (left) and John Dorahy giving the visitors a 10-0 lead in as many minutes.

The crowd of nearly 19,000 was as shocked as the Parramatta players, but it didn't take long for the fans to find their voice.

Tony Melrose put the Eels on the board with a try in the 23rd minute and further tries to Kevin

EYES ON THE PRIZES

PLAYERS have been rewarded for excellence – financially and otherwise – since the birth of rugby league. That was the essence of the breakaway from the repressive rugby union.

The best and most consistent performers have won prizes ranging from cash, watches, cars, holidays as well as the customary trophies, medals and saturation coverage in the media.

There's a colourful tale worth telling from the 1911-12 Kangaroo tour.

Australia's star halfback, **Chris McKivat**, was known for his unselfish play but in one tour game, against Coventry, the little captain decided to go it alone for a change.

A local businessman had offered an overcoat as prize for the first tryscorer. McKivat won it after a fabulous solo effort marked by a series of dummy passes, sidesteps and sprints through gaps in the defence.

'It's cold in England,' he explained later, 'and overcoats don't grow on trees.'

The early best and fairest awards series were, by and large, conducted by newspapers with a 10 pound player of the day award the common practice.

In later years, the now defunct Sydney afternoon newspaper, *The Sun*, put up a Ford car for its choice as player of the year.

In 1980 the rival *Daily Mirror* introduced the Dally M awards which were named in honour of the legendary Dally Messenger, one of the Australian game's pioneers.

The Dally Ms not only lauded the top player – and still do – but saluted the best in each of the nine field positions plus best coach, representative player and rookie of the season.

The **Rothman's Medal**, judged by the first grade referees and touch judges, became the definitive award and was first awarded to Cronulla's Terry Hughes in 1968.

Frank BURGE
Born: August 14, 1894.
Died: July 5, 1958.
Played: 1911-1927.
Clubs: Glebe, Grenfell, St George.
Position: Lock.
Weight: 13st 10lb (87kg).
Height: 6ft (182cm).
Tests: 13.
Career games: 213.
Career points: 858.

Man on Man
Frank Burge v Nik Kosef

FRANK Burge was regarded as a player way ahead of his time. He was one of the first players to recognise the value of pre-season training and he was often seen jogging from his home near the old Grace Brothers store in inner-Sydney Broadway to Coogee and back on a Sunday. Physical fitness coupled with a powerful personality allowed him to dominate the game during a 17-year career from 1911-27. At 6ft (182cm), Burge was

'Stumpy' Stevens and skipper **Steve Edge** *(left)* saw Parramatta ahead 15-10 by halftime.

The second half was an attacking extravaganza, with the ball sweeping from one end of the field to the other at breathtaking speed.

Parramatta led 19-18 late, before a Graham Eadie penalty goal edged the Sea Eagles ahead 20-19.

Finally, it was left to a field goal from Melrose to lock up the scores, with both teams earning a standing ovation as they left Cumberland for the final time.

Big Parramatta prop Bob O'Reilly dominated the game, taking most man of the match awards, but Manly's Eadie, Dorahy and Randall also put in stirring performances. 🏉

A host of great players including Tom Raudonikis, Graham Eadie, Mick Cronin (twice), Steve Rogers, Peter Sterling (twice), Wayne Pearce and Allan Langer had their names inscibed on the Rothman's Medal honour roll.

In 1997, the award was known as the Provan-Summons medal and Sydney City's Brad Fittler was a popular winner.

In 1998, the National Rugby League announced the **Dally M Medal**, sponsored by *The Daily Telegraph*, would be the code's official player of the year award.

Newcastle's Andrew Johns won in 1998 and 1999. 🏉

Birth of a club...

AUCKLAND WARRIORS

AUCKLAND Warriors entered the competition in 1995 with many expectations surrounding a team backed by an entire nation. The New Zealand side was boosted by overseas imports Greg Alexander, Phil Blake, Denis Betts and Andy Platt. The team lost their first game 25-22 against Brisbane but won two weeks later against Wests 46-12. They were stripped of those historic two points when Joe Vagana was sent on as an illegal fifth replacement. The incident came back to haunt the Warriors as they missed a place in the top eight on for and against averages. In their first year the team won 13 games and lost nine.

COLOURS: Blue and white are Auckland's representative colours. Red and green came from their first major sponsor, DB Bitter

NICKNAME: Warriors was overwhelming choice after a public competition.

---

a big man for his time and with abundant mobility, he established tryscoring records for a forward that may never be broken. With his size and training discipline it is not difficult to envisage Burge mixing it with modern day lock forwards like Nik Kosef. Size and mobility are attributes that Kosef has used to considerable advantage in his career with Manly, NSW and Australia throughout the 1990s.

Nik KOSEF

Born: June 6, 1974.
Played: Since 1992.
Club: Manly.
Position: Lock.
Weight: 15st 8lb (99kg).
Height: 6ft 2in (188cm).
Tests: 9.
Career games: 148.
Career points: 64.

THE CHAMPIONS
Premiers and runners up 1908-99

1908 **Souths** Easts	*1955* **Souths** Newtown
1909 **Souths** Balmain	*1956* **St George** Balmain
1910 **Newtown** Souths	*1957* **St George** Manly
1911 **Easts** Glebe	*1958* **St George** Wests
1912 **Easts** Glebe	*1959* **St George** Manly
1913 **Easts** Newtown	*1960* **St George** Easts
1914 **Souths** Newtown	*1961* **St George** Wests
1915 **Balmain** Glebe	*1962* **St George** Wests
1916 **Balmain** Souths	*1963* **St George** Wests
1917 **Balmain** Souths	*1964* **St George** Balmain
1918 **Souths** Wests	*1965* **St George** Souths
1919 **Balmain** Easts	*1966* **St George** Balmain
1920 **Balmain** Souths	*1967* **Souths** Canterbury
1921 **Norths** Easts	*1968* **Souths** Manly
1922 **Norths** Glebe	*1969* **Balmain** Souths
1923 **Easts** Souths	*1970* **Souths** Manly
1924 **Balmain** Souths	*1971* **Souths** St George
1925 **Souths** Wests	*1972* **Manly** Easts
1926 **Souths** University	*1973* **Manly** Cronulla
1927 **Souths** St George	*1974* **Easts** Canterbury
1928 **Souths** Easts	*1975* **Easts** St George
1929 **Souths** Newtown	*1976* **Manly** Parramatta
1930 **Wests** St George	*1977* **St George** Parramatta
1931 **Souths** Easts	*1978* **Manly** Cronulla
1932 **Souths** Wests	*1979* **St George** Canterbury
1933 **Newtown** St George	*1980* **Canterbury** Easts
1934 **Wests** Easts	*1981* **Parramatta** Newtown
1935 **Easts** Souths	*1982* **Parramatta** Manly
1936 **Easts** Balmain	*1983* **Parramatta** Manly
1937 **Easts** Souths, St George (tie)	*1984* **Canterbury** Parramatta
1938 **Canterbury** Easts	*1985* **Canterbury** St George
1939 **Balmain** Souths	*1986* **Parramatta** Canterbury
1940 **Easts** Canterbury	*1987* **Manly** Canberra
1941 **St George** Easts	*1988* **Canterbury** Balmain
1942 **Canterbury** St George	*1989* **Canberra** Balmain
1943 **Newtown** Norths	*1990* **Canberra** Penrith
1944 **Balmain** Newtown	*1991* **Penrith** Canberra
1945 **Easts** Balmain	*1992* **Brisbane** St George
1946 **Balmain** St George	*1993* **Brisbane** St George
1947 **Balmain** Canterbury	*1994* **Canberra** Canterbury
1948 **Wests** Balmain	*1995* **Canterbury** Manly
1949 **St George** Souths	*1996* **Manly** St George
1950 **Souths** Wests	*1997* **Newcastle** Manly
1951 **Souths** Manly	*1997* **Brisbane** Cronulla (*Super League*)
1952 **Wests** Souths	*1998* **Brisbane** Canterbury
1953 **Souths** St George	*1999* **Melbourne** St George-Illawarra
1954 **Souths** Newtown	

Ron COOTE
Born: 1944

20 FOLLOWED Johnny Raper as Australia's premier lock and suffered little in comparison. Long-striding attacking player and an exceptional cover defender, Coote achieved many of highest honours in game over 15 seasons. Emerged with crop of outstanding South Sydney juniors to help the Rabbitohs to four premierships in five years (1967-68, 1970-71). Transferred to Easts, 1972, and played in two more grand final-winning sides under coach Jack Gibson (1974-75). Captained Australia to victory in 1970 World Cup. Played over 250 matches at club level. 13 Tests (1967-74), Kangaroo 1967-68.

Frank BURGE
1894-1958

16 BIG man with high-running action and exceptional pace, Burge scored more tries than any forward in history of Australian game. Mainly a lock, he had ability to play second row or prop and specialised in breaking quickly from scrum to link with three-quarters. One of first to recognise need for physical fitness, Burge made regular road runs with footballing brothers Albert, Peter and Laidley. Scored 33 tries in 23 games on 1921-22 Kangaroo tour and holds Australian premiership record of eight tries in one match (1920). Scored 137 tries in 138 matches for Glebe. 13 Tests (1914-22), Kangaroo 1921-22.

Peter STERLING
Born: 1960

14 ONE of the dominant playmakers of 1980s, Sterling had ability to control proceedings like few before him. Astute mind, accurate kicking game and creative passing took him to great heights in 15-year career. Not overawed when thrown into first grade semi-final at 18, rapidly became integral part of Parramatta side that won four premierships in 1980s. Starred in consecutive undefeated Kangaroo tours 1982, 1986. Won Rothmans Medals, Dally M awards and Clive Churchill Medal and was man of match in four Origin games. 18 Tests (1982-88), Kangaroo 1982, 1986.

Duncan THOMPSON
1895-1980

19 REGARDED as a player way ahead of his time, Thompson's tactical mind and quick-thinking play often baffled his team-mates, let alone the opposition. Queensland-born, Thompson survived a bullet to his lung at Western Front in 1918 and returned home to represent Australia a year later. Joined North Sydney in 1920 and helped to inspire club's only premiership wins 1921-22. Returned to Queensland in 1924 where he helped State to dominant performances over former masters, NSW. Lightning fast from scrumbase, Thompson engineered bumper harvest of tries. 9 Tests (1919-24), Kangaroo 1921-22.

THE
Daily Telegraph

WE SELECT THE BEST OF THE CENTURY

Brian BEVAN
1924-1991

13 GREATEST tryscorer in league history, Bevan scored an astonishing 796 career tries in 695 appearances. Began with Easts in 1942, but lost to Australian game when he signed with Warrington in 1945. Freakish ability belied frail appearance. Reputedly learned devastating sidestep dodging telegraph poles in Oxford Street on his way home from SCG as child. Most famous try, once described as 'try of the century' in Wardonia Cup final in 1948 – ran 125 yards diagonally from corner to corner. Appeared in two winning Challenge Cup finals for Warrington. 16 matches for Other Nationalities (1949-55).

The Great 100

Arthur BEETSON
Born: 1945

18 FRONTROWER of unrivalled ability, Beetson was tough and skilful and one of the modern game's great personalities. Emerged from Roma in Queensland to forge remarkable career with Balmain and Easts before playing final seasons of club football with Parramatta. Debut for Australia against Great Britain, 1966, virtually winning Test in sparkling 40-minute display. Ball skills were at best when he captained Easts to premiership wins 1974-75, but best remembered for leading Queensland to victory in inaugural State of Origin match, 1980. 14 Tests (1966-74), Kangaroo 1973.

Wally PRIGG
1908-1980

17 GREATEST forward of country football, Prigg refused many offers to play in Sydney, preferring to remain in Newcastle. Transformed lock play by promoting close-passing and quick backing-up game. Notable 'firsts' include: first player to tour three times with Kangaroos, first Australian to score a try on French soil, first Novocastrian to captain Australia. Pioneer player Bill Cann rated Prigg the finest lock he had ever seen: 'He possessed two of the greatest assets for his job, an alert mind and the very best judgment'. 19 Tests (1929-38), Kangaroo 1929-30, 1933-34, 1937-38.

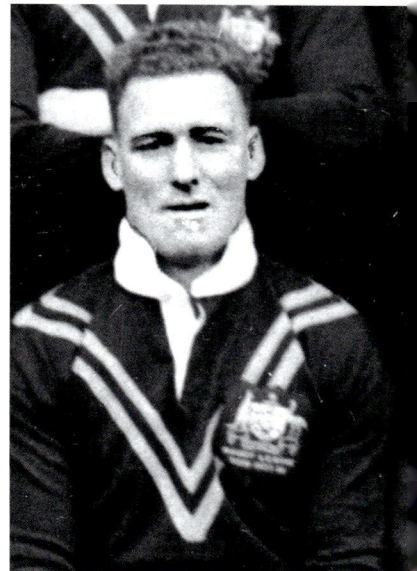

Mal MENINGA
Born: 1960

15 POWERHOUSE centre from Queensland, with astonishing list of accomplishments. Came to notice with blockbusting efforts in early Origin matches after kicking seven goals on debut (1980). Overcame series of career-threatening broken arms to achieve numerous landmarks. First player to make four Kangaroo tours and only man to captain Kangaroos twice. Played more Tests (45) and scored more points (272) than any other Australian. Holds records at Origin and club level. Captained Canberra to three premierships, retiring in triumph in 1994. 45 Tests (1982-94), Kangaroo 1982, 1986, 1990, 1994.

Harold HORDER
1894-1978

12 DAZZLING winger of early years, who scored at rate better than a try per game over 15-year career. South Sydney junior, rocketed to prominence with length-of-field try on first grade debut in 1912. Greatest feats include scoring 10 tries in space of three days for NSW in 1915, 35 tries on 1921-22 Kangaroo tour and record nine tries in four-Test series against NZ in 1919. Played in Norths' first two premiership-winning teams 1921-22, captaining 1921 side. Used pace, sidestep and swerve to bamboozle opponents. 13 Tests (1914-24), Kangaroo 1921-22.

Brian CARLSON
1933-1987

11 PRODUCT of Newcastle football, rated one of most naturally gifted of all players. Could play centre, wing or fullback with equal dexterity and represented Australia in all three. Powerfully built, Carlson was brilliant in attack – a tryscoring specialist who also possessed strong goalkicking skills. Scored nine tries in tour match in New Zealand in 1953. Represented Newcastle, City, Country, NSW, Queensland and Australia in 13 years at top level. Five overseas tours and played in World Cup campaigns of 1957 and 1960. 17 Tests (1952-61), Kangaroo 1952-53, 1959-60.

CHAPTER TEN

The Greats

BY PETER FRILINGOS

The way we were...

The Greats

TOP 10 AUSTRALIAN PLAYERS OF THE CENTURY

THE definition of impossible in rugby league would probably include the exercise of attempting to assess and then rank the talents of the game's masters.

Only two – Herbert 'Dally' Messenger and Clive Churchill – have been dubbed with the ultimate accolade of 'master' and by that test alone are entitled to be rated beside each other as the best the game has produced in this country.

If only it were that easy – decide between Messenger and Churchill for the premier position then take it from there with the help of contemporary reports, historical notes, eye-witness accounts and so on.

And when all physical information is digested, throw in that intangible factor called opinion.

There are players with bulging Test match portfolios who have not made *The Daily Telegraph's* The Great 100, so records at the game's elite level were only one of a series of areas to be considered in the determination of rankings.

So when it came down to naming the 10 best all-time players in Australia, the judging panel of Peter Frilingos, Ian Heads, David Middleton, Frank Stanton and Wally O'Connell was guided less by statistics than opinion.

Players from the last 20 years would otherwise have had an unfair advantage through their impressive representative resumes strengthened by numerous State of Origin appearances.

Origin football is now regarded by many as the equal of, or even superior to, Test matches and obviously players before 1980 did not have the chance to compete regularly at that level.

Even with the Origin factor taken into account it will be seen that only one player from that era, Wally Lewis, earned a place in the Top 10.

Golden age ... record-breaking Graeme Langlands

It's also interesting to note that the panel's choices included players from most of the decades since the game kicked off in Sydney in 1908.

That was simply the way the cards fell, it had nothing to do with making a conscious effort to nominate a player representing each era.

The 1960s, at least in the panel's judgment, turned out to be the golden age with the legendary Graeme Langlands, Reg Gasnier, John Raper and Ken Irvine making the Top 10.

And under those circumstances it's no coincidence that Langlands, Raper and Gasnier played together for St George during the club's world record 11 straight premierships from 1956 to 1966.

These men then are the stuff from which legends are made. The 10 greatest Australian players of all time.

Ken IRVINE

10

KEN 'Mongo' Irvine was one of those players who come along maybe once in a lifetime – a player who brought the crowd to its feet every time he touched the ball.

And after scoring 300 tries from 340 matches there were many spectators who made little use of their seats at venues all over the world.

In a career bursting with highlights the wing speedster, who died prematurely from leukemia in 1990 at the age of 50, will probably be best remembered for his role in Australia's Third Test win against Great Britain in 1962.

With the clock winding down and Great Britain leading 17-13 and looking like making a clean sweep of the series Irvine scored in the corner to make the score 17-16 with a kick to come.

Skipper Arthur Summons threw the ball to Irvine for the conversion kick even though he wasn't a regular kicker.

As Irvine placed the ball and stepped back to measure his walk-up referee Darcy Lawler said 'It won't go over like that, aim it more to the left' and Irvine took his advice and piloted the ball over the bar from near the sideline.

Lawler later denied he had made that comment but Irvine insisted it was right and often wrote about it in his adopted career as a sports journalist.

Irvine played with Norths from 1958 to 1971 without winning a premiership or even making a grand final.

However, those goals came in a rush when he joined Manly to win back-to-back titles in

Dave Brown congratulated by the man whose pointscoring record he broke, Dally Messenger

1972-73 to ring down a magnificent career at club and international level.

A lesser man would have called it quits on the 1967 Kangaroo tour – his third – when he suffered a serious leg injury in France that took almost a year to heal.

Some say Irvine was the fastest-ever player in league and, after he set the world professional sprint record at 9.3sec for 100 yards, it's hard to find his equal.

Once in a lifetime ... rugby league speed machine Ken Irvine

Ken IRVINE

Born: March 5, 1940. **Died:** Dec 22, 1990. **Played:** 1958-72.
Clubs: North Sydney, Manly. **Position:** Wing.
Tests: 31. **Career games:** 380.
Career points: 1256.
Career highlights: Toured three times with Kangaroos, scored most Test tries for Australia, most tries in premiership football (212), two premiership wins for Manly.

Dave BROWN

9

MODEST, genial Dave Brown was a relentless pointscorer sometimes described as 'rugby league's Bradman' in a career where records were established that may never be beaten.

The Eastern Suburbs goalkicking centre, who died at the age of 60 in 1974, still holds records for the most points on a Kangaroo tour (285 in 1933-34), most points in a first grade match (45 against Canterbury in 1938) and most tries in a season (38 in 1935).

Brown knew Dally Messenger and in the 1960s described Reg Gasnier as 'the greatest footballer I have seen'.

He was the jewel in the crown of the magnificent Easts teams of the 1930s after overcoming setbacks in his youth that would have ruined a lesser man.

As a child he lost the top of his right thumb in a gardening accident and at Waverley College aged 14 he severely injured his right arm in an accident with boiling water which left him with little use of two fingers.

Then in 1931 a strange illness left him completely bald, a traumatic event for an 18-year-old.

He was inspired to wear headgear after a teammate threw his wig out of a porthole en route to the 1933-34 Kangaroo tour.

In 1936 Brown became Australia's youngest Ashes captain at 23 years and 86 days (later beaten by Reg Gasnier) when he led the side to a 24-8 victory against Great Britain at the SCG.

Australia lost that series but Brown so impressed the Englishmen that he later signed a lucrative contract with Warrington.

Brown was a remarkable attacking player but his real strength was his ferocious tackling.

He was also an iron man who played in 32 games on the 1933-34 Kangaroo tour to equal the mark set by the great Newcastle lock Wally Prigg.

He was a much-loved and respected figure in rugby league and became NSWRL schools liaison officer in 1959.

Dave BROWN

Born: April 4, 1913. **Died:** February 24, 1974.
Career details (see page 170).
Career highlights: Australia's youngest Test captain, scored 285 points on 1933-34 Kangaroo tour, three premiership wins for Easts, premiership records for most points in one game (45) and most tries in a season (38).

‹ **161** ›

Birth of a club...

THE idea for a national rugby league team based in North Queensland surfaced in 1989 when 16,000 fans turned out to watch Brisbane play a National Panasonic Cup quarter-final in Townsville. By late 1992 a North Queensland team had been accepted into the Winfield Cup and on March 11, 1995 the Cowboys played their first game against the Sydney Bulldogs. They lost 32-16. In their first season 238,734 people attended their 11 home games. The side won only two games in their debut season.

COLOURS: Navy blue, yellow, white and grey were chosen as they depicted the North Queensland lifestyle and climate.

NICKNAME: The club board decided on Cowboys as it identified with the North Queensland beef and cattle industry and the outback.

1990-99

JUNE 30, 1990: Ten Souths players test positive to banned drugs following lightning raid by Australian Sports Drug Agency. One player is immediately dismissed.
JULY 23, 1990: NSWRL officially adopts controversial players' draft at board meeting in Sydney.
OCTOBER 27, 1990: Australia beaten 19-12 in first Test of Kangaroo tour at Wembley, the Kangaroos' first defeat since 1978.
NOVEMBER 10, 1990: Memorable last-minute try by Australian captain Mal Meninga levels Ashes series one-all in Old Trafford Test.
NOVEMBER 24, 1990: Australia secure Ashes with 14-0 win at Elland Road, Leeds.

Team man ... the 'human bullet' Vic Hey with his Wests contemporaries

Vic HEY

8 THEY called Vic Hey the 'human bullet' or the 'greatest five-eighth of all time'. At his peak in the late 1930s, Hey played for English club Leeds after being lured to England on a big-money deal that Australian clubs could not match.

Hey was a Western Suburbs boy who was promoted to first grade as a teenager and he became an important contributor to the Magpies' premierships in 1930 and 1934 and their runners-up result in 1932.

Back from the 1933-34 Kangaroo tour where he left a lasting impression on English clubs, Hey was going from strength to strength and in 1936 he was in Australia's side for the Ashes series.

After that season he said farewell to Australia and, after signing on with Leeds for £1250 a season, spent the next 11 years in England which included stints with Dewsbury and Hunslet.

While playing for Leeds the *Yorkshire Post* writer Alfred Drewery said of Hey: 'He is almost 13 stone of dynamic energy, as quick off the mark as a bullet and with a sidestep like a fairy.'

He led Leeds to consecutive Challenge Cup wins against Halifax in 1941 and again the following year.

Back in Australia as coach of Parramatta, he played for another season before quitting in his mid-30s because he found the grounds too hard after the lush English surfaces.

His crowning glory as a coach came in the Ashes

series of 1950 and 1954 when he led Australia to victories against the old enemy. In 1950 in the slush at the SCG Australia won the third Test when Ron Roberts scored that celebrated try on the only dry patch on the famous old ground.

It was Australia's first Ashes victory at home for 30 years and Australian skipper Clive Churchill called Hey his 'inspiration'.

Vic HEY

Born: November 18, 1912. **Died:** April 11, 1995. **Played:** 1933-49. **Clubs:** Western Suburbs, Toowoomba, Leeds, Dewsbury, Hunslet, Parramatta. **Position:** Five-eighth. **Tests:** 6. **Career games:** 307*. **Career points:** 427*. **Career highlights:** Toured with Kangaroos 1933-34, two Ashes series against England, played in first league match in France, one premiership win for Western Suburbs, two Challenge Cup victories for Leeds.
*Not including Toowoomba

Bob FULTON

7 BOB 'Bozo' Fulton combined athleticism, attacking genius and gamesmanship to mould a spectacular career as a centre and five-eighth between 1966 and 1979.

Fulton's style has often been compared to Dally Messenger's because they were both brilliant individualists specialising in scoring tries in seemingly impossible situations.

Testimony to his try-scoring prowess is the 147 premiership touchdowns he scored, fifth behind legendary winger Ken Irvine, Terry Lamb, Harold Horder and Andrew Ettingshausen.

Fulton would do anything to win and often used his wits and sometimes flippant approach to achieve that end.

A prime example came on the 1978 Kangaroo tour when Fulton led Australia against Great Britain in the second Test at Headingley, Leeds after the tourists had lost the first Test.

Struck in the chest by Great Britain prop Brian Lockwood, Fulton crashed to the turf as though struck in the head by a stiff-arm tackle.

Referee Billy Thompson immediately dismissed Lockwood and playing a man short Great Britain were no match for the Australians, losing 14-6.

Fulton was so convincing that Australian trainer Alf Richards raced on to the field certain he was seriously injured.

In the third Test Fulton's acting ability was not needed as he shredded the Great Britain defence to set up Australia's 15-5 win to clinch the series.

Manly would never have won the 1973 grand final against Cronulla without Fulton's individual brilliance in what ranks as the most vicious premiership decider on record.

Twice when the chips were down Fulton blew the Cronulla defence apart with surging bursts through tackles and around groping defenders to ensure the Sea Eagles won back-to-back titles.

Whether it was for Manly, Easts, NSW or Australia, Fulton always played with the same level of intensity – he simply detested the thought of losing and that philosophy motivated a highly successful career both as a player and a coach.

Bob FULTON
Born: December 1, 1947.
Played: 1965-79.
Clubs: Wollongong Wests, Manly, Warrington, Easts. **Position:** Five-eighth, Centre. **Tests:** 20.
Career games: 361*.
Career points: 907*.
Career highlights: Toured twice with Kangaroos, captained 1978 touring side, three premiership wins for Manly, including one as captain, 147 tries at club level.
*Not including Wollongong Wests

Manly's attacking genius Bob Fulton

1990-99

MARCH 15, 1991: Unlimited interchange rule attracts hail of protest after Manly-Brisbane match features 41 separate interchanges. Rule amended after just one month.
APRIL 3, 1991: NSWRL general manager **John Quayle** reveals Canberra in breach of salary cap when they won 1990 title. Financial crisis threatens club.
JUNE 12, 1991: The 'king' of Origin, Wally Lewis, announces retirement from rep football after leading Queensland to another series win.
SEPTEMBER 6, 1991: League's draft defeated by unanimous vote of full bench of Federal Court.
SEPTEMBER 22, 1991: In their 25th season, Penrith break through for first grand final victory.
NOVEMBER 7, 1991: Channel Nine win television rights to cover game for three years at cost of $24 million.
APRIL 6, 1992: All-time great Peter Sterling announces retirement after recurrence of serious shoulder injury.
MAY 18, 1992: Auckland admitted to 1995 premiership. Teams from North Queensland, Perth and South Queensland admitted later to 20-team competition.
JUNE 21, 1992: Tragic death of 20-year-old Penrith player Ben Alexander in car accident.
AUGUST 23, 1992: Brisbane play last match at Lang Park, then move to 60,000 capacity ANZ Stadium in 1993.
SEPTEMBER 27, 1992: Brisbane become first interstate side to win premiership, beating St George 28-8.
OCTOBER 18, 1992: World record crowd for league international of 73,631 watch Australia beat Great Britain 10-6 in World Cup final.

Birth of a club...

EX-SUPER League boss John Ribot was given the task of setting up and part-owning a rugby league franchise in Victoria.

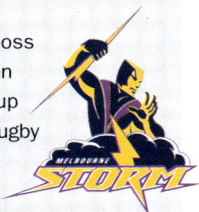

The Storm entered the competition in 1998 when the game was unified once again.

The club played their first game against Illawarra on March 14 at WIN Stadium, scoring an upset 14-12 victory.

The debut side was made up of players from nine different teams, including six from the defunct Hunter Mariners.

The team performed beyond expectations, winning a premiership in their second season.

COLOURS: Blue and white, the colours of Victoria. Purple and gold were added after consultation with fashion designers

NICKNAME: The Storm was chosen after a reader competition in Melbourne's *Herald-Sun* newspaper.

I was there...

'Reg Gasnier was the most exciting centre I ever saw. 'Gaz' could set himself to do whatever he wanted to do on a football field – and do it. He could have played anywhere in the backline and made a good job of it. He regularly made unwinnable games winnable. He timed his runs to perfection and rarely ran at a man. It was always into open territory. His acceleration was legendary, the catalyst for dozens of tries. A brilliant individual, he also looked after his wingers with superb passes. Reg Gasnier stood out in an age when there were plenty of top-class centres. He was one of a kind.'

St George legend **Norm Provan**

Wally LEWIS

6 ONLY one player in the game's history has had a bronze statue erected at the scene of his greatest triumphs. Under the circumstances it's hardly surprising Queensland and Australia's Wally Lewis was nicknamed 'King Wally' or the 'Emperor of Lang Park'.

The statue of Lewis stands at the southern end of Suncorp Stadium (nee Lang Park) presiding over State of Origin matches, just as he did as a player in that arena from 1980 to 1991. Lewis played in the first State of Origin game in 1980 and as Queensland's captain in 30 of his 31 Origin appearances dominated interstate football like no other player.

The fact that he also captained Australia on the unbeaten 1986 Kangaroo tour on the way to representing his country 33 times to some people is merely a sidebar to his glittering career with the Maroons.

Lewis's spectacular talent on the football field was matched by his penchant for controversy fuelled by his quixotic tilts at officialdom.

That attitude often divided the league world into pro and con Lewis factions which he often used to motivate himself and his Queensland players to do battle with NSW.

He made his Test debut against New Zealand in 1981 but failed to impress some critics and after being named vice-captain of the 1982 Kangaroos missed a place in the Test sides with Parramatta's Brett Kenny winning the No 6 jumper.

That was the start of a number of conspiracy theories Lewis fomented, including his omission from the 1990 Kangaroo squad over a disputed injury ruling by team doctor Nathan Gibbs.

Before missing that trip Lewis had captained Australia in 23 consecutive Tests and was without peer as the world's leading player.

He said at the time he was ruled out of the tour because he would have surpassed records by Clive Churchill (captain for 24 Tests) and Reg Gasnier (played 36 Tests) – a claim debunked by the ARL and the national selectors.

Lewis managed to combine the bulk of a second-rower with his natural gifts of speed and immense strength and the ability to control games like few players before him or since.

Wally LEWIS

Born: December 1, 1959. **Played:** 1978-92.
Clubs: Brisbane Valleys, Wakefield Trinity, Wynnum-Manly, Brisbane Broncos, Gold Coast. **Position:** Five-eighth. **Tests:** 33. **Career games:** 398. **Career points:** 683. **Career highlights:** Toured with two undefeated Kangaroo outfits, captain of 1986 team, captained Australia in 23 Tests, captained Queensland in 30 out of 31 State of Origin matches, man of match eight times at Origin level.

One of a kind ... the man who "invented" cover defence Johnny Raper and (below) *that* bowler hat

John RAPER

5 JOHNNY Raper was and is one of a kind, on and off the rugby league field.No player in the history of the game was able to burn the candle at both ends then play devastating football in the first 10 minutes of a match and remain just as formidable in the final 10 minutes.

Raper had two seasons with the now defunct Newtown club from 1957 before joining St George and playing 11 seasons at Kogarah during the club's golden era.

Apart from his obvious athleticism and sheer ability, Raper was a rugby league revolutionary who set the standard for lock forward play that every player since has attempted to emulate.

Raper invented the art of cover-defending and his sweeping runs across field to cut down flying wingers with horizontal tackles became the centrepiece of his amazing repertoire.

From early on, Raper became a fitness fanatic, reckoning if he still had plenty of energy in the last few minutes of a game his opponents would likely be out of petrol.

And, because he liked to play just as hard off the field as on, his fitness credo was to help maintain his position as Australia's most admired performer for 13 years.

Testimony to his talent came early in his career with Newtown when he consistently played lock, five-eighth, centre and second row.

In his first year with St George in 1959, the season Saints didn't lose a game, Raper played five-eighth in the grand final.

It was to be the first of eight grand finals with Saints and his performance earned him a place on the 1959-60 Kangaroo tour along with a host of other young hopefuls including Reg Gasnier and Ken Irvine.

Raper made the second of his three Kangaroo tours in 1963-64 and in the second Test at Swinton the league world saw Raper at his best.

He didn't score as Australia sealed the series with a 50-12 win over Great Britain but created most of the side's 12 tries with a passing and running display said to have been one of the most dominant witnessed at that level.

Four years later he was to have his finest moment in the international arena when he captained Australia to Ashes victory in the third Test, also at Swinton, while carrying a cheekbone fracture.

It was on that tour that Raper became known as the 'Man in the Bowler Hat' after being accused of striding through the snow in the English village of Ilkley wearing nothing but a bowler hat.

Raper was not the culprit but was happy to wear the tag and has since used it to his advantage commercially.

Johnny RAPER

Born: April 12, 1939. **Played:** 1957-74. **Clubs:** Newtown, St George, Newcastle Wests, Kurri Kurri. **Position:** Lock (early career at five-eighth). **Tests:** 33. **Career games:** 400. **Career points:** 318. **Career highlights:** Three Kangaroo tours, starring performance in record 50-12 Test win against Great Britain (1963), captained Australia to 1968 World Cup win, eight premiership wins for St George.

1990-99

MARCH 28, 1993: Bumper crowd of 51,517 turn out for Brisbane's first match at ANZ. Premiers beaten 12-8 by Parramatta.

SEPTEMBER 24, 1993: Sydney wins Olympic bid, meaning league will at last have 80,000-plus capacity stadium.

MARCH 2, 1994: Rumours of breakaway competition reported following deteriorating relations between NSWRL and Brisbane.

MAY 23, 1994: Down 12-4, Queensland stage gripping fightback in last five minutes of opening Origin match with **Mark Coyne** scoring match-winner in final minute.

JUNE 8, 1994: Australian record crowd of 87,161 turn out at MCG for second Origin match. NSW win dour game 14-0.

JULY 26, 1994: News of 'Super League' competition surfaces. NSWRL general manager John Quayle concedes privately run competition feasible.

SEPTEMBER 11, 1994: Special police task force investigates allegations of match fixing involving Souths. Rabbitohs cleared after six-week investigation.

SEPTEMBER 25, 1994: Canberra captain Mal Meninga ends club career on winning note when he leads Raiders to 36-12 win over Canterbury, their third premiership. Meninga makes history when named captain of Kangaroos (first player to tour four times and first player to lead two tours).

OCTOBER 20, 1994: ARL chairman **Ken Arthurson** warns Brisbane they face expulsion from premiership over Super League involvement.

FEBRUARY 6, 1995: All 20 premiership clubs reject News Limited proposal for a Super League in 1996. Intervention of media magnate Kerry Packer changes course of meeting.

The way we were...

1995: Pay TV arrives in Australia. Australian film *Babe* becomes huge box office hit. **Pope John Paul II** makes first Australian visit in nine years.

1996: Englishman Peter Ryan appointed NSW Police Commissioner. Thirty-five people die in Port Arthur massacre, gunman Martin Bryant arrested. Australia wins nine gold, nine silver and 23 bronze medals at Atlanta Olympics. Ivan Milat found guilty of murdering seven backpackers and given life sentence.

1997: World stock markets in turmoil as Asian currencies plunge. **Diana, Princess of Wales**, dies in car accident in Paris. Unmanned US spacecraft lands on Mars. Martina Hingis, 16, wins three of the four Grand Slam singles titles. John Denver dies in plane crash.

The Daily Telegraph
SPECIAL EDITION
DIANA DIES

1990-99

MARCH 10, 1995: Expanded 20-team ARL competition kicks off with Brisbane playing Auckland at Ericsson Stadium. North Queensland, South Queensland and Perth Reds make competition debuts.

MARCH 30-31, 1995: Onset of ARL-Super League war. News Limited launches court action against ARL and begins lightning raids in Perth, Townsville, Brisbane, Canberra and Sydney signing players to lucrative SL contracts.

APRIL 2, 1995: Backed by Kerry Packer, the ARL respond to the News raids by signing more than 50 players to inflated contracts.

Dally MESSENGER

4 RUGBY league may not have established itself so quickly early on if Herbert 'Dally' Messenger had decided against switching to the new code from rugby union.

Messenger was a freak footballer, a centre whose ingenuity and ability to produce the unorthodox made him a class apart from all other players.

Fans flocked to see every game he played because often he would beat the whole field with a dazzling run or kick-and-chase to amaze both spectators and opponents.

Messenger played the first league games against A H Baskerville's New Zealand All Golds and so impressed the Kiwi management they asked him to join their tour to England.

He agreed to tour and became a sensation by scoring 146 points – over 100 more than any other member of the team.

The following year Messenger captained Australia on the first Kangaroo tour of 1908-09 and was the new code's first Test captain on Australian soil in 1910.

So magnetic was his pulling power that when the first Kangaroo tour ran into financial difficulties in England, signs reading 'Messenger is playing today' outside grounds ensured full houses.

It was said his ability as a goalkicker and his speed and agility attracted a £1500 offer from soccer club Tottenham Hotspur, the rough equivalent of $1 million today.

He declined the offer and later scored a try in the second Test of that 1908 tour, later described this way by an English sportswriter:

'Messenger was the hero, securing the ball in midfield the Australian captain dodged, swerved and beat man after man. It seemed an impossible feat for him to get through but player after player fell in attempting to tackle him and Messenger finished a glorious exhibition by placing the ball between the goal posts.'

A picture of Messenger hangs in the NSW Leagues Club with no name inscribed below. The caption simply reads 'The Master'.

Dally MESSENGER

Born: April 12, 1883. **Died:** November 24, 1959. **Played:** 1907-13. **Club:** Eastern Suburbs. **Position:** Centre. **Tests:** 10 (7 for Australia, 3 for New Zealand). **Career games:** 140. **Career points:** 998. **Career highlights:** Only player to tour with the Kiwis and Kangaroos, captained Australia in first two Tests against Great Britain, three premiership wins for Easts, rugby league's first true champion.

Reg GASNIER

3 TAGGED 'Puff the Magic Dragon' and the 'Prince of Centres' for his breathtaking exploits on the field, Reg Gasnier has an aura as a champion centre for St George and Australia as strong today as it was between 1959 and 1967.

Gasnier played only a handful of games for St George in 1959 before being selected for NSW and Australia.

Testimony to his genius came early that year when he had actually played more games for NSW and Australia than for St George.

Gasnier was one of a kind – no other player had his astonishing acceleration and body swerve and chances are his like will never be seen again.

His reputation preceded him in England on the 1959-60 Kangaroo tour and fans waiting in the biting cold at Widnes for his first appearance were soon left in no doubt he was a special player.

The first time Gasnier touched the ball was when he scooped up a dropped pass 60m away from the Widnes line.

With his head back in trademark style Gasnier effortlessly accelerated, swerved through a gap then dashed away under the posts.

He scored three tries that night and he backed up with another three against Oldham before scoring a treble in his Test debut against Great Britain at Swinton.

There was a touch of magic about all three tries but it was his creation of a try for winger Brian Carlson which led critics to speculate they had seen the most finely-crafted Test try ever.

Gasnier broke the line inside his own quarter, dummied and almost imperceptibly changed his pace before giving Carlson a clear run to the line.

Gasnier went on to play 36 Tests and probably his finest hour came in the second Test at Swinton on the 1963-64 tour that saw Australia clinch the series 2-0.

After scoring three tries in the first Test he produced two slashing touchdowns as Australia blew Great Britain away 50-12.

Reg GASNIER

Born: May 12, 1939. **Played:** 1959-67. **Club:** St George. **Position:** Centre. **Tests:** 36. **Career games:** 233. **Career points:** 719. **Career highlights:** Three Kangaroo tours including one as captain, hat-trick of tries on Ashes debut, six premiership wins with St George, 127 tries in 125 games for Saints.

The magical Dragon Reg Gasnier

1990-99

APRIL 6, 1995: Great Britain and New Zealand leagues isolate the ARL internationally by signing with SL. Pacific nations Papua New Guinea and Fiji soon follow suit.

MAY 15, 1995: A team of virtually unknown Queenslanders triumph 2-0 in the opening Origin match at the SFS. Coach Paul Vautin lifts the Maroons to stunning series cleansweep.

MAY 23, 1995: Canterbury players Jarrod McCracken and Jim Dymock join teammates Dean Pay and Jason Smith in turning backs on SL contracts.

SEPTEMBER 24, 1995: Canterbury (playing as the Sydney Bulldogs) complete remarkable year when they defeat Manly 17-4 in grand final.

SEPTEMBER 25, 1995: Justice James Burchett, in Federal Court, hears opening arguments in the ARL-News Limited case, which will decide control of rugby league in Australia.

OCTOBER 28, 1995: Australian side depleted by absence of Super League-aligned players triumph 16-8 over England in the final of the Centenary World Cup in England.

JANUARY 22, 1996: NSW Government announce plans for a 110,000 capacity, $463 million **Olympic Stadium** at Homebush Bay.

FEBRUARY 23, 1996: SL's challenge to club loyalty contracts is ruled out of order by Justice Burchett. Orders banning SL until 2000 are formalised.

I was there...

'Dave Brown's greatest strength was his ability to stay on his feet. He was very rarely caught with the ball. He just knew the precise moment to pass and invariably it was to a teammate in a better position. He had plenty of speed and the ability to beat his man a number of ways. Brown was a freakish pointscorer in his own right but those who played around him scored more than their share of tries. He was inspirational in those wonderful Easts teams of the 1930s and his bald head made him a huge personality wherever he played.'

Former top player and league broadcasting icon **Frank Hyde**

1990-99

MARCH 22, 1996: SL clubs forfeit opening round of ARL competition as rebel players consider their options. Six matches are scrapped.

MAY 23, 1996: SL appeal begins before full bench of Federal Court.

OCTOBER 4, 1996: Full bench of Federal Court unanimously overturn Justice Burchett's decision to ban Super League, freeing way for rebel competition in 1997.

Graeme LANGLANDS

2 CLIVE Churchill once described Graeme Langlands as the greatest all-round player he had seen. Praise like that from 'The Little Master', the game's number one player, says it all about the skinny kid from Wollongong who became an Australian and St George legend.

It was only fitting this year that Langlands was elevated to the same level as Churchill when, along with Wally Lewis, he became one of the game's six Immortals.

'Changa' Langlands got his first big break in 1962 when Les Johns pulled out of the Country Firsts team to meet City through injury.

His performance in that game sparked a bidding war between St George and Manly and while the Sea Eagles offered more money he signed on the dotted line with the famous red and whites.

Thus began an enduring love affair between a champion player and a great club which was to last for 14 seasons.

Langlands joined Saints towards the end of their world record 11 straight titles (1956-66) but he was as much a part of the St George legend as Raper, Gasnier, Provan and Walsh.

Capable of playing anywhere in the backline at any level of football, Langlands had a unique right-foot sidestep that left the game's best tacklers all over the world clutching thin air.

Blistering pace, a silky-smooth running action, prolific goalkicking skills and a venomous desire to win completed a world-class package.

He went on to play 227 games for Saints, scoring 1554 points from 86 tries and 648 goals.

He played 34 Tests in a 13-year international career (1963-75), scoring 17 tries and 69 goals for 189 points.

In the second Test at Swinton in 1963, won 50-12 by Australia to wrap up the Ashes series, Langlands scored a record 20 points from two tries and seven goals – a mark that stood until Michael O'Connor's 22 points at Old Trafford in 1986.

Touring three times with the Kangaroos to England and France he was Australia's captain-coach on the last tour in 1973 but had to hand over the fullback job to Manly rookie Graham Eadie after injuring his hand.

He played in three World Cup series – 1968, 1972 and 1975 – captaining the last two.

In the days before State of Origin football Langlands played 33 games for NSW, scoring 137 points from 19 tries and 40 goals.

Cast aside by the selectors during the 1974 Ashes series in Australia he made a triumphant comeback to lead Australia to victory at the SCG in the third Test.

On the way to beating Great Britain 22-18, Langlands became the first player to top 100 points in Ashes Tests and was chaired from the field by teammates with the crowd chanting 'Changa ... Changa'.

A wayward pain-killing needle hit a nerve in his groin before the 1975 grand final, making him little more than a passenger against Eastern Suburbs.

That problem highlighted the injured champion's decision to wear white boots as the Roosters ran up a record 38-0 scoreline.

It was not quite the end of a glittering career but a sad footnote for a player whose place in the pantheon of heroes can never be denied.

Graeme LANGLANDS

Born: October 2, 1941. **Played:** 1962-76. **Clubs:** Wollongong, St George.
Position: Fullback, Centre. **Tests:** 34.
Career games: 320*. **Career points:** 2120*.
Career highlights: Three Kangaroo tours including one as captain, 45 Test and World Cup matches, four premiership wins with St George, record 1554 points for Saints.
*Not including Wollongong

Enduring love affair ... an airborne Graeme Langlands scores a spectacular try against Parramatta at the SCG

Greatest all-round champion... 'The Little Master', South Sydney's Clive Churchill

Clive CHURCHILL

1

'No player, not even Dally Messenger, could have improved on the display of Churchill.' That comment came from leading official John Quinlan who had followed the code closely since its inception.

Quinlan was speaking after watching Churchill play in a club game against Newtown in 1952 and his thoughts on the champion fullback were to be repeated by many others in Australia, England and New Zealand.

Former ARL chairman Harry 'Jersey' Flegg first saw Churchill play at the age of 12 in a schoolboys representative match at the SCG.

Churchill had come to town from Newcastle and the chairman said: 'I see a youngster I predict will one day become an international and captain Australia in Test football.'

Many years later after Flegg's prediction had become reality the chairman upped the ante in praising Churchill.

'Churchill was the greatest all-round champion the rugby league code has known,' Flegg said.

Dubbed 'The Little Master' because Messenger was 'The Master' in the game's early days, Churchill was much more than a tough, though diminutive, fullback renowned for his speed, agility and courage.

Churchill revolutionised fullback play by injecting himself into the attack to make the extra man and set up wingers headed by Ian Moir, his partner at Souths and for Australia.

The skinny kid from Newcastle played 99 consecutive representative games before being dropped in controversial circumstances, made four Kangaroo tours as a player and one as coach and captained Australia to Ashes series victories in 1950 and 1954.

Whether it was tackling rampaging forwards head-on and driving them backwards, kicking goals from seemingly impossible positions or producing touches of genius to win games, Churchill was unique.

Former Test forward Bernie Purcell says of his Souths teammate Churchill from the fabulous 1950s sides that he always managed to come up with something different.

'I remember one game when he had to retrieve the ball in-goal from a kick with four opposition players chasing him across the line,' Purcell recalled.

'Churchill scooped up the ball and, just when they were about to tackle him in-goal, he wrapped one arm around a goal post and swung around it full circle.

'The chasers were so mesmerised by the event that they just stood there with their mouths open while Churchill charged back upfield.'

In 1955, with Souths coming from near last at the end of the first round in pursuit of their third straight title, Churchill broke his wrist playing against Manly.

Because Souths could not afford to lose another game and hope to make the grand final, Churchill had a painkilling injection at halftime and convinced the club doctor to fashion a makeshift splint from paddle pop sticks and the cardboard cover of an exercise book.

He played through the game with one arm hanging limply by his side yet kicked the winning conversion from the sideline. An inspired Souths went on to win the competition and help cement the Churchill legend.

Clive CHURCHILL

Born: Jan 21, 1927. **Died:** Aug 9, 1985. **Played:** 1946-61. **Clubs:** Central Newcastle, South Sydney, Norths Brisbane, Moree. **Position:** Fullback. **Tests:** 34. **Career games:** 298*. **Career points:** 412*. **Career highlights:** Captained Australia to first Ashes win in 30 years (1950), 24 Tests as captain, toured three times with Kangaroos as player, 99 consecutive representative games, five premiership wins with Souths.
*****Not including Central Newcastle, Norths Brisbane, Moree**

1990-99

NOVEMBER 11, 1996: John Quayle resigns as chief executive of NSWRL and ARL and is followed soon after by NSWRL and ARL chairman Ken Arthurson. Former Balmain hooker **Neil Whittaker** succeeds Quayle.

MARCH 1, 1997: SL competition kicks off with matches in Brisbane and Townsville.

MAY 19, 1997: NSW outlast Queensland 23-22 in final of SL's Tri-series. The 104-minute, extra-time, marathon is longest game of rep football ever played.

JUNE 11, 1997: NSW wrap up ARL Origin series with 15-14 win over Queensland at MCG.

AUGUST 31, 1997: After only three seasons South Queensland Crushers play final match, thrashing Wests 39-18.

SEPTEMBER 17, 1997: SL announce new Victorian franchise to be known as Melbourne Storm.

SEPTEMBER 28, 1997: Newcastle perform grand final miracle when try to winger **Darren Albert** in final seconds secures 22-16 victory over Manly. A week earlier Brisbane down Cronulla 26-8 in SL grand final.

NOVEMBER 5, 1997: League world rocked by death of high-profile former international Peter Jackson.

DECEMBER 19, 1997: Historic series of meetings at SFS brings peace deal between ARL and SL and National Rugby League is formed. SL clubs Hunter Mariners and Perth Reds disbanded to produce 20-team competition for 1998.

The way we were...

1998: Violence escalates in Kosovo, Yugoslavia. President Clinton admits relationship with **Monica Lewinsky**, Starr report released. Six sailors die in Sydney-Hobart yacht race. Banned human growth hormone found in Chinese swimmer's baggage at Sydney Airport. Cricketers Shane Warne and Mark Waugh admit accepting money from Indian bookmaker during 1994 tour of Pakistan and Sri Lanka.

1999: Sydney battered by hail in Australia's worst natural disaster. Kosovo refugees arrive in Australia. Tony Lockett breaks Gordon Coventry's all-time AFL goal record. Australia wins cricket World Cup. GST bill passes through Parliament. Australian troops lead UN peace-keeping force to East Timor after independence vote.

I was there...

'To many, Johnny Raper was the greatest player rugby league has known and it was a pleasure to be the man who eventually succeeded him at Test level. We roomed together on a Kangaroo tour and that was an experience I'll never forget. He was a great role model for youngsters: he played the game fair, he was a brilliant cover defender and support player, and he had the knack of being able to control the play. I was quite a few years younger but he taught me a lot and I owe him heaps.'

Souths and Easts great **Ron Coote**

Man on Man
Dave Brown v Terry Hill

THE playing styles of 1930s idol Dave Brown and modern-day international Terry Hill typify the extremes of the old game and the new. Brown and Hill both played in the centres, both represented their country in nine Test matches and both wore the Tricolours of Eastern Suburbs. That is where any comparison begins and ends. Brown was a footballing artist, a master of positional play, whose all round skills made him one of the game's greats. Hill achieves his objectives in a completely different manner. Where Brown's game was built on finesse, Hill uses power to achieve his ends. Size, strength and speed are the bywords of the modern game and Hill is blessed with these attributes.

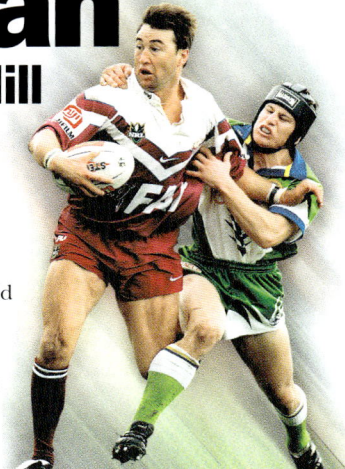

Dave BROWN
Born: April 4, 1913.
Died: February 24, 1974.
Played: 1930-41.
Clubs: Easts, Warrington.
Position: Centre.
Weight: 14st (89kg).
Height: 5ft 10in (178cm).
Tests: 9. **Career games:** 254.
Career points: 1502.

Terry HILL
Born: January 22, 1972.
Played: Since 1990.
Clubs: Souths, Easts, Wests, Manly.
Position: Centre.
Weight: 15st 10lb (100kg).
Height: 6ft 1in (186cm).
Tests: 9. **Career games:** 216.
Career points: 380.

WHAT A GAME!
NORTHS v EASTS 1921

NORTH Sydney's team that won the club's only premierships in 1921 and 1922 *(pictured opposite)* are recognised among the greatest club sides in history.

The star-studded Norths outfit had a powerful pack of forwards, a crafty halfback in Duncan Thompson and two legendary wingers in Harold Horder and Cec Blinkhorn.

Early in the 1921 season, Norths faced a test of their premiership credentials against a classy Eastern Suburbs side. It was round six and the stage was set for a classic encounter at the Sydney Cricket Ground, with both teams coming into the match undefeated.

The game was the talk of the town all week and a crowd of 44,818 – the first crowd in excess of 40,000 in the code's history for a club game – poured into the ground on Saturday afternoon.

The game began with a series of kicking duels, with the Tricolours fullback 'Snowy' Rigney landing an early field goal.

But Norths were keen to capitalise on their pace out wide and it wasn't long before Thompson broke away, sending Blinkhorn over. That put the Bears ahead 3-2 but two penalty goals to Easts winger Rex Norman gave Easts a 6-3 halftime lead.

After the break he added another goal before Thompson put Norths within striking distance with a penalty goal, making the score 8-5 and setting the stage for a thrilling finish.

Norths attacked in waves for the final 20 minutes, only to be repelled by last-ditch Easts defence.

In the final minute, Norths finally found the try they had worked so hard to score.

Secondrower Alf Faull burst through, sending Horder into the clear. Horder juggled the pass for

Team of the Decade...
1990-1999

BY the 1990s, league had evolved into a game of power and pace. At elite level, the game's exponents were finely tuned and highly skilled athletes. This team presents a mouth-watering blend of the game's finest qualities. The raw power of players like Sailor, Clyde, Sironen and Lindner, the high artistry of Brasher, Ettingshausen and Renouf and genius of men such as Daley, Fittler and Langer ensured Australia remained unchallenged as the leading force in world league. Laying the foundation were the 'hard yards' men, players who drove their bodies beyond the call of duty.

Laurie Daley

Fullback: Tim BRASHER (Balmain, Souths).
Wingers: Andrew ETTINGSHAUSEN (Cronulla), WENDELL SAILOR (Brisbane, Leeds).
Centres: Laurie DALEY (Canberra), Steve RENOUF (Brisbane).
Five-eighth: Brad FITTLER (Penrith, Sydney City).
Halfback: Allan LANGER (Brisbane).
Lock: Bradley CLYDE (Canberra, Canterbury).
Secondrowers: Paul SIRONEN (Balmain, Villeneuve), Bob LINDNER (Wests, Illawarra, Oldham).
Frontrowers: Glenn LAZARUS (Canberra, Brisbane, Melbourne), Paul HARRAGON (Newcastle).
Hooker: Steve WALTERS (Canberra, Nth Queensland, Newcastle).

over 10 metres, finally knocking it backwards.

Hooker George Green, in support, scooped up the loose ball and crawled two metres to the line, levelling the scores at 8-all.

Horder had the chance to win the game for Norths after the siren but his sideline conversion swung just wide of the posts.

The match confirmed both teams' status as the clubs to beat for the title, with Norths going on to take the honours and Easts finishing runners-up.

1990-99

MARCH 13, 1998: NRL competition commences. Brisbane beat Manly 22-6 in opener before 39,000 fans at ANZ Stadium

APRIL 24, 1998: Australia play first fully-fledged international since 1994, but are beaten 22-16 by NZ in Auckland.

JUNE 12, 1998: Game rocked by drugs scandal when Newcastle's Robbie O'Davis and then Wayne Richards, Adam MacDougall and Melbourne's prop Rodney Howe return positive samples.

AUGUST 22, 1998: Gold Coast and Adelaide play final premiership matches.

SEPTEMBER 23, 1998: St George and Illawarra announce historic first joint venture. NRL prepares 17-team draw for 1999.

SEPTEMBER 27, 1998: Brisbane win first NRL premiership, beating gallant Canterbury side 38-12.

MARCH 6, 1999: World record league crowd of 104,583 attend double-header at Stadium Australia to launch NRL.

APRIL 28, 1999: Brisbane captain Allan Langer announces shock retirement. Paul Harragon, Glenn Lazarus, Steve Walters and Paul Langmack follow suit.

JULY 27, 1999: Balmain and Wests football club members vote overwhelmingly to form joint venture for 2000 season.

SEPTEMBER 26, 1999: World record crowd broken for second time when 107,961 attend grand final at Stadium Australia. In only second season, Melbourne stun St George-Illawarra 20-18.

OCTOBER 9, 1999: Manly members vote to form joint venture with insolvent North Sydney Bears.

OCTOBER 15, 1999: South Sydney ejected from competition after NRL release final premiership criteria standings.

TEAM OF THE CENTURY

FOR THE RECORD

RUGBY League's growth in Australia has been documented throughout the century by a media with an insatiable appetite.

Newspapers in the pioneer years chronicled the first steps of the brash, rebel professional code which dominated headlines after breaking away from rugby union.

It became the working man's game and league's new batch of heroes and their deeds filled countless column inches.

The first radio broadcast was made in 1924, bringing the game's action and excitement to the masses with a brand new immediacy.

In 1953 legendary caller **Frank Hyde** made his league debut on the airwaves with his colourful broadcasts from around the suburbs, interstate and eventually the world.

Hyde's trademark description of goalkicks – 'it's long enough, high enough, if it's straight, it's there. Straight between the posts ...' – was done to cater for blind listeners.

Hyde did not have the match-calling caper all to himself.

His great friend Ernest 'Tiger' Black had a strong following on 2KY and as the years rolled on, ex-referee Col Pearce starred behind the mike.

That trio were succeeded by the likes of John O'Reilly (2BL), Ray Warren, Greg Hartley, Peter Peters (2GB), and modern callers Ray Hadley (2UE) and Peter Wilkins (2BL).

SELECTING the finest 13 Australian players of the 20th Century is a near impossible task. Our panel of judges were charged with this onerous responsibility as part of their selection of the game's Great 100 players.

Each judge independently ranked his leading 100 players in order and the votes were pooled to produce the final list of Australia's greatest 100 players of the century.

From these rankings we determined the Team of the Century.

Using the rankings as the basis, the selection of the top fullback, the top hooker or the top halfback was a formality.

The position went to the player ranked highest in the top 100.

The difficulty arose when high-ranking players with utility value such as Graeme Langlands, Brian Carlson, Frank Burge and Ron Coote were involved.

Langlands, for instance, was probably better known as a fullback, but his displays at centre on the 1963-64 Kangaroo tour mean he could cover two positions.

But would his abilities as a centre be enough to earn him a place ahead of the man they called 'The Master', Dally Messenger? Our judges agonised over the decision, before giving Langlands the nod.

The wing position produced a similar conundrum.

Should Brian Carlson, a player of outstanding ability in any of the outside back positions (wing, centre, fullback), win a place ahead of wing specialist Harold Horder? The judges thought not.

The second row produced another headache.

Could our high-ranking lock forwards such as Frank Burge, Wally Prigg or Ron Coote win a place in front of lower-ranked specialist secondrowers such as Norm Provan and Bob McCarthy? What about an old-timer in George Treweek, surely he was good enough to win a place in Australia's greatest ever team? In the end, a compromise was reached.

Burge, the game's most prolific tryscoring forward, won a place alongside legendary St George secondrower Norm Provan.

Although Burge was best known as a lock, there are many instances where he starred at secondrow or even prop.

After much gnashing of teeth and the burning of midnight oil, the judges emerged with Australia's greatest ever XIII.

The end result is an outstanding team of all talents – and one the judges feel will endure the test of time.

Fullback
Clive CHURCHILL (1)

Wingers
Ken IRVINE (10), Harold HORDER (12)

Centres
Reg GASNIER (3), Graeme LANGLANDS (2)

Five-eighth
Wally LEWIS (6)

Halfback
Peter STERLING (14)

Lock
Johnny RAPER (5)

Secondrowers
Frank BURGE (16), Norm PROVAN (32)

Frontrowers
Arthur BEETSON (18), Duncan HALL (26)

Hooker
Ian WALSH (25)

Final positions in The Great 100 are in brackets.

LASTING TREASURE

HARRY 'Mick' Kadwell loved the game of rugby league and until his death in late October, 1999, was considered a living treasure.

The longest surviving Kangaroo tourist at 96, the grand old Rabbitoh held fond memories of the game he says gave him his start in life.

'League has been very, very good to me,' the man who toured as a utility back with the 1929 Kangaroos told *The Daily Telegraph* just before his death.

'It gave me the start in life I needed and I am greatly indebted to the game for that.'

Kadwell's early years growing up in suburban Surry Hills were harrowing. As the eldest of 10 children, he was forced to leave school at the age of 13 – there just wasn't enough money coming in to provide for the family.

The young Kadwell toiled daily at a Chinese market garden and supplemented his meagre income by selling newspapers on a city street corner.

'I got seven or eight bob a week,' he said, 'And, as you can

imagine, that didn't go very far with so many mouths to feed.'

Kadwell had a relatively late start in rugby league with the Redfern United juniors.

Small in size but extremely quick and gifted with his hands, it didn't take long for Souths to scout his potential.

He rose to first grade in 1927 and never looked back in a brief but sparkling career that ended up at St George in 1930.

As a child, Kadwell saw the great Dally Messenger in action for Eastern Suburbs.

'Dally wasn't a footballer, he was a wizard,' he recalled. 'He had the ability to manoeuvre opposing players into certain positions and almost invariably, they'd go for the wrong man.

'I've seen most of the good ones and Dally was probably the brainiest footballer league has seen.

'Everything he did, he did as 'The Master'. No silly passes, no missed tackles. When Dally Messenger got the ball, something was going to happen. You could rely on it.'

Kadwell followed the evolution and expansion of the code closely down through the years.

Even though he didn't attend many matches in his later years, he followed the game closely through the newspapers, radio and television.

'I think modern league is in pretty good shape,' he said in his last interview. 'It gets a bit too physical at times but the excitement is still there in the really big games.

'Today's players are just as good to watch as those of my day and the officials seem to be showing wisdom by streamling the competition.

'Rugby league will continue to be our favourite sport beyond the year 2000.'

And so say all of us.

FOR THE RECORD

Australian television picked up the league ball and ran with it from 1961.

The first black and white telecasts were on the primitive side but football fans could not get enough of the action.

As TV became more sophisticated, so did its telecasts. Huge advancements in technology made it a brilliant spectacle on the small screen with the really big games becoming ratings bonanzas.

TV produced its own batch of league personalities including commentators Ron Casey, **Rex Mossop**, Allan Marks, Graeme Hughes, and Ray Warren.

Newspapers and magazines have increasingly devoted more space to league coverage to satisfy readers' hunger for news.

Fine reporters including Tom Goodman, Claude Corbett, Jim Mather, George Crawford, and E E Christensen set high standards for those who followed including Bill Mordey, Peter Muszkat and Mike Gibson, to name but a few.

Today's pen, notebook (and tape recorder) men have carried on their forebears' lofty standards.

Photographers and artists are also an integral part of newspaper coverage as news and views on The Greatest Game of All is gathered and presented 'for the record'.

Indebted ... Harry 'Mick' Kadwell, who until his death in October, 1999, was the longest living Kangaroo tourist (left) and the South Sydney dynamo of the late 1920s (above)

Photo: Roy Haverkamp

Other books by Harper*Sports*

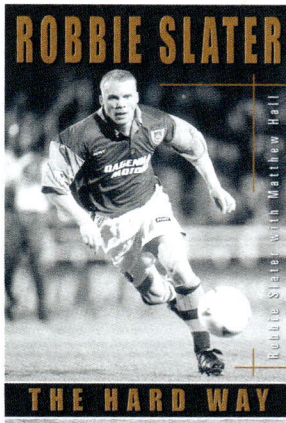

Robbie Slater: The Hard Way
By Robbie Slater with Matthew Hall

Robbie Slater was the heart and soul of the Socceroos for over a decade of international football and the first Australian to win a Championship medal in the English Premier League. *The Hard Way* is the no-holds-barred story of one of Australian soccer's true legends — a man who always put his body and heart on the line, no matter what the odds.

ISBN 0 7322 6483 9

Atlas of Australian Surfing: Traveller's Edition
By Mark Warren

For more than a decade, *Mark Warren's Atlas of Australian Surfing* has been the must-have book for every Australian surfer. Now, for the first time, it has been published in a convenient and durable paperback format. Supported by stunning colour photos and all-new location maps, this is an essential read for surfers and all lovers of the Australian coastline.

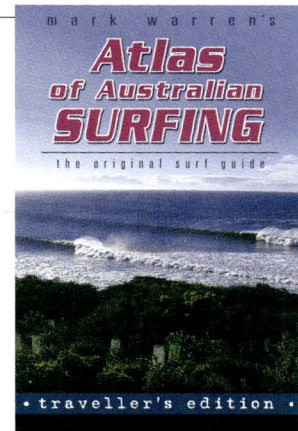

ISBN 0 7322 6731 5

One-Day Cricket: Playing the One-Day Game
By Adam Gilchrist with John Townsend

One-Day Cricket: Playing the One-Day Game is essential reading for anyone wanting to improve their cricket skills. The Australian one-day wicketkeeper and opening batsman, Adam Gilchrist, shares his advice on how to play the one-day game — from batting, bowling and keeping wicket to fielding positions and tactics for captains.

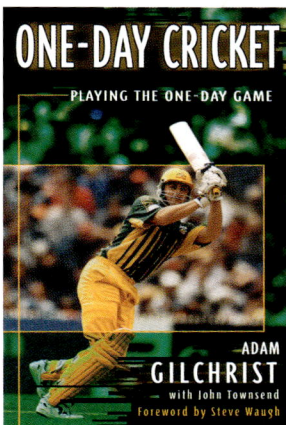

ISBN 0 7322 6713 7

Tumble Turns: An Autobiography
By Shane Gould

Shane Gould blazed a trail into history, breaking a dozen world swimming records and winning five Olympic medals at Munich in 1972, yet her career lasted just three years. At 13, she became a household name, at 16 she retired and almost disappeared. Not forgotten.

In this amazing autobiography, Shane tells a story of success, failure, warmth and happiness, fear and love.

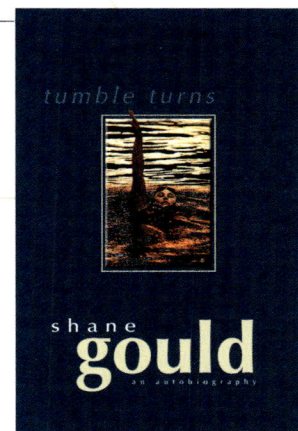

ISBN 0 7322 6761 7

No Regrets: A Captain's Diary
By Steve Waugh

No Regrets — Steve Waugh's sixth diary — is the story that began in one of cricket's most unlikely locations, and ended in glory at Lord's, the home of cricket.

It is a celebration of one of the most extraordinary and successful sporting odysseys in the history of Australian sport and a wonderful souvenir for all those dedicated fans who braved the late nights to share a wonderful year in the game and watch Australia bring home the World Cup.

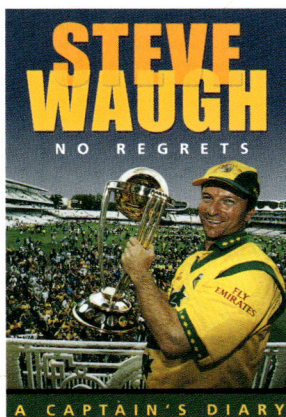

ISBN 0 7322 6452 9

Visit the HarperCollins website @ http://www.harpercollins.com.au

RUGBY LEAGUE 2000

By David Middleton

Rugby League 2000 — **in its 13th year** — is, without doubt, the most comprehensive yearbook on league. Packed with of fantastic photographs and statistics, this fabulous book also includes a preview of the upcoming season, a review of the 1999 season, the most comprehensive all-time records sections ever compiled, and a club-by-club guide to the modern game. *Rugby League 2000* also features interviews and reviews, news stories and an extensive interview with Glenn Lazarus, the captain of current premiers Melbourne Storm.

Written by respected rugby league journalist, statistician and historian David Middleton, *Rugby League 2000* is the most up-to-date book on the game today, making it an absolute must for any league fan.

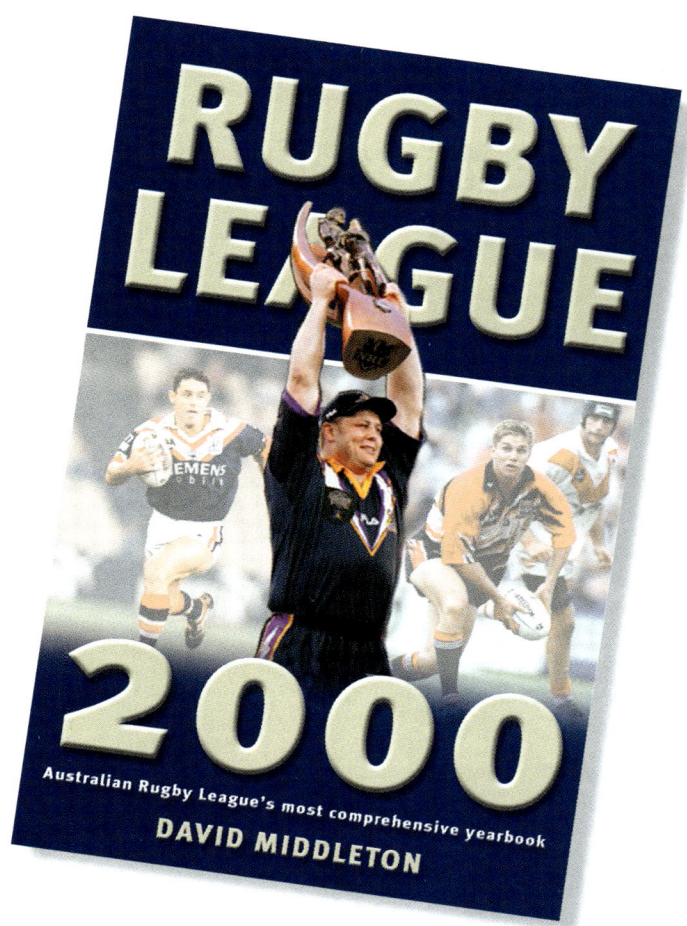

The Daily Telegraph **HarperSports**

Visit the HarperCollins website @ http://www.harpercollins.com.au